William Hayes Ward

Abraham Lincoln

Tributes from his Associates, Reminiscences of Soldiers, Statesmen and Citizens

William Hayes Ward

Abraham Lincoln
Tributes from his Associates, Reminiscences of Soldiers, Statesmen and Citizens

ISBN/EAN: 9783337136871

Printed in Europe, USA, Canada, Australia, Japan

Cover: Foto ©ninafisch / pixelio.de

More available books at **www.hansebooks.com**

ABRAHAM LINCOLN

TRIBUTES FROM HIS ASSOCIATES

REMINISCENCES OF SOLDIERS, STATESMEN
AND CITIZENS

WITH INTRODUCTION BY

THE REV. WILLIAM HAYES WARD, D.D.

NEW YORK: 46 EAST 14TH STREET
THOMAS Y. CROWELL & COMPANY
BOSTON: 100 PURCHASE STREET

COPYRIGHT, 1895,
BY "THE INDEPENDENT."

COPYRIGHT, 1895,
BY T. Y. CROWELL & CO.

Norwood Press:
J. S. Cushing & Co. — Berwick & Smith.
Norwood, Mass., U.S.A.

CONTENTS.

	PAGE
INTRODUCTION	ix

By the Rev. WILLIAM HAYES WARD, D.D., Associate Editor of *The Independent*.

FOUR GLIMPSES OF PRESIDENT LINCOLN 1

Unfriendly New York — "We shall beat them, my son" — Receives the Renomination.

By the late GEORGE WILLIAM CURTIS. From an unpublished letter to Professor R. R. WRIGHT of the Georgia Industrial College.

A WONDER AND A MYSTERY 4

His Wisdom and his Tenderness.

By the Hon. HENRY L. DAWES, lately United States Senator from Massachusetts.

THE STORY OF THE ASSASSINATION 9

Told by One on the Stage — How Wilkes Booth escaped — The Chamber of Death.

By W. J. FERGUSON, one of the Players at Ford's Theatre.

AN UNPUBLISHED LETTER FROM LINCOLN'S LAW PARTNER . 17

Lincoln on Education — His View of Woman's Rights — An Early Reformer.

By W. H. HERNDON, Esq.

LINCOLN'S FAITH IN PRAYER 22

After Gettysburg.

By General JAMES F. RUSLING, LL.D.

CONTENTS.

	PAGE
RECOLLECTIONS OF ABRAHAM LINCOLN	26

History of his First Visit to New York and New England — New Facts, with Incidents and Stories.

By HENRY C. BOWEN, Editor, Publisher, and Proprietor of *The Independent*, and one of its Founders in 1848.

SOME REMINISCENCES OF ABRAHAM LINCOLN . . . 35

Lincoln's Visits to the Army — "The Skeared Virginian" — A Man to be reverenced.

By Major-General OLIVER OTIS HOWARD, U.S.A. (Retired).

LINCOLN'S VIGIL 41

The Defeat of Chancellorsville.

By WILLIAM O. STODDARD, Private Secretary to Abraham Lincoln.

INCIDENTS OF PRESIDENT LINCOLN'S SYMPATHY . . . 50

The Boy who robbed the Mails — The Exchange of Prisoners — The Boy who wanted to be a Page — Close Districts.

By the Hon. ALEXANDER H. RICE, formerly Member of Congress and Governor of Massachusetts.

A DISTINGUISHED EDITOR'S RECOLLECTIONS . . . 57

A Whisky Bill — Lincoln as an Editorial Writer.

By MURAT HALSTEAD, Editor of *The Brooklyn Union*.

HOW LINCOLN WAS WARNED OF THE BALTIMORE ASSASSINATION PLOT 60

How he entered Washington.

By FREDERICK W. SEWARD, Author of the "Life of William H. Seward."

THE CAREER OF ABRAHAM LINCOLN 66

His Character as a Man — His Place in History.

By the Hon. GEORGE S. BOUTWELL, Ex-Secretary of the Treasury.

FROM LIBBY PRISON 92

The South feared Lincoln's Renomination.

By General NEAL DOW.

CONTENTS.

	PAGE
PRESIDENT LINCOLN'S KNOWLEDGE OF HUMAN NATURE: A CRITICAL STUDY	94

By the Hon. THOMAS L. JAMES, Ex-Postmaster-General.

AN HOUR WITH PRESIDENT LINCOLN 102

By FRANK B. CARPENTER, Author of "Six Months in the White House."

REMINISCENCES OF ABRAHAM LINCOLN 108

Lincoln's Reception to Tom Thumb — His Favorite Books of Humor — In his Coffin.

By GRACE GREENWOOD.

LINCOLN AS A STORY TELLER 116

By General EGBERT L. VIELE.

LINCOLN — AFTER THIRTY YEARS 125

By THEODORE L. CUYLER, D.D.

LINCOLN'S MOST CONSPICUOUS VIRTUE 130

From a Confederate General.

By the Hon. JOHN T. MORGAN, U.S. Senator from Alabama.

ABRAHAM LINCOLN AS SEEN BY A LIFELONG DEMOCRAT . 132

After going through Baltimore.

By Colonel B. F. WATSON, of the Massachusetts Sixth Regiment.

THE HOUR OF HIS THANKSGIVING 146

"A Thundering Old Glory" — The News of his Assassination — Angry Crowd at the Sub-Treasury.

By the Hon. L. E. CHITTENDEN, Ex-Registrar of the Treasury.

GOD IN LINCOLN 151

Lincoln in New Orleans — Attends a Slave Auction.

By DAVID GREGG, D.D., Pastor of the Lafayette Avenue Presbyterian Church, Brooklyn.

CONTENTS.

	PAGE
LINCOLN'S KINDNESS OF HEART	155

Pleading for a Deserter.
By JOHN D. KEENAN, Esq.

A TELEGRAPHER'S REMINISCENCE 157

Lincoln in the Telegraph Office — The Nomination of Andrew Johnson — Mr. Lincoln's Fears.
By CHARLES A. TINKER, Esq., Superintendent Eastern Division, Western Union Telegraph Company.

LINCOLN AND THE SLAVE TRADER GORDON 167

Refusing a Reprieve.
By ETHAN ALLEN.

A THEATRICAL MANAGER'S REMINISCENCES . . . 169

Interview with Wilkes Booth — Effect upon Edwin Booth.
By Colonel WILLIAM E. SINN, of the Park Theatre, Brooklyn, N.Y.

SOME TRAITS AND SAYINGS OF ABRAHAM LINCOLN . 175

His Self-Control — His Foresight — His Sympathy.
By WAYLAND HOYT, D.D.

LINCOLN IN HARTFORD 182

The Yeoman Orator — Refuses Wine — Names the Republican Clubs — Discusses his Secretary of the Navy.
By DANIEL D. BIDWELL, Editor of the Hartford *Evening Post*.

ABRAHAM LINCOLN'S BIRTHDAY 185

Senator Hoar's Comparison — A Negro's Tribute to Lincoln.
By R. R. WRIGHT, President of the Georgia Industrial College.

PERSONAL RECOLLECTIONS OF ABRAHAM LINCOLN . . 188

By HENRY W. KNIGHT.

LINCOLN AS A RHETORICAL ARTIST . . . 194

How he learned to demonstrate.
By AMOS W. PEARSON, Editor of the Norwich, Conn., *Bulletin*.

CONTENTS.

	PAGE
TYPE OF THE AMERICAN PEOPLE	197

The Destroyer of Slavery — Abraham Lincoln, 1865–1895.
By F. B. SANBORN, Author of "Life of John Brown."

RECOLLECTIONS OF ONE WHO STUDIED LAW WITH LINCOLN. 200

By JOHN H. LITTLEFIELD, Author of Lecture, "Personal Recollections of Abraham Lincoln."

MR. LINCOLN AT THE COOPER INSTITUTE . . . 207

A Critical View.
By HENRY M. FIELD, D.D., Editor of *The Evangelist.*

WHAT GENERAL SHERMAN THOUGHT OF LINCOLN . . 210

The Noblest of Men — Nature's Orator.
By the Rev. GEORGE W. PEPPER, Captain and Chaplain of the Eightieth Ohio Volunteers.

AS LINCOLN APPEARED IN THE WAR DEPARTMENT . . 214

By ALFRED B. CHANDLER, President and General Manager, Postal Telegraph Company.

LINCOLN AND THE ABOLITIONIST RIOTS . . . 224

To prevent his Inauguration.
By AARON M. POWELL.

LINCOLN AND CHARLES A. DANA 227

By DAVID HOMER BATES, General Manager Bradstreet's Agency, New York.

LINCOLN'S FAREWELL TO SPRINGFIELD 232

Trust in Divine Guidance.
By GEORGE W. F. BIRCH, D.D.

A SIDE-LIGHT AND AN INCIDENT 234

Lincoln's Description of Sheridan.
By CHARLES HAMLIN, late Adjutant-General United States Volunteers.

CONTENTS.

	PAGE
REMINISCENCES OF LINCOLN AS A LAWYER	237

Incidents of his Practice in Illinois — Interesting Cases — A Notable Address to a Jury.

By the HON. LAWRENCE WELDON, Judge of the United States Court of Claims.

INCIDENTS RECALLED IN WASHINGTON 256

Recollections of Ex-Secretary McCulloch and Mrs. McCulloch and Judge Shellabarger.

By JANET JENNINGS.

MR. LINCOLN IN NEW YORK 261

His Addresses in New England — "Right makes Might."
Compiled from Correspondence.

ANECDOTES OF LINCOLN 268

Stories about him — Choice Stories by him — Some of his Apt Illustrations — His Epigrammatic Sayings.

LINCOLN'S SECOND INAUGURAL ADDRESS . . . 293

INTRODUCTION.

This volume is not one man's view, nor two men's view, of Abraham Lincoln. It is no portrait biography by a single admirer giving a single picture of the most picturesque, perhaps the most noble, character in American history. It is a portfolio of portraits, one of them, careful and labored, by Ex-Secretary of the Treasury Boutwell, others, vivid and striking snap-shots by men on whose memory some single interview had impressed itself as a great event in their lives; others, single scenes in which President Lincoln was the prominent figure.

All these together supply a grand composite picture, the separate parts all blending in one harmonious whole, and supplying such a complete, many-sided view of the man as has never before been given to the American people.

It is the charm of such a multiple presentation of Mr. Lincoln's character, that in all these separate views of it, given here by more than forty men and women, there is nothing that breaks the harmony of the whole. From every side at which we are called to look upon his character we see something noble. He is small nowhere. It is as if a hundred vessels were approaching the peak of Teneriffe from as many directions, and from each the mountain is seen rising lofty above the level of the sea.

Such a writer as his private secretary, Mr. W. O. Stoddard, saw him close at hand every day, knew him intimately, saw him in his most familiar moods, and watched his bitterest struggles with the adverse fortunes which, in threatening to destroy the Union, first struck at his heart; but he can remember nothing but one noble hero, carrying with anxious, yet cheerful, but almost supernatural strength the weight of a Nation's hope, the burden of a Nation's fate. Just such a man they also saw who met him but once, perhaps on some tender errand of mercy, always great, however simple, playful, or anxious.

This series of reminiscences extends from his early manhood, before any one imagined his future fame, till the very hour of his death. It is fortunate that his law partner, Mr. Herndon, and his associates in his early experiences at the bar, Judge Weldon and Mr. Littlefield, have been able to give such interesting accounts of his activity in his profession and in politics while he was yet unknown to the world. And, passing those years of fame and coming to that last terrible night that put the whole country in mourning, it is equally fortunate that Mr. W. J. Ferguson, who was one of the players at Ford's Theatre on that tragic night, has been persuaded to break his long silence on the subject and tell the story of the assassination as he saw and knew it; also that Colonel Sinn, who, as theatrical manager at the time, knew and met Wilkes Booth, can tell so much of the latter.

Perhaps the serious side of Mr. Lincoln's character is made more prominent in these papers. The public has heard too much of Lincoln as a story-teller, and has come to think of him as at times almost dropping into buffoonery. General Viele speaks of him as a story-teller, and others do so incidentally, and it is well to hear their testimony that he had no patience with any story whose wit was only vulgarity. But it will be observed that the prevailing impression made by Mr. Lincoln on those who met him was that of a burdened and weary anxiety, as of a man who carried a load which he could rest on no other man's shoulders, and whose physical nature could bear the spiritual burden only as he sought mental relief in that relaxation of joke and story which he could so much enjoy.

A number of writers, among them Henry C. Bowen, Daniel D. Bidwell, and Dr. Henry M. Field, describe how Mr. Lincoln first made the acquaintance and captured the hearts of his friends in the East, after his public discussion with Mr. Douglass, and so became an acceptable candidate for the nomination as President. After his election he entered Washington unexpectedly, by a different route from that announced, in a way that gave occasion for much criticism. Major Seward tells just what was the occasion of this surprising change of plan and route, and how his father, Secretary Seward, sent him to meet Mr. Lincoln and warn him to avoid Baltimore and escape a plot to murder him, just before his inauguration. Not three weeks later the Massachusetts Sixth fought its way through Baltimore, the first armed regiment to reach Washington, and Colonel Watson, of that regiment, tells the interesting story of his interviews with the President at the time.

Original testimony as to Mr. Lincoln's religious faith is offered by General Rusling, taken from Lincoln's own mouth. But that story should be very carefully collated with the wonderful story of perhaps the same occasion told by Mr. Stoddard. The two together will make it clear what was the Higher Arm on which, in the time of his greatest depression, our beloved President leaned with a faith that gave him assured certainty that the cause of Country and Liberty must prevail at last.

For the lighter touches that fill in the vivid picture of Mr. Lincoln's character, the reader will turn to the skilful hands of the late George William Curtis; of Grace Greenwood; of General O. O. Howard; of the journalist, Murat Halsted; of the artist, Frank B. Carpenter, who spent six months in the White House, painting the picture of the signing of the Emancipation Proclamation; of Governor Rice of Massachusetts; of Charles A. Tinker, who spent hours with him in the telegraph office of the War Department; of Henry W. Knight, who was his body-guard in his walks at midnight from the War Department to the White House; of Albert B. Chandler and David H. Bates, whose duty it was to translate the cipher messages from the field for the President and Secretary Stanton; and of Secretary Hugh McCulloch, of the Treasury; and Mrs. McCulloch, whose reminiscences have been taken down by Janet Jennings.

Besides these writers there are others who speak more of Lincoln's character as he appeared to them. Secretary Boutwell's chapter is really nothing less than a grand oration, which surveys the whole man and his position in the Nation's history. Similarly, but at less length, he is viewed by Senator Dawes, General Neal Dow, Ex-Postmaster-General James, Senator Morgan of Alabama, Dr. Theodore L. Cuyler, the Hon. L. E. Chittenden, Dr. David Gregg, Dr. Wayland Hoyt, Mr. Amos W. Pearson, and other writers.

I believe that no man can fail, from reading these

various chapters, as full of thrilling interest as of shrewd character-sketching, to gain a very complete and correct view of what was the inner life of the later of the two men whose names head the list of those whom our country will ever delight to honor. George Washington stands first as the Father of his Country, and his place no one can take. Neither can any one take the place in our love and reverence of our Martyr President, on whom God put the no less weighty task of preserving the American Union, and the equal honor of emancipating the slaves. These chapters will be a fund of information for future historians, but more valuable as bringing the man Lincoln down from the pedestal of his fame into the humble homes of the people whose homely simplicity he never lost.

These chapters, with the appended anecdotes and characteristic sayings of Mr. Lincoln, first appeared in a special "Lincoln Number" of *The Independent* of April 4, 1895.

WILLIAM HAYES WARD.

I called with his friend, Mr. Isaac N. Arnold, representative for Congress from the Chicago district in Illinois. Mr. Lincoln received us in his office — the large room on the second floor, next to that in which the Cabinet meetings are held. He was dressed in black and wore slippers. On a table at his side were maps and plans of the seat of war; and pins with blue and gray heads represented the position of the soldiers on both sides. He had a weary and anxious look in his sad eyes, and a tenderness of tone in talking that was very touching. He spoke without bitterness toward any person or party, and with the air of a man bearing a most solemn responsibility.

When we rose to leave, Mr. Lincoln accompanied us to the door of the room, and as he shook my hand and said good by, he said with a paternal kindness and evident profound conviction: "We shall beat them, my son — we shall beat them." But the air and tone with which he said the words were so free from any unworthy feeling that the most resolute and confident of his opponents would have been deeply impressed.

Again I saw him when, as one of the Committee of the Baltimore Convention, to announce to him his renomination in 1864, I went with my associates to the White House. Mr. Lincoln received us in the East room; and, standing at one side of the room, not at the end, while we formed a semicircle before him, he put on his spectacles and, drawing a manuscript from his pocket, read his little speech of acceptance. Afterward, by appointment of the committee, I wrote a formal letter, to which he returned a reply which was published. The letter itself, written by a secretary, and signed in a firm, legible hand, "Abraham Lincoln," not the usual A. Lincoln, is in my possession.

Last of all, near the New York Hotel, in Broadway, where I had first seen him passing on his way to Washington, I saw his coffin borne along through the immense and reverent throng of the great city on its way to Illinois. The whole country knew then how great and good a man it had lost, the only American whom we name and revere with Washington.

A WONDER AND A MYSTERY.

HIS WISDOM AND HIS TENDERNESS.

BY THE HON. HENRY L DAWES,

LATELY UNITED STATES SENATOR FROM MASSACHUSETTS.

MR. LINCOLN was always to me both a wonder and a mystery. From the day I first saw him, on the morning in which he surprised all Washington by his unexpected and unexplained appearance at the railroad depot while every one else supposed him quietly asleep in Harrisburg, through all the subsequent four years of marvellous achievement, he was to me a study. I could never quite fathom his thoughts, or be quite sure that I saw clearly the line along which he was working. But as I saw how he overcame obstacles and escaped entanglements, how he shunned hidden rocks and steered clear of treacherous shoals, as the tempest thickened, it grew upon me that he was wiser than the men around him. He never altogether lost to me the look with which he met the curious and, for the moment, not very kind gaze of the House of Representatives on that first morning after what they deemed a pusillanimous creep into Washington. It was a weary, anxious look, of one struggling to be cheerful under a burden of trouble he must keep to himself, with thoughts afar off or deep hidden which he could not impart even to the representatives of the nation to whose Chief Magistracy he had been called and for whom he was to die. I met him many times after this; but it was never my good fortune to meet him on any of the few occasions in all his after life when the sky was so clear and the prospect so cheering as to lift from him the burden of anxiety and distress which so constantly pressed upon him. Indeed, it was in times of the deepest concern that I saw most of him, and therefore when his face, which was always a title-page, most clearly revealed the painful strain of the life he lived. Others were more fortunate in falling under the fascinating influences of the *natural* man on those few occasions when trouble spared him for a brief interval, lifting its weight from off the springs and impulses of his real life. These were the lights which set off the shades of the four years' picture otherwise painfully sombre.

Every one, however, came away from his presence, whether it was when he was in his serious or lighter mood, impressed with his stature as a man. That which all the world, looking back over the vista of thirty years upon the great events of that period, now concedes with entire unanimity, grew by slow degrees, but more clearly every hour, to be the conviction of those who stood about him, and saw what manner of man he was. The world sees now, what contemporaries were reluctant to believe, that the nation had no other man for the place to which he was assigned by the Great Disposer of those events.

It would be almost a waste of words to bring up anew to the minds of those who have studied the agencies of different men most conspicuous in the bringing about the great achievements of Mr. Lincoln's time, the many proofs of a clearness of foresight, an unerring judgment dissipating mists and clarifying doubts, and a wisdom astonishing the wisest, which met perils and solved problems and adjusted complications which appalled and confounded the wisest and most patriotic of those around him. Those called to hold up his hands as counsellors found him calmer and clearer-sighted than they, and more than one in command of armies under him pronounced him the ablest strategist of the War. It was intuition, not learning or experience, that guided his pen in reshaping Mr. Seward's first instructions to Mr. Adams, our Minister to England, and saved the nation from an untenable attitude toward the rebel States, upon which hostile Europe was making haste to seize. It was political wisdom passing that of any other man which enabled him to hold in check the too ardent, and at the same time hold up the too timid and faint-hearted, while he worked out, without convulsion, the solution of the problem of emancipation. Reconstruction, though not accomplished in his lifetime, was certainly held, under his guiding hand, free from the disasters which came upon it when the reins fell from his grasp. The political sagacity of no other man was ever equal to that which enabled him to gather around him in earnest support of his administration, rivalries, opposing purposes, conflicting theories, and implacable enmities, which would have rent asunder any other administration. No one like him could turn aside, so that they hurt him not, the shafts of malice and detraction, or like him could compose strifes and poultice heart-burnings till enthusiasm drove out sulkiness. Whether it was in the small things or in the great things with which he had to deal, he was equally matchless. And all this was born in him. Neither education nor experience nor example had anything to do with the production of this great central, controlling force in the greatest of all the crises that ever came upon the nation. His development kept pace with the multiplying exigencies which confronted him, and he was never found wanting. He grew wiser and broader and stronger as difficulties thickened and perils multiplied, till the end found him the wonder in our history. His last public utterance, only three days before his death, when, taking the nation into his confidence as never before, he spoke of the controlling motive of the past, to what it had brought the nation thus far, and what was yet to be done, all put forth with a simplicity and power of speech no other man possessed, stands unchallenged in the light of thirty years of subsequent study and experience of what was gained and what was lost when power passed into other hands.

I love to think of him, however, as the man open to human and humane influences, pained by the distress and sorrow which filled the land, shedding tears over the terrible sacrifice of life which was the price paid for victories that filled others with exultation. No familiarity with the horrors inseparable from war ever so hardened the softest and tenderest heart that ever beat in the breast of man that it did not bleed in a hospital, that it did not rebel against the necessity which compelled him to deny the importunities of sorrowing fathers and broken-hearted mothers whose sons had fallen within the enemy's lines, or were languishing in prisons beyond his reach. The desolation and woe which followed the work forced upon him saddened every waking hour of his life from the day that terrible work began.

This is the Abraham Lincoln I saw most frequently, and who comes back most vividly to my mind as the anniversary of the day approaches when his life and work came to such a tragic end.

PITTSFIELD, MASS.

THE STORY OF THE ASSASSINATION.

TOLD BY ONE ON THE STAGE — HOW WILKES BOOTH ESCAPED — THE CHAMBER OF DEATH.

BY W. J. FERGUSON,

ONE OF THE PLAYERS AT FORD'S THEATRE.

ONLY four actors are now alive who performed in the play of "Our American Cousin," which President Lincoln was witnessing on the night when he was so cruelly assassinated. These actors are Harry Hawke, E. A. Emerson, John Matthews and myself. The play referred to is a comedy-drama, and was written by the late Dion Boucicault. The leading male character, Lord Dundreary, is an English dude, whose peculiarities are a drawling accent and great intellectual vacuity. This character, on the occasion referred to, was played by Mr. Emerson, who afterward retired from the stage, and who for years has been a cotton planter near Richmond, Va. He has always refused to say anything on the subject of the assassination. Just before this presentation of the play it may be interesting to note that it was presented in other cities, and the character of Dundreary was successfully portrayed by Commissioner W. S. Andrews, of New York, who was at one time a member of Edwin Booth's company. The second leading character, Asa Trenchard, a straightforward, honest Yankee, was played by Harry Hawke, who is still in the profession, and is located somewhere in the West. This character has been made famous by Mr. Joseph Jefferson, who has played it many times. Mr. Matthews, who played a subordinate character, is in New York, no longer playing, but connected in an official capacity with the benevolent organization known as "The Actors' Fund of America."

I was a very young man, almost a boy, at the time of this national tragedy about which I have often refused to speak. I will, however, break silence on this occasion for a great weekly journal like the New York *Independent*, which proposes, as I am informed, to give a symposium of reminiscences of the lamented Abraham Lincoln. Being quite young at the time of the assassination, the facts, as they appeared to me, were indelibly impressed upon my memory, never to be effaced; for I believe it is a well-recognized principle of memories that, as age advances, we remember best the remarkable occurrences that happened in our youth.

It was my first season on the stage. I was what was termed the call-boy. The call-boy is a messenger for the stage manager, and is often assigned to play some simple part. One part of his duty is to call the hours of the acts. A half-hour before the raising of the curtain he goes to the orchestra room and says "Half-hour," meaning that in half an hour the curtain will be raised. Before each act of the play he goes to each dressing room, raps at the door and says "Half-hour," or "Fifteen minutes," as the case may be, meaning there is that much time before the raising of the curtain. This position of call-boy, by the way, has since then been done away with.

A young man who was playing a small part in the

piece was ill on the day of the assassination, and Miss Laura Keene, who was the star in the piece, asked me to take his part. When she came to the theatre at night, as I had a scene with her, she rehearsed me in it. In that way I happened to be on the side of the stage behind the scenes with her. To put it in theatrical parlance, she and I were standing at the right first entrance, at the prompter's box, directly opposite the box in which the President sat.

The performance was to be for the benefit of Miss Laura Keene; and the President, together with General Grant and other prominent men, had been invited, and were expected to be present. The private box adjoined the dress circle and had two doors, as it was sometimes, by a partition, converted into two boxes. These doors opened into a dark passage, closed by a door at the end of the dress circle. During the day, or previously, it is said that the assassin or some accomplice had bored gimlet holes in the box doors, enlarged by a penknife on the inside sufficiently to survey the position of the parties within at the moment of action. The hasps of the locks, which were on the inside of the box doors, had been weakened by partly withdrawing the screws, so that a man could easily press them open if locked. Mr. Lincoln's chair was in the front corner of the box, furthest from the stage; that of Mrs. Lincoln was more remote from the front, and near the column in the centre. In the box with the President and Mrs. Lincoln were Major Henry R. Rathbone and Miss Clara H. Harris, daughter of Senator Harris.

It was during the second scene of the third act that the shot was fired. "May Meredith" was on the stage doing a quiet piece of monologue, which is always listened to by the audience in silence. Suddenly the sharp report of a pistol rang through the house. At the moment the pistol shot did not attract my attention because the "property man" (the employé having charge of pistols, guns, etc., used in plays) was in the habit of discharging old firearms in the alley back of the theatre (the theatre being on a level with the street), in order to reload them. But not more than a second or two had elapsed after the firing of the shot before a man (Booth) jumped from the private box on to the stage. The crash of his fall quickly caused me to turn. Meanwhile — to record my mental impression — as I had had charge of placing books, manuscripts and papers on a desk that was to be used in the following scene, and which was just back of the scene on the stage, the thought occurred to me that the desk had, in some way, been overturned and the papers all displaced. "More work for me," I murmured to myself.

But as I looked on the stage, I saw Booth kneeling on one knee, the position in which he had fallen. The spur on his riding-boots had caught in the flag with which the box was draped and thrown him in that position when he alighted. The boards used on a theatrical stage are quite narrow, about two and a half inches wide. We afterward discovered that there was a semicircle cut by his spur just below the President's private box from whence he had jumped.

Booth (for I recognized him instantly) rose at once and quickly ran across the stage as if nothing had happened. Inside of thirty seconds he ran across, past the prompt box and then out of the stage door, which was on a level with the stage and opened on an alley.

For a moment the audience seemed to be spellbound. There was a deathly silence. You could have heard a pin drop. I instinctively imagined what had occurred. I looked up at the President's box, and saw him with his head leaning on his breast. He always sat with his back toward the audience. He was a very plain, unostentatious man, never wanted his coming to the theatre to be announced, and never cared for any demonstration of applause when he came in.

According to my recollection it is not true, as some of the newspapers reported, that Booth, as he jumped on the stage, cried out: "*Sic semper tyrannis!*" He jumped up from his knee and ran rapidly across the stage in my direction. I retreated two steps to give him plenty of room to pass me. He ran out into the alley where his horse was standing. It was shown afterward that he had taken a stable in the rear of the theatre, having hired a fine bay mare from a man named James Pumphrey. The horse was saddled and ready to mount, as he had ordered the bridle not to be taken off. All this was done so quickly that those in the theatre could hear the horse's hoofs rattling over the cobblestones down the alleyway — tramp, tramp, tramp, until the sound of their rattling hoofs quickly died away in the distance. It seemed as if for a minute or more there was a dead silence in the audience. There was no crying out. Suddenly a movement was made; the actors behind the scenes crowded on the stage, persons in the front of the house crowded the orchestra and tried to reach the stage. Then some one said: "Booth!" and the cry was taken up, louder, and still louder: "Booth!" "*Booth!*" "BOOTH!"

After the excitement was over, some blood was found on the dress of Miss Laura Keene, and some of the sensational newspapers took pains to chronicle that the blood of the martyred President was on the dress of an actress. That is not the fact. The truth is, the President did not bleed at all, at least while he was in the theatre, from which he was quickly removed. The wound was on the left side of the head behind, on a line with and three inches from the left ear. It is true that blood was found on Miss Keene's dress, but it came from Major Rathbone. It seems that as Booth ran across the box the Major attempted to seize him. But Booth wrested himself from the Major's grasp and made a violent thrust at him with a large knife which he carried in his hand. The Major parried the blow by an up-stroke, and received a wound several inches deep in his left arm between the elbow and the shoulder. He afterward said that the orifice of the wound was about an inch and a half in length, and extended upward toward the shoulder several inches. The wound bled very profusely, so much so that after he had assisted in carrying the President to the house across the street from the theatre where he died, the Major fainted away in the hall and had to be taken in a carriage to his residence. It was the blood from Major Rathbone's wound that, in the midst of the excitement that followed, when actors and audience crowded the stage, got on Miss Keene's dress.

I am sorry to say that after this great tragedy, Miss Keene, in her travels throughout the country, would exhibit this dress and claim that it was stained with the blood of the President. To say nothing about the want of decency or good taste of such a proceeding, it was, as I have shown, contrary to the fact. Harry Hawke, in his statement of the occurrence, says that when Booth gained the stage he slipped, but got up on his feet in a moment and brandished a large knife. He looked toward Mr. Hawke, who recognized him as John Wilkes Booth.

As he ran toward Mr. Hawke, the actor says he thought he had designs upon him, and so he ran off the stage and up a flight of stairs. I was in the box directly after the assassination, and saw that the President did not bleed. He was quickly carried downstairs and across the street to the house I have mentioned, where he was placed in a bedroom in an extension on the first or parlor floor of the house. It was a small room, ornamented with prints on the wall, the familiar one of Landseer's, a white horse, hanging directly over the bed. The wound in the President's head did not begin to bleed until some time toward morning. So the blood of the martyred President did not "bedabble the robes of an actress."

I had seen Booth on the afternoon of the fatal evening. At about three o'clock he passed by in front of the theatre. I passed the time of day, and he remarked that he was not feeling very well; he said, he had pleurisy. He went down the street to cross and then walked up toward the White House. For three months before he had not been seen about the theatre. Among the profession he was supposed to be engaged in oil speculations. He had not been acting that season, and was very much interested in the oil excitement in Pennsylvania.

The house where the President was taken, across the street from the theatre, was occupied by a family named Peterson. The President died in this house about half-past seven the following morning. The son of Mr. Peterson and I were chums. When the President was carried in the house I went to the basement, where I was admitted, and went upstairs to the room where the President had been taken. I saw him lying on the bed. And it is a singular fact that perhaps has never been published, but I had seen John Wilkes Booth lying on that same bed, a little over three months before, smoking a pipe. The house was a sort of rendezvous for actors, and members of theatrical companies often rented furnished rooms there.

After this sad event the theatre was closed for an indefinite period, and it was never opened again as a theatre. It is a singular fact, having no significance except among those who were superstitiously inclined, but the building fell to the ground on the day that Edwin Booth died. The truth is that the theatre was never properly constructed, and its fall can easily be accounted for from natural causes.

New York City.

AN UNPUBLISHED LETTER FROM LINCOLN'S LAW PARTNER.

LINCOLN ON EDUCATION — HIS VIEW OF WOMAN'S RIGHTS — AN EARLY REFORMER.

BY W. H. HERNDON, ESQ.

[The venerable W. H. Herndon, who for twenty-five years was Abraham Lincoln's law partner, and knew him better than perhaps any man now living, wrote the following — a letter to Mr. John C. Henderson, of this city, giving facts which are an interesting and valuable contribution to the history of one of America's most celebrated statesmen.]

You request me to state to you what were the feelings, sentiments and ideas of Mr. Lincoln touching the great subject of public — universal — education of the people, especially in America. I became acquainted with Mr. Lincoln in 1834, while he lived in New Salem, in Sangamon County, in this State (Illinois), and knew him well from 1834 to the day of his death; and I ought to know his feelings, sentiments and ideas on this subject. I know what he has really said on the question of education, and I know what he has written on it; he has said to me, and to others in my presence and hearing, that "universal education should go along with and accompany the universal ballot in America; that the very best, firmest and most enduring basis of our Republic was the education, the thorough and the universal education of the great American people; and that the intelligence of the mass of our people was the light and the life of the Republic." This I have heard him say in *substance* over and over, again and again. Mr. Lincoln was conscientiously just, truthful and honest, and hence thought that every other person was just, truthful and honest; but in this belief he was often sorely disappointed. He had an infinite faith — trust — in the people, and in their instinct of, and mental insight into, the fundamentals of government. He trusted the people, and saw no creature made purposely to rule them without their consent. He looked to the great mass of men for the right, and had full faith in the honesty and capability of the people for self-government. As a politician and a statesman he took no steps in advance of the great mass of our people. Before he acted on any great political or other question touching the people's interest, he took notes, made observations, felt the public pulse; and when he thought that the people were ready he acted, and not before. At times I thought that he was timid, overcautious; but in the end he was right and I was wrong. Mr. Lincoln's ideas were that men do not of themselves make events, but that events make men. Hence he waited with a cautious patience, a philosophic judgment, on the constant and regular flow and logic of them.

Give Mr. Lincoln his own time and he was a man of great common sense, which he applied to the daily and practical affairs of men; he was not a genius, but was better; he was a good man, an honest man, a sound man, and an upright and downright one. When he once formed an opinion he never took a backward step. What I have said to you herein marked him somewhat as a politician and a statesman. Mr. Lincoln trusted in the people and appealed to them, and they in their turn trusted and appealed to him. Neither was disappointed.

If what I have stated to you is correct, *truthful*, then Mr. Lincoln must have written something on the subject of education. If he had faith in the people — if he thought that universal education should go along with and accompany the universal ballot; and if he thought that the strongest, firmest and most enduring basis of a Republic was the thorough and universal education of the great mass of our people, then he must have taken a firm stand on this great question, and so he did. Let me explain. Mr. Lincoln became a candidate in this State (Illinois) in 1832, for the Legislature. It was then and continued for years to be a custom for the respective candidates to issue a handbill — a program of the principles which they would advocate if elected to the honorable position. According to that universal and long-settled custom here in this State, Mr. Lincoln did on the ninth day of March, 1832, issue his handbill, containing the things — subjects and laws which he would advocate in the Legislature, if elected. Mr. Lincoln travelled around the country, saw the people, and asked them to support him for the causes which he advocated on the stump and in his handbill. In that handbill he uses these exact words:

"Upon the subject of education, not promising to dictate any plan or system respecting it, I can only say that I view it as *the* most important subject which we as a people can be engaged in. That every man may receive at least a moderate education and thereby be enabled to read the histories of his own and other countries, by which he may duly appreciate the value of our free institutions, appears to be an object of vital importance even on this account alone, to say nothing of the advantages and satisfaction to be derived from all being able to read the Scriptures and other works, both of a religious and moral nature, for themselves.

"For my part, I desire to see the time when education — and by its means, morality, sobriety, enterprise and industry — shall become much more general than at present, and should be gratified to have it in my power to contribute something to the advancement of any measure which might have a tendency to accelerate the happy period."

Mr. Lincoln was defeated in 1832, but was elected in 1834 to the Legislature. I have been informed, but do not know of my own knowledge, that Mr. Lincoln most heartily supported every measure which came before the Legislature touching the question of the people's education and common schools. I have been told this by a member of the Legislature of this State in 1834–35. I believe it. In short, on this question, Mr. Lincoln's ideas of the education of the people were practical; he wished the people educated and enlightened on practical questions for a practical life and an immediate, practical end. He was a practical man in all the ways and walks of life. Mr. Lincoln was not a great general reader, but was a special one. When he wished to know anything he hunted it up and dug it out to the small, fibrous end of the very taproot. I say that Mr. Lincoln was a practical man, and hence he was a special man; that is, he worked for a practical and paying end. He did not much care to know anything that he would have no use for. Politics was his constant study and newspapers his ever present library. Mr. Lincoln was the great practical — the embodiment of caution and prudence. "Take him all in all, and we shall not soon see his like again."

As remarked, many, many times before, Mr. Lincoln had a keen, quick sense of the eternal right and just. Seeing that Woman was denied in *free* America her right to the elective franchise, being the equal but the other side — the other and better half of man — he always advocated her rights — *yes, rights.* In the year 1836 Mr. Lincoln issued a kind of handbill, making a declaration of some things which he wished and would advocate, and among them were these — I quote his words:

"I go for *all* sharing the privileges of the Government *who assist in bearing its burdens.* Consequently, I go for admitting *all* whites to the right of suffrage *who pay taxes* or bear arms, by no means excluding *females.*

"If elected I shall consider the *whole* people of Sangamon my constituents, as well those who oppose as those that support me."

Mr. Lincoln was twenty-three years of age when he issued his first handbill in 1832, and twenty-seven when he issued the one in 1836. When Mr. Lincoln once, as said before, on due consideration, took a step forward, he never took one backward. He would at any time have supported and advocated and voted for woman's rights. Though he believed in woman's rights, he thought the time probably had not yet come to openly advocate the idea before the people. He said: "This question is one simply of time."

SPRINGFIELD, ILL.

LINCOLN'S FAITH IN PRAYER.

AFTER GETTYSBURG.

BY GEN. JAMES F. RUSLING, LL.D.

OF course, secession was a miserable sophism, and the Southern Confederacy based on slavery was an anachronism. It was a pirate-ship in the nineteenth century. It sailed under the curse of both God and man, and was sure to sink or be sunk in due time. But whether we could have made such a good fight against it as we did, with any other chief and leader than President Lincoln, may well be doubted. It is true, he did not have the culture and prestige of Mr. Seward; but he had real breadth and sagacity, fine moral fibre, and was pre-eminently a man of his age and time.

It may be his early beliefs were unsettled and variable; but it is certain that our great War, as it progressed, sobered and steadied him, and that in the end he came to accept as the rule of his life "to do justice, to love mercy, and to walk humbly before God." As striking evidence of this, I beg to give a significant conversation of his in my presence, in July, 1863, in Washington, D. C., on the Sunday after the battle of Gettysburg. General Sickles, of New York, had lost a leg on the second day at Gettysburg, while in command of the Third Corps, and arrived in Washington on the Sunday following (July 5th). As a member of his staff, I called to see him, and while there Mr. Lincoln also called, with his son Tad, and remained an hour or more. He greeted Sickles very heartily and kindly, of course, and complimented him on his stout fight at Gettysburg, and then, after inquiring about our killed and wounded generally, passed on to the question as to what Meade was going to do with his victory. They discussed this *pro* and *con* at some length, Lincoln hoping for great results if Meade only pressed Lee actively, but Sickles was dubious and diplomatic, as became so astute a man. And then, presently, General Sickles turned to him, and asked what he thought during the Gettysburg campaign, and whether he was not anxious about it?

Mr. Lincoln gravely replied, no, he was not; that some of his Cabinet and many others in Washington were, but that he himself had had no fears. General Sickles inquired how this was, and seemed curious about it. Mr. Lincoln hesitated, but finally replied: "Well, I will tell you how it was. In the pinch of your campaign up there, when everybody seemed panic-stricken, and nobody could tell what was going to happen, oppressed by the gravity of our affairs, I went into my room one day and locked the door, and got down on my knees before Almighty God, and prayed to him mightily for victory at Gettysburg. I told him this was his war, and our cause his cause, but that we couldn't stand another Fredericksburg or Chancellorsville. And I then and there made a solemn vow to Almighty God that if he would stand by our boys at Gettysburg I would stand by him. And he *did*, and I *will*. And after that — I don't know how it was and I can't explain it — but soon a sweet comfort crept into my soul that things would go all right at Gettysburg, and that is why I had no fears about you."

He said this solemnly and pathetically, as if from the very depths of his heart, and both Sickles and I were deeply touched by his manner.

Presently General Sickles asked him what news he had from Vicksburg. He answered, he had none worth mentioning, but that Grant was still "pegging away" down there, and he thought a good deal of him as a general and wasn't going to remove him, though urged to do so; and "Besides," he added, "I have been praying over Vicksburg also, and believe our Heavenly Father is going to give us victory there too, because we need it, in order to bisect the Confederacy and have the Mississippi flow unvexed to the sea." Of course he did not know that Vicksburg had already fallen, July 4th, and that a gunboat was soon to arrive at Cairo with the great news that was to make that Fourth of July memorable in history forever.

He said these things very deliberately and touchingly, as if he believed thoroughly in them. Of course, I do not give his exact words, but very nearly his words, and his ideas precisely. He asked us not to repeat what he said — at least, not then — lest "people might laugh, you know." But his tragic death, and the long lapse of years since, and his imputed infidelity if not atheism, would seem to justify my speaking now. General Sickles also well remembers the above conversation, and gave the substance of it in a recent after-dinner address in Washington, but not so fully as the above. Of course, he could not be expected to recall it so well, "done to the death" as he then nearly was. Altogether, we Americans may well be proud of Abraham Lincoln. If not our first American, he is at least only second after George Washington; and he will go down to history an honor and a credit to human nature. In any other age he would long since have been canonized as Abraham the Just or St. Abraham the Good. On this the thirtieth anniversary of his assassination let us devoutly say of him, as was said of that good knight of old:

> "His good sword is rust,
> His bones are dust,
> His soul is with the saints,
> We trust."

TRENTON, N. J.

RECOLLECTIONS OF ABRAHAM LINCOLN.

HISTORY OF HIS FIRST VISIT TO NEW YORK AND NEW ENGLAND — NEW FACTS, WITH INCIDENTS AND STORIES.

BY HENRY C. BOWEN,

Editor, Publisher and Proprietor of the "Independent," and one of its Founders in 1848.

In 1858 Abraham Lincoln was nominated at Springfield, Ill., by the Republican State Convention as the candidate for United States Senator from Illinois in place of Stephen A. Douglas, who desired re-election to that office afterward. Lincoln challenged Douglas to canvass the State with him and publicly discuss the question of slavery. This discussion attracted the attention of the whole American people to Mr. Lincoln as a man of great intellectual and oratorical power — a splendid, keen, quick-sighted platform speaker. His speeches during that campaign were reported and read in every part of the country. They were noticeable for their brilliant and humorous illustrations, which made them very effective. I read most of these speeches with interest, and they made a deep impression on my mind. The fresh and aggressive style of Lincoln led me then to think that he had a brilliant political future of great value to the Republican Party.

During the winter of 1859 several young men in New

York, including Mr. Joseph H. Richards, who was then in my employ and connected with the *Independent* as its publisher; Mr. S. W. Tubbs, receiving teller of the Park Bank; Mr. S. M. Pettingill, a well-known advertising agent, and the Hon. James A. Briggs, decided to arrange for a lecture to promote a benevolent object — supplementary to a course in Brooklyn. They wanted a man who would draw a crowd and make the lecture a success, they said, and asked me if I could name such a man.

I knew Mr. Lincoln by reputation, as a lawyer, before his platform contests with Douglas in Illinois. He had been employed by my firm — Bowen & McNamee — on several occasions. We found him to be able, efficient and successful. I gave it as my decided opinion that Mr. Lincoln would be the best man to fill Cooper Institute. The expense would be large in bringing him here from Illinois; but the young men decided to take the risk of inviting him. The compensation offered was $200, which included all his expenses. The proposal made to him was promptly accepted, and on Mr. Lincoln's arrival in New York he came directly to my office, where I was very glad to receive him. I had never seen him before. His personal appearance surprised me somewhat.

The introductory conversation was quickly over, and he immediately made himself at home, completely covering the sofa, which was quite too small and short for his extended figure. I soon saw he was a talker. He bubbled over with stories and jokes, and speedily convinced me that I had made no mistake in recommending him as a lecturer. After an hour's talk I asked him where he was stopping in the city, and he said he had a quiet room in the Metropolitan Hotel where he could have a chance to think. I invited him to be my guest in Brooklyn; but he declined, saying he was afraid he had made a mistake in accepting the call to New York, and feared his lecture would not prove a success. He said he would have to give his whole time to it, otherwise he was sure he would make a failure, in which case he would be very sorry for the young men who had kindly invited him. This interview was on Saturday. I then said: "Will you come to Brooklyn and attend church with me on Sunday?" He said he would be very glad to do so. He asked where I attended church. I told him Plymouth Church; and he said he would like to hear Mr. Beecher, and that he would come over in good time. I then invited him to dine with me after the morning service. He said he would do so. Soon after ten o'clock on Sunday morning he appeared at the door of the church where I was waiting for him, and I escorted him to my pew. His presence in the church was unknown to anybody. A few moments before the service commenced I introduced him to Mr. Horace B. Claflin, who sat in the next pew behind me. He talked with him a moment, and then Mr. Claflin turned round and spoke to his neighbor in the adjoining pew; and I am pretty sure that within ten minutes a large proportion of the audience knew Mr. Lincoln was present. The sermon seemed to interest him very much, and after the meeting closed I invited Mr. Beecher — on a slip of paper — to come down and speak to Mr. Lincoln. He did so, and the interview seemed to attract the attention of the audience, who remained, almost in a body, to look at the distinguished stranger from Illinois. All seemed anxious to shake hands with him, and hundreds did so. Finally he said: "I think, Mr. Bowen, we have had enough of this show, and I will now go with you." We started from the church, passed through the crowd and went to my house. When we got to the front steps he said: "Mr. Bowen, I guess I will not go in." My reply was: "My good sir, we have arranged to have you dine with us, and we cannot excuse you." His reply was: "Now, look here, Mr. Bowen, I am not going to make a failure at the Cooper Institute to-morrow night, if I can possibly help it. I am anxious to make a success of it on account of the young men who have so kindly invited me here. It is on my mind all the time, and I cannot be persuaded to accept your hospitality at this time. Please excuse me and let me go to my room at the hotel, lock the door, and there think about my lecture."

The lecture which Mr. Lincoln was to give on Monday evening was fairly well advertised; but the young men, who greatly desired his success — mainly, for financial reasons — did not seem to be very enthusiastic, Mr. Richards said, about the result.

The evening came, and everybody was apparently astonished to see a crowded house. The speech, which was mostly on slavery and kindred topics, was regarded a most wonderful success; it seemed to please everybody. He presented point after point in such a fair, happy and telling way, that he made an army of friends at once; even the proslavery men present — attracted there to see the man who had the reputation of whipping Douglas — went away saying: "Well, I like that man, if I don't agree with him." "He is a good fellow, anyway." "He doesn't make you mad as Garrison and Phillips do," etc. More *zealous* Republicans were probably made within twenty-four hours after the delivery of that speech than existed before in the whole city. The *Tribune* and other newspapers reported his speech fully, and very little was said in any quarter against it. Within two days letters and telegrams came pouring in from all quarters inviting Mr. Lincoln to lecture. The Hon. Hugh H. Osgood, of Norwich, Conn., made the first application to Mr. Lincoln for a lecture in that city. He had obtained the names and influence of most of the leading men in Norwich to aid him, and it was at once decided that Mr. Lincoln should go East, speaking in New Haven, Hartford, Norwich, and also at Providence. Within ten days Abraham Lincoln was everywhere, in Republican circles, spoken of and applauded for his boldness and wisdom and was pronounced the "coming man" and a great acquisition to the ranks of outspoken antislavery men.

The following May, at the Republican National Convention, which, fortunately for Mr. Lincoln, met at Chicago, he was made the candidate of the party for President. While he was popular and well spoken of in all quarters, very few believed that he would be nominated, and I was among them. My choice was William H. Seward for President, and Abraham Lincoln for Vice-President. The convention was greatly excited; the friends of Seward were legion, and they did their very best to secure his nomination. Mr. Seward obtained on the first ballot $173\frac{1}{2}$ votes, Mr. Lincoln, 102, and the remainder were much scattered. At the second ballot, it seemed certain that Mr. Seward would triumph by a very large majority. But when the vote was taken, it showed $184\frac{1}{2}$ for Seward and 181 for Lincoln. The third ballot gave Mr. Lincoln $231\frac{1}{2}$ votes — only two short of the number required to nominate him — when, before the result was declared, enough Ohio and New England votes were promptly given to nominate him. But that mere majority was not permitted to stand on the record, for State after State wheeled into the Lincoln ranks, and, amid immense enthusiasm, he was made by a unanimous vote, on the motion of the Hon. Wm. M. Evarts (Seward's strongest friend), the Republican candidate for President; and in due time he was elected the first Republican President of the United States.

In a long and private conversation with President Lincoln during a whole evening at the Soldiers' Home, during the week of his inauguration, he gave me a history of his feelings and anxieties during the campaign. He said he had "gone his whole length" for the Republican Party (six feet and four inches, I thought), and he felt that the nation was thoroughly aroused and enthusiastic, as never before, for the overthrow of slavery and the establishment of freedom throughout the land. He was sure, he said, "from the word go," after his nomination that he would be elected.

In November, on the day of the election, he said he was calm and sure of the result. The first news he received, mostly from New York, was unfavorable, and he felt a little discouraged. Later the dispatches indicated a turn in the tide, and when he learned of his election he said his heart overflowed with thanksgiving to God for his providential goodness to our beloved country. He continued: "I cannot conceal the fact that I was a very happy man," and then he added, with much feeling, "Who could help being so under such circumstances?" He then said that "the enthusiastic greetings of his neighbors and friends during the evening, at the Club," together with the numerous telegrams which poured in upon him, "well-nigh upset him with joy." At a late hour he left the Club rooms and went home to talk over matters with his wife. Before going to the Club that evening to get the election news as it came in, he said: "I told my wife to go to bed, as probably I should not be back before midnight. When at about twelve o'clock the news came informing me of my election I said: 'Boys, I think I will go home now; for there is a little woman there who would like to hear the news.' The Club gave me three rousing cheers, and then I left. On my arrival I went to my bedroom and found my wife sound asleep. I gently touched her shoulder and said, 'Mary'; she made no answer. I spoke again, a little louder, saying, 'Mary, Mary! *we are elected!*' Well," continued the President, "I then went to bed, but before I went to sleep I selected every member of my Cabinet, save one. I determined on Seward for my Secretary of State, Chase for Secretary of the Treasury, Welles, whose acquaintance I made in Hartford, for Secretary of the Navy, and Blair and others for the other positions; but I was induced to make one or two changes when I got to Washington. My Cabinet, however, was substantially fixed upon that night. I wanted Seward, for I had the highest respect for him and the utmost confidence in his ability. I wanted Chase, also; I considered him one of the ablest, best and most reliable men in the country and a good representative of the progressive, antislavery element in the party." In a word he said he "wanted all his competitors to have a place in his Cabinet in order to create harmony in the party."

In 1862 Mr. Beecher and Mr. Tilton, who had then, by contract, the sole editorial control of the paper, while I retained direction only of the financial and other business departments, felt it to be their duty, against my wishes, to criticise President Lincoln for "not moving more rapidly in suppressing the Rebellion." At one time, while General McClellan was the leader of our armies in Virginia, the editors, believing that the great body of the people demanded more activity, spoke out plainly, and perhaps too much so, about the "slow course of the President." Mr. Lincoln felt deeply grieved by these criticisms in the *Independent* and spoke about it to a mutual friend — the Hon. Schuyler Colfax — supposing, as he did, that I was then the sole owner and editor of the paper. Mr. Colfax — then a leading Republican Congressman from the West — lost no time in writing me on the subject. My reply to him was that I did not control the editorial columns of the *Independent* except in the business departments, and requested him kindly to state that fact to the President. He did so immediately, but thought I had better let the President know this by a personal interview — if I could go to Washington — or, if not, by letter. I went immediately to Washington and called without delay at the White House. An immense crowd was there, and after waiting an hour or more, I came to the conclusion that there was no chance of seeing the President that morning. The city was then in the greatest excitement — as was the whole country — about the news from the battle-fields; and I saw that the poor man had enough on his mind to crush him, without my adding a feather's weight to his troubles. I started to go to my hotel, when, in passing out of the reception room, I met the President face to face, on his way from his office downstairs to his luncheon. He grasped my hand and said: "Well, well! is this you? What can I do for you?" I commenced to tell my errand, when he broke out in the most tender and touching words, saying: "Mr. Bowen, I now know your position; it is all right. I am sorry you troubled yourself to come here. Pray don't bother yourself a moment"; and with many kind words he pressed my hand, and we parted.

Never after that interview did the President have occasion to criticise the *Independent* for deviating from its uniform course in doing all in its power to sustain and encourage him in his efforts for the suppression of the Rebellion. Such measures, however, were soon adopted by him as led the people of the whole North, and particularly the newspapers, to see that President Lincoln meant to do his duty faithfully, that he was pushing the conflict as rapidly and wisely as it was safe to do.

New York City.

SOME REMINISCENCES OF ABRAHAM LINCOLN.

LINCOLN'S VISITS TO THE ARMY — "THE SKEARED VIRGINIAN" — A MAN TO BE REVERENCED.

BY MAJOR-GEN. OLIVER OTIS HOWARD, U. S. A. (RETIRED).

It was not my good fortune to have known Abraham Lincoln before I took my regiment, the Third Maine Volunteers, to Washington, and encamped it on Meridian Hill, near the Columbian College, the first week of June, 1861. The officers of the regiment, after our arrival, took great pains to have a good evening parade about sundown on every fair day; and so, as to Burnside's encampment of his Rhode Island Brigade, in another part of Washington, and Butterfield's Twelfth New York on Franklin Square, visitors from the city every evening came in carriages to witness the exercises. Sometimes Cabinet officers and members of Congress sat in their carriages and observed us while the parade went on. Mr. Lincoln himself came two or three times and looked on with evident interest; but before I had finished my part of receiving and conducting the exercise he had ridden away, so that I did not then make his personal acquaintance.

A little later there was some consultation of army leaders by Cabinet officers in the presence of Mr. Lincoln at the White House, and I was among them. At that time I must have been introduced to the President, but think only in a hurried way, as we came together into the middle room and immediately took seats. Several officers took part in the conversation. I remember only that Mr. Seward answered a proposition from me in such a way that it made me feel very small and very young. I now only recall the fact of a young man's mortification and his resolution thereafter to hearken diligently and say little.

The next occasion when I observed Mr. Lincoln was after I had been promoted to a brigadier-general (September, 1861); and while waiting orders at Washington, McClellan had a grand review, and I crossed the long bridge and went over beyond the Arlington Heights to view the handling of the troops on that occasion. I met some old army acquaintances with ladies, also looking on from a nice position. As I approached I was made to feel that my presence among these old-time friends was not welcome. These ladies and all about them were in sympathy with the Rebellion and laughed at me as a new-fledged brigadier on the Yankee side. Mr. Lincoln's curious appearance on horseback, with his long stirrups and his hat apparently on the back of his head, was the cause of all sorts of satirical and unkind remarks among my neighbors. As I already esteemed him highly I quickly left them. It was while returning to Washington after that parade that an officer complained to Mr. Lincoln of Gen. W. T. Sherman, who had threatened to shoot him for some misconduct, if he repeated the offence. Mr. Lincoln told the officer in a quiet whisper aside, that Sherman was a man of his word and might do it. Surely the officer must not again give him the occasion.

I think that I must have seen Mr. Lincoln at different

times when he came to the Army of the Potomac on the Peninsula, but no public reception now impresses me like that given him in the fall of 1862 at Harper's Ferry. We had passed through the not very decisive battle of Antietam. My division, the second of Sumner's corps, had cleared the field of wrecks and disabled animals, and buried the dead. It had then marched on and caught up with the main army, encamped about that historic pocket — what the French would properly call a *cul de sac* — Harper's Ferry. Mr. Lincoln had with him at this time quite a staff. An officer who rode by his side during the review of the troops, besides McClellan, was the already distinguished Western general, McClernand. He seemed then to have a grievance against Grant. From some remarks dropped I have always thought that at that time he had just been relieved from the command of his Thirteenth Corps, and wanted to be restored, or to have another equivalent, or better, assigned him. What struck me by the persistence of McClernand was the conviction that Mr. Lincoln must have continued worry, and be forced to exercise extraordinary patience under the ever-reiterated grievances of old friends and acquaintances.

As the generals and handsome staff officers escorted the President near to my front I joined the reviewing party. Mr. Lincoln rode along in silence, returning the salutes. As soon as the solemn review was over, he lightened up. Noticing Major Whittlesey of my staff receiving some order from me and riding off, some one said to Mr. Lincoln, as he noticed and spoke of Whittlesey's fine figure and splendid horsemanship, "that Major was before the War a minister!" Mr. Lincoln smiling, rejoined: "He looks more the cavalier than the clergyman!" When we passed through a field where a few stumps remained cut rather high up, he contrasted that sort of stumping with that in Illinois, and told an incident concerning chopping trees by some public man, which I did not quite hear. Suddenly we saw a little engine named "The Flying Dutchman" fly past us on a railroad track. Mr. Lincoln seeing it and hearing a shrill, wild scream from its saluting whistle, laughed aloud. He doubtless was thinking of John Brown's terrorism of a few years before, for we were near the famous engine-house where John Brown was finally penned up and taken; for, referring to the locomotive, Mr. Lincoln said: "They ought to call that thing 'The Skeared Virginian'!"

Sprightly as he was in story-telling and in conversation about what he saw around him, he looked to me, as soon as he relapsed into silence, very careworn and very sad. Our victory at Antietam was too little decisive to meet the desire of his heart.

My next interview with Mr. Lincoln was in the spring that succeeded Fredericksburg. I had been assigned by him to the Eleventh Army Corps and was encamped near Brook's Station, a small hamlet on the railroad north of Falmouth. It was in April, 1863, soon after I had gone up there to assume command from the Second Corps, which was located nearer the Rappahannock. My corps was reviewed in the usual manner by Mr. Lincoln, accompanied by General Hooker and a small host of attendants. The corps presented a fine, brilliant appearance along the hills and slopes. The Germans were remarkable for their neatness on parade and for the soldierly salutes which never failed to attract attention. I was congratulated by observing officers upon such a splendid command. Mr. Lincoln said nothing till just as he was finishing the review, when he remarked to me, inquiringly: "How is it, General Howard, that you have so large a part of your command over there?" He referred to those who appeared to be off duty, and were on the slopes opposite to those in the ranks. Of course, I explained as well as I could how the old guard, the quartermaster's men, the orderlies, cooks and other essential details, had come out to see the President. Mr. Lincoln smiled, and said, gently: "That review yonder is about as big as ours!" His evident criticism was a wholesome one to the young corps commander. Those altogether too large "details" were always a source of great weakness to us in time of battle.

I had my new tent wonderfully pitched by my German pioneers. The approach was a corridor of evergreens. Mr. Lincoln came around to see it, and to chat with me alone for a few minutes. He was now very kind and fatherly. He took notice of my tablets, hung against the rear tent-pole inside. The one for the day, I think, was the beginning of the Twenty-third Psalm: "The Lord is my Shepherd; I shall not want."

I had reason to remember this occasion afterward. After Chancellorsville, several officers high in command, some aspiring, went to Mr. Lincoln at the White House and besought my removal. At General Hooker's tent one day I was made to understand something of this hostile action. I said then, substantially, to Hooker, during a formal visit to his tent: "Whatever you think of doing, I will hereafter simply mind my own business and obey orders." But as I rode back the few miles to my headquarters I was dreadfully depressed. On entering my tent I looked up and saw that strong promise,

"The Lord is my Shepherd." "Yes," I said, "why didn't I think of it?" Mr. Lincoln's decision and his flattering remark soon after this were brought to me: "He is a good man. Let him alone; in time he will bring things straight." I felt that Mr. Lincoln's heart beat in sympathy with mine, and I reverenced him greatly. I loved him.

After Gettysburg I received from him a remarkable letter. It was in response to mine urging the advantages of keeping the army under our new commander, General Meade. That letter was long ago published in the *Atlantic Monthly*. You will remember how two divisions of my corps and two of Slocum's, with our corps organizations preserved, were detached in September, 1863, after Rosecrans's battle of Chickamauga, and sent by rail far West to his neighborhood, with General Hooker commanding the whole detachment. Mr. Lincoln and I, just before my departure, had quite a lengthy talk in his office room at the White House. He had a fine, "well-mounted" map hung upon a firm framework. Mr. Lincoln took me to this map, and questioned me about East Tennessee. He told me how loyal the people of that region were, and asked my opinion about getting our forces in there, so as to hold the country permanently. Just as I was leaving I asked him where he obtained his map, showing him mine. "Here, General," he said, "take this. Yours will do for me. Mine will be better for you, as it will stand more wear and tear."

His parting words I cannot recall, but the impression of them was never effaced. They gave me a knowledge of his confidence and a belief in his personal interest and affection. Abraham Lincoln was worthy to be trusted and to be loved by all his countrymen.

Portland, Ore.

LINCOLN'S VIGIL.

THE DEFEAT OF CHANCELLORSVILLE.

BY WILLIAM O. STODDARD,

Private Secretary to Abraham Lincoln.

They seem far away and almost unreal, as if they had never been, those long, overheated years with Lincoln in the White House. Very few remain of the men whose names and faces are associated in memory with the events of that time. Yet it often seems strange, unnatural, to find that the people met and talked with in every-day life, all of them who are of less than middle age, are but vaguely informed concerning those events and the actors in them. Probably most of these must, indeed, be forgotten, they were so many and there is so much else that this generation must needs study and always assume to know.

One tall figure, however, still stands forth, distinctly visible always, as if it belonged to the present as much as to the past and would march along forever, keeping step, shoulder to shoulder, with the continuous history of the Republic.

Lincoln cannot be forgotten. He is even better and better understood by thinking men. But there seems to be floating around, in the minds of many, something of the idea so curiously presented by one of the dead President's old Illinois neighbors:

"Linkin?" said the prairie man; "oh yes, I knowed him. Knowed his folks, too. They was torn-down poor. He wasn't much up to the War; that was what made him. Tell ye what, they wouldn't let on so much 'bout him now, 'f he hadn't been killed. That helped him, powerful. People kind o' sympathized with him, ye know. It made him pop'lar. He saved suthin' w'ile he was President, but I don't reckon he left much proppity. Oh yes, I knowed Linkin."

In strong contrast with this crude scepticism is the marvellous keenness of the general popular instinct which then recognized, accepted, trusted and sustained its God-appointed leader. That he was of God's appointment must be apparent to any man whose creed contains a confession of a living God, mindful of human affairs.

It may be noted, without any surprise whatever, that many intelligent persons who had associated with Lincoln in his earlier years were never, to the end, able to see anything but what may be called their first mental photographs of him, badly taken, on defective negatives. These were at best but surface pictures and contained only something of the man as he was seen before, say, the year 1858. One of his oldest, most intimate professional associates and latest biographers, for instance, was hardly acquainted with him at all; for he did not even see him after 1860.

During long years prior to the War, the actual growth of so deep and strong a nature was necessarily hidden, even from himself; and when its disclosure came, through trial after trial, there was something of surprise attaching to each successive manifestation of capacity. His slow and somewhat ponderous inability to hesitate; his apparently overconfident readiness to accept responsibilities; his forward stride to grapple unflinchingly with unknown, untellable difficulties, were only the unexpected expressions of his silent consciousness of power. This subtle, unformulated assertion of the strength that was in him was itself a serious offence, often, to men who thought they knew him, but did not, and to others who could not believe it possible for any man to do the things which he undertook and accomplished.

One remarkable feature of his development, or of its expression, was the suddenness with which, in 1861, he ceased to be a party man, or merely the head of a party, and became the man of the nation. It was true that his party itself underwent a change, welding in with the great mass of American patriotism, but its after relations with him contained little or no mere partisanship. It was once said of a President elect: " Well, he was big enough for so small a State as ours [his own]; but I'm thinking he'll show kind o' thin when you come to spread him out over the whole country." The thin spot in Lincoln's spreading out has not yet been discovered.

When he went to Washington, in 1861, and the first great army from the North and West poured in around him, with their haversacks crammed with recommendations for appointment to office, there was yet another large tribe who were sorely astonished and disappointed. They had known him years and years, had heard him tell stories and try law cases, or they had even higher claims upon him, and they wondered at the heartless ingratitude with which he ignored them in making his appointments. They never forgave him; for they could not and would not understand that to him the public service was first, and personal relations not so much second as simply somewhere else. He did not even make his own father a brigadier nor invite Dennis Hanks to a seat in his Cabinet.

Lincoln's work as President and, to a certain extent, as General-in-Chief in charge of the military operations which were already not only inevitable but actually progressing, began even before his election. It is no exaggeration to say that thenceforward his toil did not cease until the end. When not asleep he was at his task.

The White House then, the Executive Mansion as it is otherwise described, was much simpler and narrower in its official staff and management than it is now. Part of it was a family residence, but all the rest, including the reception rooms, was merely a workshop. There were a few days, truly, in the spring of 1861, while Washington City was a frontier post, almost cut off from the North, that the great East Room was a camp, perhaps a fort, garrisoned at night by a regiment of office seekers who had provided themselves with rifles and were prepared to defend the citadel of their prospects for appointment.

It was a remarkably silent workshop, considering how much was going on there. The very air seemed heavy with the pressure of the times, centring toward that place. There was only now and then a day bright enough to send any great amount of sunshine into the house, especially upstairs. It was not so much that coming events cast their shadows before, although they may have done so, as that the shadows, the ghosts, if you will, of all sorts of events, past, present and to come, trooped in and flitted around the halls and lurked in the corners of the rooms. The greater part of them came over from the War Office, westward, in company with messengers carrying telegraphic dispatches. Troops of them used to follow Stanton or Halleck right into Lincoln's rooms. Seward, too, was sometimes a gloomy messenger; but he was always diplomatically cheerful about it, and nobody could tell by his face but what he was bringing good news. The President could receive any kind of tidings with less variation of face or manner than any other man, and there was a reason for it. He never seemed to hear anything with reference to itself, but solely with a quick forward grasping for the consequences, for what must be done next. The announcement of a defeat or disaster did not bring to him the blow only, but rather the consideration of the counterstroke. When the cannon ball struck Charles the Twelfth in the head, it did not kill him so quickly that his sword was not half drawn before he fell.

Lincoln's characteristic as a worker was his persistency, his tirelessness; and for this he was endowed with rare toughness of bodily and mental fibre. There was not a weak spot in his whole animal organism, and his brain was thoroughly healthy; his White House life, therefore, was a continual stepping from one duty to another. There was also what to a host of men was a provoking way of stepping over or across unessential things, with an instinctive perception of their lack of value. Some things that he stepped over seemed vastly important to those who had them in hand, but at the same time he discovered real importances where others failed to see them.

He had vast capacity for work, and also the exceedingly valuable faculty of putting work upon others. He could load, up to their limit or beyond it, his Cabinet officers, generals, legislative supporters, and so forth. He could hold them responsible, sharply; but he never really interfered with them, "bothered them," at their work, or found undue fault with its execution. A false idea obtained circulation at one time concerning his hardness, his exacting dealings with his immediate co-workers and subordinates. Perhaps this arose from the numerous changes made in his civil and military appointments. He was the very reverse of exacting. For illustration, I do not know or believe that he ever found fault with one of his private secretaries in all the onerous and delicate duties with which they were charged. I know that during all the years of my own service he never uttered a criticism or expressed a disapproval, and yet such a mass of work could not possibly have all been perfect. He was the most kindly and lenient of men, even when, through days and days of gloom and overwork, he would pass us, invariably, without speaking, as if we were not there, until business gave us the right to speak.

Did he never at any time reel or stagger under his burden? Oh yes, once. He could feel a hit or a stab at any time; but the things which hurt him, that made him suffer, that were slowly killing him, as he himself declared, did not interfere with the perpetual efficiency of his work. If there were hours when despondency came and when he doubted the result, the final triumph of the national arms, he did not tell anybody; but there was one night when his wrestle with despair was long and terrible.

In the opinion of Edwin M. Stanton, concurred in by other good judges, the darkest hour of the Civil War came in the first week of May, 1863. The Army of the

Potomac, under General Hooker, had fought the bloody battle of Chancellorsville. The record of their dead and wounded told how bravely they had fought; but they were defeated, losing the field of battle, and seventeen thousand men. The Confederate commanders acknowledged a loss of only thirteen thousand, but their Army of Northern Virginia was dreadfully cut up. How severe a disaster this costly victory had been to them could not be understood by the people of the North.

The country was weary of the long war, with its draining taxes of gold and blood. Discontent was everywhere raising its head, and the opponents of the Lincoln administration were savage in their denunciations. Many of his severest critics were men of unquestionable patriotism. The mail desk in the Secretary's office at the White House was heaped with letters, as if the President could read them. He knew their purport well enough without reading. He knew of the forever vacant places in a hundred thousand households before Chancellorsville. If more than a third of each day's mail already consisted of measureless denunciation; if another large part was made up of piteous pleas for peace, for a termination of the long murder of the Civil War, what would it be when tidings of this last slaughter should go out and send back echoes from the heart-stricken multitude? Had not enough been endured, and was there not imminent peril that the country would refuse to endure any more? This question was, perhaps, the darkest element in the problem presented to Mr. Lincoln; for the armies, east or west, were ample in force and ready to fight again.

There were callers at the White House the day on which the news of the defeat was brought; but they were not the customary throng. Members of the Senate and House came, with gloomy faces; the members of the Cabinet came, to consult or to condole with the President. There were army and navy officers, but only such as were sent for. The house was as if a funeral were going forward, and those who entered or left it trod softly, as people always do around a coffin, for fear they may wake the dead.

That night, the last visitors in Lincoln's room were Stanton and Halleck. They went away together in silence, at somewhere near nine o'clock, and the President was left alone. Not another soul was on that floor except the one secretary, who was busy with the mail in his room across the hall from the President's; and the doors of both rooms were ajar, for the night was warm. The silence was so deep that the ticking of a clock would have been noticeable; but another sound came that was almost as regular and ceaseless. It was the tread of the President's feet as he strode slowly back and forth across the chamber in which so many Presidents of the United States had done their work. Was he to be the last of the line? The last President of the entire United States? At that hour that very question had been asked of him by the battle of Chancellorsville. If he had wavered, if he had failed in faith or courage or prompt decision, then the nation, and not the Army of the Potomac, would have lost its great battle.

Ten o'clock came, without a break in the steady march, excepting now and then a pause in turning at either wall.

There was an unusual accumulation of letters, for that was a desk hard worked with other duties also, and it was necessary to clear it before leaving it. It seemed as if they contained a double allowance of denunciation, threats, ribaldry. Some of them were hideous, some were tear-blistered. Some would have done Lincoln good if he could have read them; but, over there in his room, he was reading the lesson of Chancellorsville and the future of the Republic. Eleven o'clock came, and then another hour of that ceaseless march so accustomed the ear to it that when, a little after twelve, there was a break of several minutes, the sudden silence made one put down letters and listen.

The President may have been at his table writing, or he may — no man knows or can guess; but at the end of the minutes, long or short, the tramp began again. Two o'clock, and he was walking yet, and when, a little after three, the secretary's task was done and he slipped noiselessly out, he turned at the head of the stairs for a moment. It was so — the last sound he heard as he went down was the footfall in Lincoln's room.

That was not all, however. The young man had need to return early, and he was there again before eight o'clock. The President's room door was open and he went in. There sat Mr. Lincoln eating breakfast alone. He had not been out of his room; but there was a kind of cheery, hopeful, morning light on his face, instead of the funereal battle-cloud from Chancellorsville. He had watched all night, but a dawn had come, for beside his cup of coffee lay the written draft of his instructions to General Hooker to push forward, to fight again. There was a decisive battle won that night in that long vigil with disaster and despair. Only a few weeks later the Army of the Potomac fought it over again as desperately — and they won it — at Gettysburg.

MADISON, N. J.

INCIDENTS OF PRESIDENT LINCOLN'S SYMPATHY.

THE BOY WHO ROBBED THE MAILS — THE EXCHANGE OF PRISONERS — THE BOY WHO WANTED TO BE A PAGE — CLOSE DISTRICTS.

BY THE HON. ALEXANDER H. RICE,

Formerly Member of Congress and Governor of Massachusetts.

It happened that a mercantile firm in Boston had an office boy whose duty, among other things, was to take the mail to and from the post office. This boy was fresh from the country and was dazzled by the apparent wealth of everybody in the city, without having any very definite ideas of how competency is attained; and seeing his opportunity to get money from the letters entrusted to him, he yielded to the temptation and fell into the habit of thus stealing money, was detected, convicted and imprisoned; but the employers of the boy and the jury that convicted him felt kindly disposed, and joined with the boy's father, after some months had elapsed, in an effort to obtain the boy's pardon. As his offence was against the National Government, the application must, of course, be made to the President. For that purpose the father appeared in Washington equipped with a petition for the pardon of his son which was numerously signed by the jurors and many citizens of Massachusetts, and asked me to accompany him to the White House, which I did, and introduced him to the President, to whom also I handed the petition. Mr. Lincoln put on his spectacles, threw himself back in his chair and stretched his long legs to their utmost extent, and thus read the document. When finished, he turned to me and asked if I met a man on the stairs going down as I came up, and I said that I did. "Well," said Mr. Lincoln, "he was the last man in this room before you came and his errand was to get a man pardoned out of the penitentiary, and now you come to get a boy out of jail. I am bothered to death," said he, "about these pardon cases; but I am a little encouraged by your visit. They are after me on the *men*, but appear to be roping you in on the *boys*. What shall we do? The trouble appears to come from the courts. Let's abolish the courts, and I think that will end the difficulty. And it seems as if the courts ought to be abolished, anyway; for they appear to pick out the very best men in the community and send them to the penitentiary, and now they are after the same kind of boys. According to that man's testimony who was just in here, there are few men so upright as his client; and I don't know much about boys in Massachusetts, but according to this petition there are not many such boys as this one outside the Sunday-schools in other parts of the country." Then assuming more gravity he asked the father what he intended to do with the boy if released; and the reply was that the boy had had quite enough of the city and would be content to go upon the farm where he would hereafter stay. The President finally said that if a majority of the Members of the Massachusetts delegation in Congress would sign the petition, he would then pardon the boy. This was done, and I never heard of the boy afterward.

After the Congressional election, in 1862, my seat in Congress was contested by an estimable old gentleman who differed from his constituents, and with the evidence in the case, by supposing that he and not I was elected to the Congress. The matter of contest was reported upon by the Committee on Elections in my favor, and their report was affirmed by the House. At the next following election my old friend and myself were again opposed to each other as candidates, and I led him at the polls nearly 4000 votes; to be more exact, by 3600+. It is remarkable how fully apprised of the trend of politics in different localities Mr. Lincoln kept himself. With all his labors and anxieties he kept his finger always upon the public pulse and appeared to know the "close districts" and the "certain" ones throughout the country. On my return to Washington, after that election, I chanced one day to pass the White House just as the President was coming out, and he hailed me, saying: "Well, your district is a good deal like a jug, after all — the handle is all on one side." He then proceeded to tell me that he was at the War Department when a dispatch came in saying that Rice was re-elected by more than three thousand plurality, and Mr. Lincoln said to those present, That can't be, for he has one of the closest districts in the country. While they were commenting upon the matter another dispatch from another source came saying, Rice elected by nearly four thousand plurality. Well, said Mr. Lincoln, if that is the way in which the doubtful districts are coming in he guessed he would not stop to hear from the certain ones.

There is a certain recognized order of precedence of admission when calling upon the President of the United States; the Vice-President will be first admitted, if present, then members of the Diplomatic Corps, Cabinet Ministers, Justices of the Supreme Court, Senators, members of the House of Representatives, and so on. It happened at one time that the late Senator Henry Wilson and myself called to see President Lincoln on a joint errand; and for that reason, I, who was a member of the House of Representatives, could be admitted with the Senator. After we had waited some little time in the anteroom, we were at length admitted; and as the door to Mr. Lincoln's room opened, a small boy, perhaps twelve years old, slipped into the room between the Senator and myself. After the customary salutations the President appeared to be absorbed in the lad, and said, "And who is the little boy?" an inquiry which neither the Senator nor myself could answer. The lad, however, immediately replied that he was a good boy who had come to Washington in the hope of obtaining a situation as page in the House of Representatives. The President began to say to the boy that he must go to Captain Goodnow, the head doorkeeper of the House, as he himself had nothing to do with such an appointment; upon which, the lad insisted that he was a *good boy*, and pulled from his pockets a recommendation from the supervisors of his town, the minister of the parish and others, stating also that his mother was a widow and pleading the necessities of the family. The President called the boy nearer to him, took his recommendation and wrote upon the back of it as follows:

"If Captain Goodnow can give this good little boy a place he will oblige   A. LINCOLN."

This he passed to the boy, who seemed visibly to grow in height as he read it, and strode toward the door buoyed with hope. The incident was tender, dramatic and pathetic.

At the beginning of the War, when President Lincoln called for seventy-five thousand troops, a certain student in a theological school in Massachusetts at once volunteered and went to the front. He was a private, but his courage and patriotism soon won promotion for him; and he was shockingly wounded and suffered long in hospital, and was finally sent home to recuperate. There was a standing regulation in the army that no communication should be made between the opposing forces, yet both sides disregarded it; and even the authorities at Washington depended not a little upon the information gathered from Southern newspapers obtained through these exchanges between soldiers of the opposing armies. After Captain Burrage (for that was his name) had sufficiently recovered from his wounds, he again joined his regiment at the front just as orders had been issued to enforce the prohibition of all exchange of newspapers. Of this special order he was ignorant, and seeing the rebels in front signalling for an exchange he went forward having only one newspaper while they had two; he took the two and gave in exchange the one he had and promised to bring another later in the day. When he again went to the front to deliver the promised paper the rebels perfidiously dragged him within their lines and carried him off to Richmond. For disobedience of orders the Washington authorities took away his commission and reduced him to the ranks, while the rebels incarcerated him and gave him only prison fare and privileges. This state of things greatly told against his health and caused his wounds to break out afresh and otherwise incommoded him. While I was at home during a recess of Congress, Captain Burrage's friend stated these facts to me and begged my interposition to have him exchanged. On my return to Washington I sought the President and began to state the facts to him, when he interrupted me by saying that it was all he could do and more to hear cases in *classes,* and that he really could not hear *individual* cases however meritorious. I saw the difficulty and so told him, but at the same time said, that I felt persuaded that if he could hear that case he would esteem it exceptional and especially worthy of his attention, whereupon he asked me to proceed with the statement giving in detail facts not necessary here to recite. When I had finished my story, he said: "I wish you would go over to the War Department and state this case to General Wadsworth [who had charge of the exchange of prisoners] and say to him from me that if he can effect the exchange of Captain Burrage without injustice to other men of his rank, I wish him to do so." I then reminded the President that when captured Burrage was a captain and held as such by the rebels, but that he had since been reduced to the ranks, and we could only give a private soldier in exchange for him while the rebels would probably demand a captain. To this the President replied that if General Wadsworth should raise that point I might tell him that if he (Wadsworth) could take care of the exchange part he guessed he (the President) could take care of the rank part. I fulfilled my errand to General Wadsworth, and he said he could easily effect the exchanges provided he could be allowed to give a captain for Burrage. I then told him what Mr. Lincoln had said about the "rank part," and that I would immediately return to the White House and inform Mr. Lincoln of what he had said. I did so, and Burrage was in Washington in less than a fortnight afterward. This story will illustrate the patience and sympathy which Mr. Lincoln gave to every interest of the soldiers, whether in the service or in captivity.

A DISTINGUISHED EDITOR'S RECOLLECTIONS.

A WHISKY BILL — LINCOLN AS AN EDITORIAL WRITER.

BY MURAT HALSTEAD,

Editor of "The Brooklyn Union."

I BECAME acquainted with President Lincoln through an old and somewhat peculiar farmer, named "Sol" Meredith. He introduced me to the President on one occasion when he was in the West. Old "Sol" Meredith during the War was the commander of the Iron Brigade at Gettysburg. In the West he had been a farmer, raising all kinds of agricultural products, making a specialty of breeding horses, mules and other live stock.

As a journalist, in a general way, I supported Mr. Lincoln; at the same time I was occasionally inclined to agree with those who were criticising him, but, later on, it became clear to me that he seemed to be doing pretty well. There was a time when nearly everybody criticised him, the Republicans the worst of all.

I remember particularly a speech he made in Cincinnati about 1858, from the balcony of the building where the post office now stands. I went up there for the purpose of hearing a part of the speech, and to get an impression of the man; but I was so much interested that I remained throughout the whole address. The speech was of no particular importance so far as its relation to public affairs was concerned, but in one particular it was quite pathetic. Lincoln, it will be remembered, was born in Kentucky, and in this speech he referred to his native State, remarking that he had never before made an address so near his early home. And it is a singular fact that in all his public career he never appeared as a public speaker in Kentucky.

When I was in Washington I used to see him looking through a spyglass out of a window in the White House at the Confederate flag which was kept flying from the hotel at Alexandria, where young Ellsworth was killed at the outbreak of the War. He seemed to study this flag through his spyglass; it seemed to have for him a kind of baneful fascination.

Once I saw him in the White House yard when a Wisconsin regiment was marching along. The special thing that attracted my attention was that, as they were passing along, he shed tears.

When he was in Cincinnati, and made the speech to which I referred a moment ago, some of the younger Republicans called at his rooms at the Burnett House. They sent downstairs for a box of cigars and a bottle of whisky. In some way they neglected the matter, and the whisky was charged to Mr. Lincoln in his hotel bill. This displeased him very much. There was considerable correspondence between him and the young Republicans about the matter. I saw some of his letters, and I can only say that I have a general impression that they were well written and strictly to the point. The fact was that he did not know anything about the liquor, and the parties referred to had had it all to themselves. When Lincoln became President, the recollection of this incident was anything but pleasant to the Republican gentlemen who were connected with it. They were good enough fellows personally, but, as members of the reigning political party, knowing that the experience had been exceedingly unpleasant to Mr. Lincoln, they doubtless many a time wished that the incident had never occurred, and hoped for the time when other and more important matters would crowd it out of Mr. Lincoln's recollection.

It is a curious fact that my correspondent during the Springfield Convention in 1860 was Henry Villard, afterward the wealthy railroad man. I employed him for ten years, and he was a very good newspaper man. His letters from Springfield were exceptionally good and indicated pretty plainly Mr. Lincoln's views. He sent me a manuscript editorial that Mr. Lincoln had written for the Springfield *Journal* after he was elected President. It had been strongly contended by some that Lincoln should take into his Cabinet some men who were not Republicans. This letter was written in Lincoln's quaint style, and, in a hypothetical way, showed that he could only take for his Cabinet advisers those who affiliated with the Republican Party.

BROOKLYN, N. Y.

HOW LINCOLN WAS WARNED OF THE BALTIMORE ASSASSINATION PLOT.

HOW HE ENTERED WASHINGTON.

BY FREDERICK W. SEWARD,

Author of the "Life of Wm. H. Seward."

The most important and interesting recollection I have of President Lincoln is in regard to the warning I carried to him of the plot to assassinate him in Baltimore. The story of this event is reproduced from my Life of Secretary Seward.

I was in the gallery of the Senate Chamber shortly after noon one Thursday, in February, 1861, when one of the pages touched my elbow, and told me that Senator Seward wished to see me immediately. Going down, I met him in the lobby. He handed me a letter he had just written to Mr. Lincoln, enclosing a note from General Scott. He said:

"Whether this story is well founded or not, Mr. Lincoln ought to know of it at once. But I know of no reason to doubt it. General Scott is impressed with the belief that the danger is real. Colonel Stone has facilities for knowing, and is not apt to exaggerate. I want you to go by the first train. Find Mr. Lincoln wherever he is. Let no one else know your errand. I have written him that I think he should change his arrangements, and pass through Baltimore at a different hour. I know it may occasion some embarrassment, and, perhaps, some ill-natured talk. Nevertheless, I would strongly advise him to do it."

The train, a tedious one, brought me into Philadelphia about ten o'clock at night. I had learned from the newspapers and the conversation of my fellow-passengers that the party of the President-elect would spend the night at the Continental Hotel, where he would be serenaded.

Arriving at the hotel I found Chestnut Street crowded with people, gay with lights, and echoing with music and hurrahs. Within, the halls and stairways were packed, and the brilliantly lighted parlors were filled with ladies and gentlemen who had come to "pay their respects." A buzz of animated conversation pervaded the throng, and, in its centre, presentations to the President-elect appeared to be going on. Clearly, this was no time for the delivery of a confidential message. I turned into a room near the head of the stairway, which had been pointed out as that of Mr. Robert Lincoln. He was surrounded by a group of young friends. On my introducing myself, he met and greeted me with courteous warmth, and then called to Col. Ward H. Lamon, who was passing, and introduced us to each other. Colonel Lamon, taking me by the arm, proposed at once to go back into the parlor to present me to Mr. Lincoln. On my telling him that I wanted my interview to be as private and to attract as little attention as possible, the Colonel laughed and said:

"Then I think I had better take you to his bedroom. If you don't mind waiting there, you'll be sure to meet him, for he has got to go there some time to-night; and it is the only place I know of where he will be likely to be alone."

This was the very opportunity I desired. Thanking the Colonel, I sat and waited for an hour or more in the quiet room that was in such contrast with the bustle outside. Presently Colonel Lamon called me, and we met Mr. Lincoln, who was coming down the hall. I had never before seen him; but the campaign portraits had made his face quite familiar. I could not but notice how accurately they had copied his features, and how totally they had omitted his careworn look, and his pleasant, kindly smile. After a few words of friendly greeting, with inquiries about my father and matters in Washington, he sat down by the table under the gaslight to peruse the letter I had brought. Although its contents were of a somewhat startling nature, he made no exclamation, and I saw no sign of surprise in his face. After reading it carefully through, he again held it to the light and deliberately read it through a second time. Then, after musing a moment, he looked up and asked:

"Did you hear anything about the way this information was obtained? Do you know anything about how they got it?"

No; I had known nothing in regard to it till that morning, when called down by my father from the Senate gallery.

"Your father and General Scott do not say who they think are concerned in it. Do you think they know?"

On that point, too, I could give no additional information, further than my impression that my father's knowledge of it was limited to what had been communicated to him by Colonel Stone, in whose statements he had implicit confidence.

"Did you hear any names mentioned? Did you, for instance, ever hear anything said about such a name as Pinkerton?"

No; I had heard no such name in connection with the matter — no name at all, in fact, except those of General Scott and Colonel Stone.

He thought a moment, and then said:

"I may as well tell you why I ask. There were stories or rumors some time ago, before I left home, about people who were intending to do me a mischief. I never attached much importance to them — never wanted to believe any such thing. So I never would do anything about them in the way of taking precautions and the like. Some of my friends, though, thought differently — Judd and others; and without my knowledge they employed a detective to look into the matter. It seems he has occasionally reported what he found; and only to-day, since we arrived at this house, he brought this story, or something similar to it, about an attempt on my life in the confusion and hurly-burly of the reception at Baltimore."

"Surely, Mr. Lincoln," said I, "that is a strange corroboration of the news I bring you."

He smiled and shook his head.

"That is exactly why I was asking you about the names. If different persons, not knowing of each other's work, have been pursuing separate clues that led to the same result, why, then it shows there may be something in it; but if this is only one story, filtered through two channels, and reaching me in two ways, then that doesn't make it any stronger. Don't you see?"

The logic was unanswerable; but I asserted my strong belief that the two investigations had been conducted independently of each other, and urged that there was enough of probability to make it prudent to adopt the suggestion, and make the slight change in hour and train which would avoid all risk.

After a little further discussion of the subject Mr. Lincoln rose and said: "Well, we haven't got to decide it to-night anyway, and I see it is getting late." Then, noticing that I looked disappointed at his reluctance to regard the warning, he said, kindly: "You need not think I will not consider it well. I shall think it over carefully, and try to decide it right; and I will let you know in the morning."

At the breakfast table the next day the papers had the report of Mr. Lincoln's remarks on raising the flag at Independence Hall early that morning. One sentence in them had a deeper meaning than his auditors guessed. Adverting to the principle embodied in the Declaration of Independence, he said:

"If this country cannot be saved without giving up that principle, I was about to say, I would rather be assassinated on the spot than surrender it."

Shortly after breakfast Colonel Lamon met me in the hall, and, taking me aside, said that Mr. Lincoln had concluded to do as he had been advised. He would change his plan so as to pass through Baltimore at a different hour from that announced. I hastened to the telegraph office and sent to my father a word, previously agreed upon, on receiving which he would understand that his advice had been taken.

Accordingly he was at the railroad station in Washington on Saturday morning, with E. B. Washburne, of Illinois, when Mr. Lincoln and Colonel Lamon, very much to the surprise of all the bystanders, got out of the night train from Philadelphia.

Writing home that day, Seward said:

"February 23d.

"I was advised on Thursday morning of a plot in Baltimore to assassinate the President-elect on his expected arrival there to-day. I sent Fred to apprise him of it. After Fred had done this, and induced a change in Mr. Lincoln's program, he went to New York to meet Anna and bring her here this evening.

"The President-elect arrived *incog.* at six this morning. I met him at the depot; and after breakfast introduced him to the President and Cabinet, and then I proceeded with him to call on General Scott. After that we rode an hour. I met him again at half-past one. He is very cordial and kind toward me — simple, natural and agreeable."

NEW YORK CITY.

F

THE CAREER OF ABRAHAM LINCOLN.

HIS CHARACTER AS A MAN — HIS PLACE IN HISTORY.

BY THE HON. GEORGE S. BOUTWELL,

Ex-Secretary of the Treasury.

There are two aspects in which Mr. Lincoln may be considered — his character as a man and his place as a historical personage.

In the thirty years since the death of Mr. Lincoln more has been written and spoken of him and of his doings than was ever written and spoken of any other American in the same period of time.

Of Mr. Lincoln's predecessors, Washington and Franklin occupy the largest space in the historical and biographical literature of the country; but in these thirty years the name, career and fame of Mr. Lincoln have given occasion for a volume of such writings quite equal in magnitude to all that has been written of either Washington or Franklin during the century which is now closing.

This peculiarity in the posthumous fame of Mr. Lincoln is realized most distinctly when we consider that his official life was embraced in the brief period of six years, while the distinguished services of Washington and the public career of Franklin alike covered the larger part of a half century.

The writers of books and essays have not created the popular interest in whatever relates to Mr. Lincoln, although these writings may have extended the interest and intensified its force. First of all, there was in the life and conversation of Mr. Lincoln a line of action and thought which attracted the "plain people," as the masses were characterized by him; and, therefore, whatever relates to Mr. Lincoln appeals to those masses, who, in America, constitute the main body of readers. In his life there was much of pathetic interest, and his tragic death raised him to the rank of a martyr in the cause of liberty.

Thus in his life and in his death, Mr. Lincoln was an attractive personality; but his chief title to enduring fame must rest upon his service, his pre-eminent service, in the causes of liberty and the Union. It is not enough to say that in his office as President the opportunity came to him to save the Union and to emancipate millions from slavery. Another man as President might have done as much; but Mr. Lincoln so conducted affairs during the period of the War that no stain rests upon him, so conducted affairs that the nation is not called upon to make explanations, nor to invent apologies.

In the methods and agencies for the prosecution of the War, in the command of the armies, in the conduct of our foreign relations, in the various projects for negotiations with the rebel authorities, in emancipation, and in the measures leading up to emancipation, he was the subject of harsh criticisms, always by Democrats, and not infrequently, and often in public, by Republicans, and by leading Republicans.

In the year 1864 a hostile manifesto was issued by

discontented Republicans, whose power, however, was exhausted by the doings of the Convention which assembled at Cleveland and nominated Fremont and Cochrane for President and Vice-President of the United States. With that nomination the power of the dissentients came to an end, and without much delay the candidates retired from the field.

Now after a third of a century, and when there is a universal acclaim of praise, it is difficult for the survivors of Mr. Lincoln's contemporaries, and it may be impossible for the newer generations, to realize the fact that Mr. Lincoln was the subject of vigorous, unreasoning criticism from his political associates, and of degrading personal assaults from his political opponents.

Mr. Lincoln was not indifferent to those criticisms and assaults: but they wrought no change in his plans or general policy, nor did they provoke in him any disposition to retaliate upon his critics and opponents. Nor did he reply to the attacks made upon his policy except when those attacks imperilled the fortunes of the country.

Of this character was his letter in regard to the arrest of Vallandigham, and his letter in which he announced his purpose to save the Union either with or without slavery. These attacks were not, at his instance, the subjects of conversation, and they produced no apparent change in his countenance, or methods, or facility for business. There was, however, at all times, when not engaged in conversation, a sadness of expression in Mr. Lincoln's countenance which was truly pathetic. This expression was not induced, however, by the War and the responsibilities of office.

It was observed at Springfield, in June, 1860, when the President of the Chicago Convention made the formal announcement to Mr. Lincoln of his nomination for the office of President of the United States. He replied in a brief, formal, solemn speech. The expression of his countenance was that which it wore, when at rest, during the remainder of his life.

On the first day of August, 1862, there was a meeting at the east front of the Capitol, ostensibly in commemoration of emancipation in the British West Indies. At that meeting Mr. Lincoln made a speech, and it was devoted, chiefly, to a vindication of the administration from the charge that there had been neglect in the support given to McClellan either in men or in the supplies of war.

Again, in the early part of May, 1864, I had occasion to observe the evidence of the fact that he was not indifferent to the criticisms that had been made upon him, and especially was he not indifferent to the criticisms touching his treatment of McClellan, who, at a time, covering the year 1861 and the largest part of the year 1862, was the idol of the army and the hope of the country.

When General Grant was about to move against Lee, the President wrote a letter to Grant, in which he said, among other things, that he neither knew nor wished to know his plan of operations; but he tendered his good wishes and promised every aid which the Government could furnish.

In reply, General Grant did not unfold his plan, but in the fullest manner he expressed his satisfaction with the support that he had received, and he then said in substance, "If the results shall be less favorable than I hope and the Government expects, the fault will not be the fault of the administration."

Soon after the receipt of General Grant's letter, at an

interview with Mr. Lincoln, he took the two letters from a pigeonhole over his table and read them to me, and with special interest, as I thought, from the fact that General Grant's conduct was in contrast with the conduct of General McClellan in similar circumstances.

For several months Mr. Lincoln was subject to the assaults of the friends and of the enemies of General McClellan. For several months he retained McClellan in command and after he had reached the conclusion that his retirement was inevitable. Such was his opinion in July, 1862, certainly as soon as the Peninsula campaign was ended; and it is probable that his opinion became unalterable upon the receipt of McClellan's letter from Harrison's Landing, dated July 7th, 1862.

In that letter McClellan said:

"The responsibility of determining, declaring and supporting such civil and military policy, and of directing the whole course of national affairs in regard to the Rebellion, must now be assumed and exercised by you, or our cause will be lost."

To this advice he added the declaration that "neither confiscation of property, political execution of persons, territorial organization of States, nor forcible abolition of slavery, should be contemplated for a moment."

In furtherance of these views McClellan said:

"You will require a commander-in-chief of the Army, one who possesses your confidence, understands your views, and who is competent to execute your orders. . . . I do not ask that place for myself. I am willing to serve you in such position as you may assign me, and I will do so as faithfully as ever subordinate served superior."

The suggestions and recommendations of this letter were such that Mr. Lincoln could not fail to treat it as a proposition for the establishment of a dictatorship, with McClellan at the head of the army.

McClellan wrote under the impression that all other means of saving the Union would prove ineffectual. That he contemplated a permanent change in the character of the Government is in a high degree improbable. Assuming honesty of purpose, it showed the weakness of the man. His standing with Mr. Lincoln was undermined fatally by that letter.

Upon the reorganization of the army, following Pope's defeat, the command was given to McClellan, but reluctantly, and in the presence of many grave doubts.

McClellan was still the idol of the army, and the situation was so serious that the wishes of the army could not be disregarded.

The spell with which the army was bound to McClellan was broken by the battle of Antietam. At the close of the day he had a reserve on the left bank of the Antietam River that had taken no part in the contest, quite equal in number to the losses sustained. His failure to pursue the enemy destroyed the confidence of the army, and henceforth there was no obstacle in the removal of McClellan from the command.

The suggestions of McClellan, whatever may have been the interpretation given to the language employed, could have produced no impression upon Mr. Lincoln, beyond the conviction that the writer was deficient in those qualities that are essential to leadership when the trend of events is adverse.

To one opinion, to one purpose, Mr. Lincoln adhered from the beginning to the end. The Union was to be saved by the exercise of power within the scope of the Constitution. Hence he annulled the emancipation proclamation of Fremont and Hunter; hence he rebuked Hooker for the remark that the President ought to proclaim himself Dictator; and hence he delayed the Proclamation of Emancipation until it could be defended on the ground of military necessity.

I turn aside from Mr. Lincoln to mention an incident which opened to General Hooker his career in the army. In the month of May, 1861, I was with Senator Sumner at his lodgings at the corner of F and Thirteenth Streets, Washington, when a stranger was announced, who gave his name as Hooker, from California. He was of middle age, tall, of florid complexion, and in dress and general appearance there were indications of poverty rather than wealth. He said that he was born at Northampton, Mass., that he was educated at West Point, that he had served in the army, and that he wished for the colonelcy of a Massachusetts regiment. In furtherance of his application he said that if he could get a regiment, he would come to the command of the army and take Richmond. It might seem that such an exhibition of conceit would have precluded him from appointment; but men of military education and experience were not to be found, and without much delay he received a commission as brigadier-general.

When he came to the command of the Army of the Potomac the realization of his vain, wild boast seemed possible. His resignation on the eve of the battle of Gettysburg was due to his vanity, which led him to act before he had knowledge of the facts.

Hooker was in Washington Thursday of the week before the battle, and at a conference with the President and the Secretary of War, it was agreed to hold Harper's Ferry, which, the year before, had been surrendered with great loss of men and materials of war. Upon his return to headquarters General Hooker changed his opinion, and, without reporting to the Secretary of War, he ordered General Wilson to evacuate the post and join the main army. This order Wilson transmitted to the Secretary of War. Mr. Stanton, assuming that there had been an error in the dispatches, or a misunderstanding, countermanded Hooker's order. Thereupon Hooker, without seeking for an explanation, resigned his command. It was then that Mr. Lincoln exhibited his predominant quality of firmness and decision under trying circumstances. Hooker's resignation was accepted, and Meade was at once placed in command.

Mr. Lincoln possessed a quality called sagacity, but which in him was wisdom, or a near approach to what passes for wisdom in man.

Mr. Seward's letter of May, 1861, to Mr. Adams, in regard to the recognition by Great Britain of belligerent rights in the Confederate Government, with Mr. Lincoln's emendations, is a well-known historical document.

Mr. Lincoln changed the pivot on which the communication was made to turn. In the letter, as it came from the hands of Mr. Seward, Great Britain was arraigned upon the allegation that the proclamation was without due authority in usage or in the law of nations, and that it was a proceeding for which we might seek compensation or resort to retaliation.

As an indication of his skill, which was manifested in many of the corrections made, I mention the fact that he changed the word *wrongful* to the word *hurtful*. The word *wrongful* looks to the motive and it implies a degree of moral turpitude; while the word *hurtful* relates solely to consequences and avoids all reflection upon the motive of the actor.

When Mr. Lincoln was called to the work of criticising that important State paper, he had been three months only in office, he had had no experience in diplomacy, and his life as a lawyer, limited as his services were to topics of local and domestic concern, was in no sense a preparation for the delicate duty which he then and thus performed. In this connection the fate of that important paper may have interest.

During General Grant's first term the Seward draft, which contained Mr. Lincoln's emendations, was brought to a Cabinet meeting by Mr. Fish, then Secretary of State. The interest in the paper was so great that I proposed to have it photographed by the photographer of the Treasury. This was done. A few copies, not more than twelve, I think, were prepared, and the negative was destroyed. A copy was taken by each member of the Cabinet, and the extra copies, with the original, were taken by Mr. Fish. While there was no injunction of secrecy, I think it was understood that the photographs were not to be given to the public.

In April, 1886, there appeared in the *North American Review* a facsimile of the paper. As there were some differences between the facsimile and the photograph in my possession, I made application at the State Department for the original, that I might trace the error. I was informed that the original had disappeared.

In 1864, Mr. Chase was nominated for Chief Justice of the United States. After the nomination was made I took occasion to say to the President that I was glad Mr. Chase had been nominated. He then said: "There are three reasons why he should be appointed and one reason why he should not be. In the first place he occupies a larger space in the public mind, with reference to the office, than any other person. Then we want a man who will sustain the Legal Tender Act and the Proclamation of Emancipation. We cannot ask a candidate what he would do; and if we did and he should answer, we should only despise him for it. But he wants to be President, and if he doesn't give that up it will be a great injury to him and a great injury to me. He can never be President." Soon after the arrival of Mr. Lincoln in Washington, near the end of February, 1861, the Massachusetts delegation in the Peace Congress called upon him and recommended Mr. Chase for the Treasury Department.

In reply, he said: "From what I know and hear I think Mr. Chase is about one hundred and fifty to any other man's hundred for that place."

During the War there was a concerted movement in Congress to secure the retirement of Mr. Seward from the Cabinet. The leaders were the friends of Mr. Chase. It is probable that Mr. Lincoln had early, daily and accurate information of the movement.

Finally a delegation of the discontented called upon Mr. Lincoln and presented their views. He was prepared fully, and without intimating a purpose to resist their recommendation, he said, in substance, that his Cabinet was organized upon the idea of recognizing the various interests in the party that were represented at Chicago, and that the change suggested would involve its reorganization. Thus by a sentence was the movement controlled and the controversy ended.

Mr. Lincoln had critical tastes and a keen relish for good writings, both of poetry and prose. I recall a conversation in which he eulogized Fisher Ames as an orator, and recited an extract from his oration on the

Jay Treaty. It was known to those who were near President Lincoln that he was a careful student of the War maps and that he had daily knowledge of the position and strength of our armies. I recall the incident of meeting him on the steps of the Executive mansion at about eleven o'clock in the evening when the news had but just then reached the War Department that Grant had crossed Black River and that the army was in the rear of Vicksburg. The President was returning from the War Office with a copy of the dispatch in his hand. I said: "Mr. President, have you any news?" He said in reply: "Come in, and I will tell you."

After reading the dispatch he turned to his maps and traced the line of Grant's movements, as he then understood and comprehended those movements. That night the President became cheerful, his voice took on a new tone — a tone of relief, of exhilaration — and it was evident that his faith in our ultimate success had been changed into absolute confidence.

In the dark days of 1862 he had never despaired of the Republic. When others faltered he was undismayed. He put aside the suggestion of Mr. Seward that he should surrender the chief prerogatives of his office; he rebuked the suggestion of General Hooker that he should declare himself Dictator; and he treated with silent contempt the advice of General McClellan from Harrison's Landing, in July, 1862, that the President should put himself at the head of military and civil affairs, with a general in command of the army on whom he could rely, and thus assume the dictatorship of the Republic. He asserted for himself every prerogative which the Constitution and the laws conferred upon him, and he declined to assume any power not warranted by the title of the office which he held. He was resolute in his purpose to perform every duty that devolved upon him, but he declared that the responsibility of preserving the Government rested upon the people.

In the further attempt to deal with Mr. Lincoln as a historical personage, it is to be said that his services and fame are so identified with the organization, doings and character of the Republican Party, that something of the history of that party is the necessary incident of every presentation of his services and of his claim to rank among the leading statesmen of modern times.

In a very important sense Mr. Lincoln may be regarded as the founder of the Republican Party. He was its leader in the first successful national contests, and it was during his administration, as President, that the policy of the party was developed and its capacity for the business of government established.

The Republican Party gave to Mr. Lincoln the opportunity for the services on which his fame rests, and the fame of Mr. Lincoln is the especial inheritance of the Republican Party. His eulogy is its encomium, and, therefore, when we set forth the character and services of Mr. Lincoln we set forth as well the claims of the Republican Party to the confidence and gratitude of the country and the favorable opinion of mankind.

If it could be assumed that for the Republican Party the Book of Life is already closed, it is yet true that that party is a historical party, and Mr. Lincoln a historical personage; not less so than Cromwell, Napoleon or Washington, and all without the glamour that magnifies the careers of successful military chieftains.

Of Mr. Lincoln's predecessors in the Presidential office, two only, Washington and Jefferson, can be regarded as historical personages in a large view of history. The author of the Declaration of Independence is so identified with the history of the country that that history cannot outlast his name and fame. As the author of that Declaration, and as the exponent of new and advanced ideas of government, Jefferson was elected to the Presidency; but his administrations were not marked by distinguished ability, nor were they attended or followed by results which have commanded the favorable opinion of succeeding generations. Washington had no competitors. The gratitude of his countrymen rebuked all rivalries. He was borne to the Presidency by a vote quite unanimous, and he was supported in the discharge of his duties by a confidence not limited by the boundaries of the Republic.

It is only a moderate exaggeration to say that when Mr. Lincoln was nominated for the Presidency he was an unknown man; he had performed no important public service; his election was not due to personal popularity, nor to the strength of the party that he represented, but to the divisions among his opponents.

In 1862 when eleven hostile States were not represented in the Government, the weakness of the administration was such that only a bare majority of the House of Representatives was secured, after a vigorous and aggressive campaign, on the part of the Republican Party.

Thus do the circumstances and incidents in the formative period in Mr. Lincoln's career illustrate and adorn the events that distinguish the man, the party and the country.

I am quite conscious that in an attempt to give Mr. Lincoln a conspicuous place in the ranks of historical personages I am to encounter a large and intelligent public opinion which claims that distance in time, and even distance in space, are the necessary conditions of a wise and permanent decision. The representatives of that opinion maintain that contemporaries are too near the object of vision, that to them a comprehensive view is impossible, and that the successive generations of one's countrymen may be influenced by inherited passions, or by transmitted traditions.

Some of Mr. Lincoln's contemporaries remain, and one and all we are his countrymen, and in advance we may accept, joyfully, any qualification of our opinions that may be made in other lands, or by other ages, if qualifying facts shall be disclosed hereafter. Nearness of observation and a knowledge of the events with which Mr. Lincoln's public life was identified, may have given to his associates and coworkers opportunities for a sound judgment that were not possessed by contemporary critics and historians of other lands, and that the students of future times will be unable to command.

The recent practical improvements in the art of printing, the telegraph and the railway have furnished to mankind the means of reaching safe conclusions on all matters of importance, including biography and history, with a celerity and certainty which to former ages were unknown. In these thirty years since the death of Mr. Lincoln there has been a wonderful exposition of the events and circumstances of the stupendous contest in which he was the leading figure.

Of the minor incidents of Mr. Lincoln's career, time and research may disclose many facts not now known, which may lend coloring to a character whose main features, however, cannot be changed by time nor by criticism. The nature of Mr. Lincoln's services we can comprehend, but their value will be more clearly realized and more highly appreciated by posterity. As to the nature of those services the judgment of his own generation is final — it can never be reversed. Indeed, it may be asserted of historical personages, generally, that the judgment of contemporaries is never reversed. Attempts have been made to reverse the judgment of contemporaries in the cases of Judas Iscariot, Henry VIII and Shakespeare, but all these attempts have failed, and most signally. In our own country there have been no reversals. Modifications of opinion there have been — growth in some cases, decrease in others; but absolute change in none. The country has grown toward Hamilton and away from Jefferson. They are, however, as they were at the beginning of the century, the representatives of antagonistic ideas of government; but their common patriotism is, as yet, unchallenged.

It is the fate of those who take an active part in public affairs to be misjudged during their lives, but death softens the asperities of political and religious controversies and tempers the judgments of those who survive.

Franklin, Washington, Jefferson, Jackson, Clay and Webster, are to this generation what they were to the survivors of the generation to which they belonged, respectively.

Mr. Calhoun has suffered by the attempt to make a practical application of his ideas of government, but the nature and dangerous character of those ideas were as fully understood at the time of his death as they are at the present moment.

I pass over as unworthy of further serious consideration, the detractions and attacks, sometimes thoughtless and sometimes malicious, to which Mr. Lincoln was subject during his administration. He made explanations and replies to those detractions and attacks only when they seemed to put in peril the fortunes of the country; but when he made replies there were none found, either among his political friends or his political enemies, who were capable of making an adequate answer.

On this point we may consult his correspondence in regard to the transit of troops through Maryland, in regard to the invasion of Virginia in case the city of Washington should be attacked or menaced from the right bank of the Potomac, in regard to the suspension of the privilege of the writ of *habeas corpus*, in regard to the arrest of Vallandigham, in regard to our foreign relations, and, finally, we may consult his numerous papers in regard to the subjects for which the war should be prosecuted, and the means as well by which it could be prosecuted.

We must realize that this work was done by a man called to the head of an administration that had no predecessor, to the management of a Government distracted by civil war, its navy scattered, its treasury bankrupted, its foreign relations disturbed by a traditional and almost universal hostility to Republican institutions, and all while he was threatened constantly by an adverse public judgment in that section of country on which his hopes rested exclusively.

We must realize, also, that Mr. Lincoln had had little or no experience on the statesmanship side of his political career; that as an attorney and advocate he had dealt only with local and municipal law; that he had been separated by circumstances from a practical acquaintance with maritime and international jurisprudence;

and yet, consider further, with what masterful force he rebuked timid or untrustworthy friends who would have abandoned the contest, and consented to the independence of the seceding States in the vain hope that time might aid in the recovery of that which by pusillanimity had been lost; with what serenity of manner he put aside the suggestion of Mr. Seward that war should be declared against France and Spain, as a means of quieting domestic difficulties which even then were represented by contending armies; with what calmness of mind he laid aside Mr. Greeley's letter of despair and self-reproach of July 29th, 1861, and proceeded in the preparation of his program of military operations from every base line of the armies of the Republic; with what skill and statesmanlike foresight he corrected Mr. Seward's letter to Mr. Adams in regard to the recognition by Great Britain of the belligerent character of the Confederate States; and, finally, consider with what firmness and wisdom he annulled the proclamation of Fremont and Hunter and reserved to himself, exclusively, the right and the power to deal with the subject of slavery in the rebellious States.

In what other time, to what other ruler have questions of such importance been presented and under circumstances so difficult? And to what other ruler can we assign the ability to have met and to have managed successfully all the difficult problems of the Civil War?

It cannot be claimed for Mr. Lincoln that he had had any instructive military experience, or that he had any technical knowledge of the military art; but it may be said with truth that his correspondence with the generals of the army and his memoranda touching military operations indicate the presence of a military quality or faculty which in actual service might have been developed into talent or even genius.

His letter to General McClellan, of October 13th, 1862, is at once a memorable evidence and a striking illustration of his faculty on the military side of his career. He sets forth specifically and in the alternative two plans of operation, and with skill and caustic severity he contrasts the inactivity and delays of General McClellan with the vigor of policy and celerity of movement which characterized the campaign on the part of the enemy.

He brings in review the facts that General McClellan's army was superior in numbers, in equipment and in all the material of war. In conclusion the President said: "This letter is not to be considered as an order"; and yet it is difficult to reconcile the continued inactivity of General McClellan with the claim that he was a patriotic, not to say an active supporter of the Union.

With that letter in hand a patriotic and sensitive commander would have acted at once upon one of the alternatives presented by the President, or he would have formed a plan of campaign for himself and ordered a movement without delay, or he would have asked the President to relieve him from the command of the army.

No one of these courses was adopted, and the policy of inactivity was continued until General Lee regained the vantage ground which he had abandoned when he crossed the Potomac into Maryland. It is at this point and in this juncture of affairs that the policy of Mr. Lincoln requires the explanation of a friendly critic. The historian of the future may wonder at the procrastination of the President; he may criticise his conduct in neglecting to relieve McClellan when it was apparent that he would not avail himself of the advantages that were presented by the victory of Antietam.

The explanation is this, in substance: The army of the Potomac had been created under the eye of McClellan, and the officers and men were devoted to him as their leader and chief. They had had but slight opportunities for instituting comparison between him and other military men. After Pope's defeat the army had been unanimous, substantially, in the opinion that McClellan should be again placed in command. The President had yielded to that opinion and against his own judgment. Having thus yielded, it was wise to test McClellan until the confidence of the army and the country should have become impaired, or, otherwise, as the President hoped would be the result — until McClellan should satisfy the administration and the army that he was equal to the duty imposed upon him. Hence the delay until the fifth of November, when McClellan was relieved, finally, from the military service of the country. Of the officers who successively were at the head of the Army of the Potomac, no one ever possessed the full confidence of Mr. Lincoln until General Grant assumed that command in person.

Turning again to the civil side of Mr. Lincoln's administration we may consider the steps by which he led the opinion of the country up to the point where the nation was ready to accept the abolition of slavery in the States engaged in the Rebellion.

History must soon address itself to generations of Americans who will have had no knowledge of the institution of slavery as an existing fact. Indeed, at the present time more than one half of the citizens of the United States have no memory of the era when slavery was the dominating force in the politics of the country; when it was interwoven in the daily domestic life of the inhabitants of fifteen States; when it muzzled the press, perverted the Scriptures, compelled the pulpit to become its apologist, and when successive generations of statesmen were "brought down on an equality of servitude" before an irresponsible and untitled oligarchy.

As early as the year 1839, Mr. Clay estimated the value of the slaves at one thousand and two hundred million dollars, and upon the same basis their value in 1860 exceeded two thousand million.

This statement conveys only an inadequate idea of the power of slavery, and it presents only an imperfect view of the difficulties which confronted Mr. Lincoln in 1861 and 1862. Delaware, Maryland, West Virginia, Kentucky and Missouri were slave States, and all of them, with the exception of Delaware, were hesitating between secession and the cause of the Union. They were in favor of the Union, if slavery could be saved with the Union; but it was doubtful in all the year 1861 whether those States could be held to the "Lincoln Government," as it was derisively called, if the abolition of slavery were a recognized part of our public policy.

Nor is this even yet a full statement of the difficulties which confronted Mr. Lincoln. With varying degrees of intensity the Democratic Party of the North sympathized with the South, and arraigned Mr. Lincoln and the Republican Party for all the evils that the country was called to endure. During the entire period of the War New York, Ohio and Indiana were doubtful States, and Indiana was kept in line only by the active and desperate fidelity of Oliver P. Morton.

In the presence of these difficulties Mr. Lincoln recommended the purchase of all the slaves in the States not in rebellion; then he suggested the deportation of the manumitted slaves and the free blacks to Central America, and for that purpose an appropriation was made. Then came a proposition to give pecuniary aid to States that might make provision for the abolition of slavery. These propositions were not acted upon nor accepted by the States, and then came the statute of July, 1862, by which slaves captured and the slaves of all persons engaged in the Rebellion were declared to be free.

It is not probable that Mr. Lincoln entertained the opinion that these measures, one or all, would secure the abolition of slavery; but they gave to the slaveholders of the border States an opportunity to obtain compensation for the loss of their slaves, and the pendency of these propositions occupied the attention of the country while the formative processes were going on, which matured, finally, in the conviction that slavery and the Union could no longer coexist.

In the same period of time the country reached the conclusion that separation and continuous peace were impossible. The alternative was this: A division of the Union, slavery in the South and a condition of permanent border warfare; or, on the other hand, a Union of States, domestic peace, a Government of imperial power, with equality of citizenship in the States and an equality of States in the Union.

Thus his measures, which were at once measures of expediency and of delay, prepared the public mind to receive his monitory proclamation of September, 1862. In that time the border States had come to realize the fact that the Negroes were no longer valuable as property, and they therefore, though reluctantly, accepted emancipation as the means of ending the controversy.

To the Republicans of the North, the Proclamation was a welcome message. To the Democrats it was a result which they had predicted and against which they had in vain protested. But the controversy over slavery would not have ended with the Proclamation nor with the surrender at Appomattox.

Slavery existed in the States that had not engaged in the Rebellion, and the legality of the Emancipation Proclamation might be drawn in question in the courts. One thing more was wanted — *an Amendment to the Constitution abolishing slavery everywhere within the jurisdiction of the United States.*

The preliminary resolution was secured after a protracted struggle in Congress, and the result was due, in a pre-eminent degree, to the personal and official influence of Mr. Lincoln. In one phrase it may be said that every power of his office was exerted to secure in the Thirty-eighth Congress the passage of the resolution by which the proposed amendment was submitted to the States.

Mr. Lincoln did not live to see the consummation of his great undertaking in the cause of freedom; but the work of ratification by the States was accelerated by his death, and on the eighteenth day of December, 1865, Mr. Seward, then Secretary of State, made proclamation that the amendments had been ratified by twenty-seven of the thirty-six States then composing the Union, and that slavery and involuntary servitude were from that time and forever forth impossible within our limits.

Our example has wrought the abolition of slavery in Brazil and in the colonies of Spain and Portugal; it has led to the extermination of the transatlantic slave trade, and it has been an inspiration to the nations of Europe in their efforts to destroy the traffic in human beings on the continent of Africa.

There is an aspect of Mr. Lincoln's career which must attract attention and command sympathy. His loneliness in his office and in the performance of his duties is deeply pathetic. It is true that Congress accepted and endorsed his measures, generally, as they were presented from time to time; but there were bitter complaints on account of his delays on the slavery question, and not infrequently doubts were expressed as to the sincerity of his avowed opinions. There were little intrigues in Congress, personal rivalries in the Cabinet, and aspirations in regard to the succession.

The commanders of the Army of the Potomac, from McDowell to Meade, each and all had failed to win victories, or they had failed to secure the reasonable advantages of victories won.

Mr. Lincoln's supremacy, not of official position merely, but of character as well, was shown in his preliminary statement when he was about to read the Proclamation of Emancipation to the members of his Cabinet. He was then about to take the most important step ever taken by a President of the United States, and yet he informed the men, and the only men whose opinions he could command, by virtue of his office, that the main question was not open for discussion; that that question had been by him already decided, and that suggestions from them would be received only in reference to the formality of the document.

Our estimate of Mr. Lincoln is not lowered by the fact that he chose to act upon his own judgment in a matter of the supremest gravity, and in relation to which, and from the nature of the case, the sole responsibility was upon him. On the great question of the abolition of slavery he had formed a definite conclusion — a conclusion on which he could act, and on which he did act neither prematurely nor after unnecessary delay. The Proclamation was issued when the exigencies of the War justified its issue as a military necessity, and when, as a concurrent fact, the public mind was first prepared to receive it and to give to the measure the requisite support.

Mr. Lincoln prepared the way for the reorganization of the Government upon a new basis. Under him the old order of things was overthrown, and the introduction of a new order became possible. Through his agency the Constitution of the United States has been brought into harmony with the Declaration of Independence.

The system of slavery has perished. The institutions of the country, in a good degree, are reconciled with the principles of freedom, as applied in the affairs of government; and in these changes we find additional guaranties for the perpetuity of the Union.

Every just eulogy on Mr. Lincoln is a continuing encomium of the Republican Party. By the election of 1860 he became the head of that party, and during the four years and more of his official life he never claimed to be better nor wiser than the party with which he was identified.

From first to last he had the full confidence of the army and of the masses of the voters in the Republican Party; and of that confidence Mr. Lincoln was always assured. Hence he was able to meet the aspirations of rivals and the censures of the disappointed with a good degree of composure. To the honor of the masses of the

Republican Party it can be said that they never faltered in their devotion to the President, and in that devotion and in the fidelity of the President to the party, were the foundations laid on which the present greatness of the country rests; for great the country is, whatever may be our opinion of the causes, or our estimate of the intensity of the calamities that now afflict us.

The measure of gratitude due to Mr. Lincoln and to the Republican Party may be estimated by a comparison of the condition of the country when that party accepted power in March, 1861, with its condition in 1885 and 1893 when it yielded the administration to the successors of the men who had well-nigh wrecked the Government in a former generation. Speaking for the Republican Party we may say, "we found the Union a mass of sand; we left it a structure of granite. We found the Union a byword among the nations of the earth; we left it illustrious and envied for the exhibition of warlike powers; for the development of the nation's industrial and financial resources in times of peace; for the unwavering fidelity with which every pecuniary obligation was met; for the generous treatment measured out with an unstinted hand to the conquered foe, and, finally, for the cheerful recognition of the duty resting upon the country to enfranchise, to raise up, to recreate the millions that had been brought out of bondage."

This work was not accomplished fully in Mr. Lincoln's life; but he was the leader of ideas and policies which could have had no other proper consummation. At the end it must be said of Mr. Lincoln that he was a great man in a great place, burdened with great responsibilities, which he used for the benefit of his country and for the welfare of the human race.

Among American statesmen he is conspicuously alone. From Washington and Grant he is separated by the absence, on his part, of military service and military renown. On the statesmanship side of his career there is no one from Washington, and thence along the entire line of public men, who can be compared with him; and we may wisely commit to other ages, and perhaps to other lands, the full discussion and final decision of the relative claims of Washington and Lincoln to the first place in the list of American statesmen.

In conclusion, I repeat my estimate of Mr. Lincoln as it is registered in, or under, the corner stone of his monument at Springfield, Ill.:

"President Lincoln excelled all his contemporaries, as he also excelled most of the eminent rulers of every time, in the humanity of his nature; in the constant assertion of reason over passion and feeling; in the art of dealing with men; in fortitude, never disturbed by adversity; in capacity for delay when action was fraught with peril; in the power of immediate and resolute decision when delays were dangerous; in comprehensive judgment which forecasts the final and best opinions of nations and of posterity; and in the union of enlarged patriotism, wise philanthropy, and the highest political justice, by which he was enabled to save a nation and to emancipate a race."

FROM LIBBY PRISON.

THE SOUTH FEARED LINCOLN'S RENOMINATION.

BY GEN. NEAL DOW.

I NEVER saw Mr. Lincoln, going off to the War as I did at the beginning, and being always in the Department of the Gulf. I had no means of learning anything of what was going on in the North, being almost all the time beyond the reach of newspapers and the mails. In our Department there were but few officers who were displeased with the President for his emancipation of the slaves.

When I was in Libby Prison preparation was made to blow up the part of it which contained eleven hundred officers. Arrangements were made to do this at a moment's notice; the proof of it was abundant and conclusive. We had facilities for communication with Washington without the knowledge of the rebels. At that time there was great fear that France and England would acknowledge the Confederacy. I availed myself of my opportunities to communicate with Mr. Lincoln and assure him that eleven hundred lives could not be sacrificed to so great advantage to the country as to have us all blown up by the rebels. We were assured that we should be destroyed in that way if an attempt were made to capture Richmond, at that time almost entirely without defence. Some of our company wrote to the

Secretary of War entreating that no attempt should be made on the rebel capital.

Immediately after being exchanged for Fitz-Hugh Lee I went North, and in Washington was taken into the House of Representatives, where I was immediately surrounded by a large body of the members and business was suspended. At that time a strong effort was made in influential quarters to substitute some other candidate than Mr. Lincoln for the ensuing Presidential election. The members of the House crowded about me to know what effect such a measure would have at the South. Great was the joy of those surrounding me when I said: The rebels are now exhausted of money and men and hope; their only chance is that Mr. Lincoln may be set aside, as they would regard that as a repudiation of his policy, and are sure that peace to the Confederacy, with formal dissolution of the Union, would follow. I did not see the President, as he was absent at the moment.

PORTLAND, ME.

PRESIDENT LINCOLN'S KNOWLEDGE OF HUMAN NATURE: A CRITICAL STUDY.

BY THE HON. THOMAS L. JAMES,

Ex-Postmaster General.

It has seemed to me that Abraham Lincoln was one of those men of whom the last word can never be said. For those who have lived, doing great things for humanity, and, being dead, have left a glorious heritage to the world, are ever of fresh interest and of splendid inspiration to those who give thought to their achievements and their characters. Mr. Lincoln was one of these. A generation has passed since the country was bereaved by his untimely and bloody death; and yet there is fascination to-day in the story of his career, the study of his character, and the analysis of his qualities; and those anecdotes which are told illustrating the man have the charm of delightful romance, and are read with greater interest than the most brilliant tales of the writers of fiction.

Mr. Lincoln looked forth upon the world, as we of to-day now realize, with almost Shakespeare's eyes; and it was, perhaps, that greater quality of his, that subtle capacity to fathom the human heart, to understand its weakness and its capacities, and so understanding to be guided by them in his own direction of affairs, and in the discipline which made it possible for him in great emergencies to stand forth as a man of true greatness, which makes the consideration of him to-day as fresh, invigorating and timely as it was when those great affairs of which he was the master were occupying the country's eye.

He was essentially a poet by nature, not with that technical facility for rhythm or command of prosody by which Shakespeare was able to reveal human nature to the world with immortal sentence, and nevertheless by those homely anecdotes — most of which were of his own creation, as wide in range and as true in teaching as the Fables of Æsop — he illustrated the weaknesses and the forces of human nature with, perhaps, almost as universal a reach as did Shakespeare in his plays.

This greater quality of Mr. Lincoln's — greater in an intellectual sense — is now beginning to be understood. Years passed before even those nearest him perceived this quality; and it is probable that, as the years roll by, and critical study is given to the purely mental capacity of Mr. Lincoln, it will furnish as profound suggestion, as amazing revelation of his all-comprehending nature, as does the investigation of the works of the great dramatists. Therefore, there need be no fear that, upon the anniversaries of Mr. Lincoln's birth and death, nothing can be said of him which has not been uttered before. There will always be new suggestions, new revelations, new understandings, for of such capacity was the quality of his intellect and soul.

It was with some consciousness of this that Mr. Lincoln's associate upon the Presidential ticket, the late Vice-President Hamlin, journeyed in the dead of winter, bent with years but still of vigorous intellect, to New York City, that he might appear before the Lincoln Club on the anniversary of Lincoln's birthday, and say something which had been in his heart to say ever since, in his retirement in his distant home in Maine, he had turned to his recollections of Mr. Lincoln, in the peaceful contemplation of his old age. Mr. Hamlin, the last survivor of all those associated with Mr. Lincoln when he took the Presidency, stood before the Lincoln Club, saying that he had made the long journey that he might impress upon them a thought which had come to him, and that was that the nation should set apart the anniversary of Lincoln's birthday, that it might be inspired by a study of his character, and that able men, and plain, unlettered folk might, upon that day, give their testimony in public places of Lincoln and his service to his country.

Scholars, profound students and men of critical capacity will have abundant inspiration long after this and succeeding generations have passed away, for study into the extraordinary intellectual qualifications of this plain man of the prairies. But a greater service will be done to the American people than any that critical scholarship can furnish if, upon this and recurring anniversaries, the life and career of Mr. Lincoln are so presented that coming generations shall know what he was, what he did, and what the lessons of inspiration for the American people in these achievements are.

Thirty-four years ago last February, and only a few days after the 51st anniversary of his birthday, Mr. Lincoln stood upon the historic platform of Cooper Institute in New York. The cultured men of the metropolis had known him only through that unique repute, which his brief career, before the public eye, in the West, had furnished. Our professional men, our scholars and our clergymen had heard, through vague reports in the public prints, and through interesting sketches brought by those who had visited the West, of a lawyer of the prairies, an unconventional man, who had had no schooling, whose practice was in the rural circuit, whose companions were men not prominent in public affairs; but who had, nevertheless, met Douglas, the most impetuous, brilliant and overwhelming debater of his day, and overthrown him in a series of public addresses in those towns. They had also heard that this country lawyer, whom his friends called "Honest Abe," with patronizing suggestion, had made a speech in which he had proclaimed, before the idol of the Republicans of the East, Wm. H. Seward, had done so, the issue upon which the "Rebellion" was created and crushed. Seward, in his Rochester speech, in the summer of 1859, had declared that there was an "irrepressible conflict" between slavery and freedom in this country, and that one or the other would be victorious; and the Republicans of the East seized that laconic term "Irrepressible conflict," and made it the watch-cry of their organization. But Lincoln, two months before Mr. Seward thus crystallized the doctrine of the Republican Party, had, with finer metaphor and apter illustration, expressed the same idea; for, in his speech at Chicago, in the spring of 1859, he said in his exordium:

"A house divided against itself cannot stand. I believe this Government cannot endure half slave, half free. I do not expect the Union dissolved, I do not expect the house to fall; but I do expect it will cease to be divided. It will become all one thing, or all the other."

The politicians of the West, to whom he read this speech before he delivered it, criticised it, begging to him to make softer utterance of that truth; but he declared that it was God's truth; that the time had come for uttering it; and that the people were ready for its enunciation; and, therein, two years before he became President, he had displayed that marvellous capacity for fathoming public sentiment and of being guided by it, which was his strength during his administration.

With the repute caused by this speech in the West, Mr. Lincoln came to Cooper Union. A notable throng was gathered to hear him. The poet Bryant presided; and, in that historic second cradle of liberty, which Cooper Union is, there were gathered representatives of culture, financial power and the lofty character which makes New York of pre-eminent influence. These men eyed the tall, gaunt lawyer from the West with curious glance; and, if most of them had spoken with the truth, they would have said it was a half-humorous curiosity which brought them to that place to hear this Western lawyer; but, when he had finished that masterly address — pre-eminent in its ability, cool and remorseless in its logic, conciliatory and tender in its suggestions — no feeling of curiosity mastered that great throng, but one of profound respect and admiration, so that they asked one another, "What manner of man is this lawyer of the West, who has set forth these truths as we have never yet heard them before?" That address disclosed one of the capacities of Mr. Lincoln which we understood better afterward. It was the ability to grasp opinion as it was asserting itself among the masses of the people, and to make such perfect presentation of it as caused him to be regarded, not as a follower of opinion, but as the creator and leader of it. Often Mr. Lincoln said, "I do not lead; I only follow." But there was the genius, such as has been given to few men in this world, revealed in that following, so that it appeared like leadership.

It is this quality which those who aspire to leadership in this day and in future would do well to study. There are those who mistake their own obstinacy, deeming it but the conviction of the public; there are those who believe that, in a Republic like ours, leadership forces public opinion and does not follow it; and the political graveyards are filled with buried ambitions and crushed hopes, because of that mistake, which Mr. Lincoln never made. He had extraordinary courage; but it was not the courage of brute obstinacy or insensibility. When, a month after his inauguration, that man of supreme ability and splendid acquirements, Governor Seward, who had been chosen Secretary of State, laid before Mr. Lincoln a certain paper containing suggestions as to policy and an intimation that the President might commit to his Secretary the carrying out of that policy, Mr. Lincoln saw that the time had come when it must be shown to his Cabinet, that he could delegate no powers and responsibilities, and that he must command his administration. But it was in gentle courtesy that he took the paper from his Secretary of State, placed it in his portfolio, and, with wise and sad admonition, indicated that the policy which he proposed he would carry out; and, from that day until his death, he was the master of his official servants.

He showed courage, when, in a time of great emergency, he sent for that Western lawyer, who was not even of his political party, and asked him to enter the Cabinet as Secretary of War. There was every reason, at least personal inclination, why Mr. Lincoln should have chosen almost any other competent man than

Edward M. Stanton for that post. Stanton had been a member of Buchanan's Cabinet. Only a few years before he had met Mr. Lincoln, in the prosecution of a law case at Cincinnati; and he, with humiliating offensiveness, snubbed the country lawyer of Illinois. Yet this, and other considerations, had no more weight with Mr. Lincoln than would have been the case had they not existed. He had the courage to call a Democrat to his Cabinet, because he perceived that that man possessed those unusual qualifications which were imperative for a successful conduct of the War Department, and he knew that behind Mr. Stanton's failings of temperament, there was an absorbing love of his country and an honesty of character, such as few men possess. With Stanton he could be firm and courageous, yielding often in trifles, but masterful when there was need of it. Said Stanton to him one day: "Mr. President, I cannot carry out that order. It is improper, and I don't believe it right." And, speaking very gently, Mr. Lincoln said: "Well, I reckon, Mr. Secretary, that you will have to carry it out." "But I won't do it, Mr. President; it's all wrong." "I guess you will have to do it, Mr. Secretary"; and it was done.

In the quality of tact Mr. Lincoln has been excelled by no man who ever held high office in this country. Van Buren was tactful, but too transparently so to secure the best results. Lincoln's tact was so subtle and masterful that it seldom was perceived, and never realized until its purpose had been accomplished. But it was the pre-eminent quality of fathoming public opinion — which he believed, in the long run, always to be right, correcting itself when led into error — and becoming the absolute servant of that opinion, in which Mr. Lincoln's claim as a public servant worthy of the highest honor and gratitude rested. We see now that he was waiting for public opinion to become pre-eminent before he indicated his policy with respect to the slaves. He revoked Hunter's order in South Carolina and Fremont's in Missouri, proclamations which established freedom for the slaves in those military districts; and though he was savagely rebuked for doing so by Phillips and Garrison and the influential public men who espoused immediate emancipation, yet it was because Mr. Lincoln saw, as they did not, that the time was not ripe for such a beneficent act. He waited for a year; and when he perceived that opinion would sustain him then he, seeming to lead it, issued his Emancipation Proclamation; and in lesser matters he was always thus guided. He erred sometimes, and no one saw a mistake sooner than he himself; but it was a recent Minister to Great Britain who said "that a man who made no mistakes made nothing." Statesmen have said that he was in error when he suggested, in the closing months of his first administration, that Congress could afford to appropriate money to recompense the men of the South for the loss of their property, if by such appropriation the War could be brought to a close. But in these latter days we are not sure that Mr. Lincoln's view had not more wisdom in it than did that of those in Congress who opposed him.

NEW YORK CITY.

AN HOUR WITH PRESIDENT LINCOLN.

BY FRANK B. CARPENTER,

AUTHOR OF "SIX MONTHS IN THE WHITE HOUSE."

MR. LINCOLN'S hand was on the bell cord of his office; Louis Burgdorf, the Prussian usher, had answered his summons. Taking up a card, he said: "I will see Colonel Noteware, of Colorado, and his friends."

Leaning back in his chair he rested his head upon his hand, with an expression of great weariness. His eyes for a moment wandered to the distant Virginia horizon and the unfinished Washington monument in the foreground.

"How sleep the brave who sink to rest
By all their country's wishes blest,"

he uttered softly, as if alone with his thoughts. "How gladly would I take the place in the ranks of the humblest soldier that sleeps to-night upon the banks of the Potomac." . . . The party of three he had sent for entered — a Western Senator, a Congressman and an old Illinois friend, Colonel Noteware. Instantly, by one of those rapid transitions, characteristic of Mr. Lincoln, the wan and tired look passed away. The greeting over, he at once began to question the party concerning the recent elections in their States, contrasting the figures given with those of former years, his memory of election returns being extraordinary.

This discussion was interrupted by the entrance of Mr. Nicolay, the private secretary of the President. He held in his hand a telegram from Philadelphia stating that a man had been arrested in that city for an attempt to obtain fifteen hundred dollars on Mr. Lincoln's name. "What!" said the President, "fifteen hundred dollars upon my name! I have given no one authority for such a draft; and if I had," he added, humorously, "it is surprising that any man could get the money!" After a moment's reflection, Mr. Nicolay said he thought he knew the accused party. "Do you remember, Mr. President, a request from a stranger a few days since for your autograph, and that you gave it to him upon a half sheet of note paper? The scoundrel doubtless forged an order above your signature, and has attempted to swindle somebody." "Oh, that's the trick, is it?" said the President. "What shall be done with him?" inquired Mr. Nicolay. "Have you any orders to give?" "Well," replied Mr. Lincoln, pausing between the words, "I don't see but that he will have to sit upon the blister-bench."

A paper bearing a number of signatures was here presented to the President. It was the application of Colonel Noteware for an official position. Taking the document in his hands, Mr. Lincoln read it carefully. He evidently recognized several of the endorsements. Looking up, with a comical expression, he said: "Colonel, your friend 'B' may be a good man, a *very* good man; but he does not know how to spell your name." Taking up his pen, he corrected the error. "There," said he, "I have, by a species of forgery, made the wrong *right*. But this is not like that chap in Philadelphia who used my name to make a right *wrong!*" Folding the paper, he continued: "Noteware, this reminds me of a little story. You know General S., don't you? Well, it appears from positive evidence of his friends, certified severally before me, who have known him during the whole term of his official life, that he is one hundred and fifteen years old. Now, Colonel, in footing up the time during which *your* friends certify to having known *you*, I found that they make you out to be precisely the same age!" Here Mr. Lincoln looked up from his desk into Colonel Noteware's face, with an indescribably droll expression, and said: "But you don't *look* to be so old a man as that, Colonel."

Referring again to the petition before him, he said: "'H,' 'H,' 'H,' — who is 'H'?" Colonel Noteware replied that he was a prominent Democrat of Illinois, and lived at O. "Ah," said the President, "I know now who he is, and I know all about O. I was there in the Black Hawk war."

At this point of the interview the Senator who accompanied Colonel Noteware called Mr. Lincoln's attention to the application of a client of his for back pay for certain services he had rendered, which the President evidently did not consider just. He responded with another "little story." "Years ago," said Mr. Lincoln, "when imprisonment for debt was legal in some States, a poor fellow was sent to jail by his creditor and compelled to serve out his debt at the rate of a dollar and a half per day. Knowing the exact amount of the debt, he carefully calculated the time he would be required to serve. When the sentence had expired he informed his jailer of the fact, and asked to be released. The jailer insisted upon keeping him four days longer. Upon making up his statement, however, he found that the man was right, and that he had served four days more than his sentence required. The prisoner then demanded not only a receipt in full for his debt, but also payment for four days' extra service, amounting to six dollars, which he declared the county owed him. Now," said Mr. Lincoln, "I think that county would be about as likely to pay the claim of this man as this Government will be to pay the claim of your friend for back pay." To which the Senator replied: "I am very much of your opinion, Mr. President."

The Hon. Hugh McCulloch, the Comptroller of the Currency, was announced, with a delegation of bankers from New York. The President had resumed his seat at the desk upon the departure of his Western visitors, and was busy writing. As the party filed into the room from the corridor, Mr. McCulloch preceded them, and, leaning over Mr. Lincoln's desk, said in a low voice: "These gentlemen from New York have come on to see the Secretary of the Treasury about our new loan. As bankers, they are obliged to hold our national securities. I can vouch for their patriotism and loyalty, for, as the good Book says, 'Where the treasure is, there will the heart be also.'" Mr. Lincoln looked up quickly, with his pen in hand, and said: "There is another text, Mr. McCulloch, I remember, that might apply equally well: 'Where the carcass is, there will the eagles be gathered together.'"

An incident occurred while I was painting the picture of the Proclamation, embracing the President and Cabinet, at the White House, which caused a hearty laugh. It was the witty reply of Edward McManus, the Irish porter, who had served through every administration from the inauguration of President Polk to that of Lincoln, with whom I became a great favorite during the six months of my occupancy of the state dining-room as a studio. The painting of the President and Cabinet was about half finished when, one day, a gentleman called and asked to see "Mr. Carpenter." Edward received him most courteously, as was his manner. "Yes," he said, "we have a 'Carpenter' here; but he has been promoted by the President. He has become a 'Cabinet' maker!"

Looking over a volume of the *Congressional Globe* for 1848, I came across a story told by Mr. Lincoln which was new to me, as I presume it will be to many of the readers of the *Independent*. It occurs in a speech he made in the House of Representatives, July 27th, 1848, on the war with Mexico and the candidacy of Gen. Zachary Taylor for the Presidency, on the part of the Whigs, as against that of Gen. Lewis Cass, the Democratic candidate.

The entire speech is most characteristic of Mr. Lincoln; but I will quote only the closing paragraph, the application of which I may be permitted to say is not limited to the political situation existing at that period:

"Mr. Speaker: I see that I have but three minutes left, and this forces me to throw out one whole branch of my subject. A single word on still another. The Democrats are kind enough to frequently remind us that we have some dissensions in our ranks. Our good friend from Baltimore (Mr. McLane) expressed some doubt the other day as to which branch of our party General Taylor would ultimately fall into the hands of. That was a new idea to me. I knew we had dissenters, but I did not know they were trying to get our candidate away from us. I would like to say a word to our dissenters, but I have not the time. Some such *we* certainly have; have *you* none, gentlemen Democrats? Is it all union and harmony in your ranks? No bickerings? No divisions? If there be doubt as to which of our divisions will get our candidate, is there no doubt as to which of your candidates will get your party? I have heard some things from New York; and if they are true we might well say of your party there, as a drunken fellow once said when he heard the reading of an indictment for hog stealing. The clerk read on till he got to, and through the words, 'did steal, take and carry away, ten boars, ten sows, ten shoats and ten pigs,' at which he exclaimed: 'Well, by golly, that is the most evenly divided gang of hogs I ever did hear of.' If there is any gang of hogs more evenly divided than the Democrats of New York are about this time, I have not heard of it."

NEW YORK CITY.

REMINISCENCES OF ABRAHAM LINCOLN.

LINCOLN'S RECEPTION TO TOM THUMB — HIS FAVORITE BOOKS OF HUMOR — IN HIS COFFIN.

BY GRACE GREENWOOD.

My actual acquaintance with President Lincoln was slight, but the place it fills in my memory seems great, and is a very sacred one. During a visit to Washington, in late war time, I received an informal invitation to a reception *extraordinaire* at the White House. It was to meet Mr. and Mrs. Charles S. Stratton — "General Tom Thumb" — and his wife, Lavinia, then on their bridal tour. I suppose that Mr. Barnum, a good loyal Republican, had solicited an audience for his then most famous, comely and *comme il faut* human curiosities, and that the President and Mrs. Lincoln, with an amiable desire to share a novel little entertainment with their friends, had sent out a limited number of invitations. I think Mr. Lincoln's quick sense of fitness led him to pass over all members of their circle, so stiffened by social starch or official solemnity as to be likely to find the occasion *infra dig.*, and so, unenjoyable.

I was presented to the President and Mrs. Lincoln by Mr. Lovejoy, and was made very happy and a little proud by being received by them as already "a friend," having become known to them in their home in Springfield through my work in magazines and newspapers —

especially the *National Era*, the *Independent*, and my own publication, the *Little Pilgrim;* so I felt at home speedily.

Yet Mr. Lincoln, before I heard his sweet-toned voice, and saw his singularly sympathetic smile, was certainly an awesome personage to me. So tall, gaunt and angular was his figure — so beyond all question, plain, was his face, furrowed and harrowed by unexampled cares and infinite perplexities, while over all was a simple dignity which was more than sacerdotal — a peculiar, set-apart look, which I have never seen in any other man, never shall see.

Mr. Lincoln's dress was sombre black, unrelieved except by gloves of white or very light kid, which had a rather ghastly effect on his large, bony hands. But Mrs. Lincoln was gay enough in attire — a low-necked gown of rich pink silk, with flounces climbing high up, over a hoop-skirt trellis, and pink roses in her hair. She was not handsome, but her manner was pleasant and kindly. She must have had a good heart, after all said, for her husband loved her. She must have had a more than ordinary intelligence, for Charles Sumner respected her opinions, and he knew her well. She certainly lacked worldly wisdom, tact and judgment — fatal lackings in her case. The dizzy elevation of her storm-rocked position, and its perils, unsettled her brain in effect, and the tragedy which shook the world, cast her "quite, quite down." Most desolate and misunderstood of women was she at the last.

Of the President's household present that evening, I remember two young men, who I thought ought to make careers for themselves, not alone because they looked clever, thoughtful and scholarly, but because their daily association with Abraham Lincoln must be a liberal education in noble ideas and aims, in manliness and mansuetude. These young gentlemen were the President's son, Robert, and his secretary, John Hay.

Rather to my surprise the high-toned and austere Secretary of the Treasury, Mr. Chase, was one of the guests, coming in early, as though in boyish haste to see the show. He was then but little past his prime, and a superb looking man. With him was his darling daughter, Kate — "the prettiest Kate in Christendom" — tall, graceful, her small Greek head borne royally, her lovely, piquant face untouched by care or sorrow, her exquisite dark eyes with their heavily fringed lids, full of a certain entangling charm.

Secretary Stanton was not there, to my disappointment, as in our younger days we had been familiar friends. Doubtless he thought this occasion a bit of fooling, unsuited to this most critical and sorrowful time of the imperilled Republic, when "men must work, and women must weep," their hardest and bitterest. He always was awfully in earnest. A pun once nearly cost me his friendship, and it was a good pun, too.

That night I first saw General Butler. It appears to me that he never changed much in all the years that followed till he died, in the house next to this — only yesterday, it seems. A little heavier grew that powerful face, a little less arrogant and audacious in expression, a little balder became that masterful, low, broad head without any "bump" of veneration, till in his coffin it looked like an antique bust of an old Roman emperor of the Augustan line — hard, but grand.

As was natural, perhaps, the autocrat of New Orleans had little sympathy with the quaint Commander-in-

Chief, whose big, soft heart so often played the mischief with military discipline through a flagrant exercise of the pardoning power; but he had to respect the moral steadfastness and purity of the man.

The reception took place in the East room; and when, following the loud announcement, "Mr. and Mrs. Charles Stratton," the guests of honor entered from the corridor, and walked slowly up the long *salon*, to where Mr. and Mrs. Lincoln stood, to welcome them, the scene became interesting, though a little bizarre. The pigmy "General," at that time still rather good-looking, though slightly *blasé*, wore his elegant wedding suit, and his wife, a plump but symmetrical little woman, with a bright, intelligent face, her wedding dress — the regulation white satin, with point lace, orange blossoms and pearls — while a train some two yards long swept out behind her. I well remember the "pigeon-like stateliness" with which they advanced, almost to the feet of the President, and the profound respect with which they looked up, up, to his kindly face. It was pleasant to see their tall host bend, and bend, to take their little hands in his great palm, holding Madame's with especial chariness, as though it were a robin's egg, and he were fearful of breaking it. Yet he did not *talk* down to them, but made them feel from the first as though he regarded them as real "folks," sensible, and knowing a good deal of the world. He presented them, very courteously and soberly, to Mrs. Lincoln, and in his compliments and congratulations there was not the slightest touch of the exaggeration which a lesser man might have been tempted to make use of, for the quiet amusement of on-lookers; in fact, nothing to reveal to that shrewd little pair his keen sense of the incongruity of the scene. He was, I think, most amused by the interest and curiosity of his "little Tad," who seemed disposed to patronize the diminutive gentleman and lady, grown up and married, yet lacking his lordly inches. When refreshments were being served, he graciously superintended his mother's kindly arrangements, by which the distinguished little folk were able to take their cake, wine and ices comfortably, off a chair.

Later, while the bride and groom were taking a quiet promenade by themselves up and down the big drawing-room, I noticed the President gazing after them with a smile of quaint humor; but, in his beautiful, sorrow-shadowed eyes, there was something more than amusement — a gentle, human sympathy in the apparent happiness and good-fellowship of this curious wedded pair — come to him out of fairyland.

After they were gone I had my little talk with, or rather from, Mr. Lincoln; for, naturally, I said but little during those golden moments. He was in one of his most genial moods; and judging, perhaps, from my newspaper connections that I was not a fool, he even favored me with a few of his "little stories," which he told very simply and tersely, yet with inimitable drollery. As was characteristic of him, he evidently was most amused by one wherein the joke was against himself. As I recall it, the story ran that a certain honest old farmer, visiting the capital for the first time, was taken by the member from his "deestrick" to some large gathering or entertainment, at which he was told he could see the President. Unfortunately, Mr. Lincoln did not appear; and the Congressman, being a bit of a wag and not liking to have his constituent disappointed, pointed out Mr. R., of Minnesota, a gentleman of a particularly round and rubicund countenance; the worthy farmer, greatly astonished, exclaimed: "Is that Old Abe? Well, I du declare! He's a better-lookin' man than I expected to see; but it does seem as if his troubles had driven him to drink."

After this evening I only saw Mr. Lincoln at two of his public receptions, when the people — or torrent of humanity — surged into the White House, and swept past him, every soul-wave mirroring clear his pale, patient face, and taking a glint from his kindly eyes. Each time I was made happy by an instant and smiling recognition and a few words of special welcome.

To pass into the presence, as one of a great crowd, even, was to receive from Mr. Lincoln a real, honest, hearty handshake, which you felt to the tips of your toes. Nowadays the official fashion is less neighborly and more perfunctory. The great man touches your fingers an instant, while looking over your shoulder for the next comer, or clutches your hand any way, pulls you forward and passes you on. You *think* he has said a word or two, but you are not quite sure.

Every moment that I found it possible on those occasions to linger near Mr. Lincoln, I spent in studying the face of the man on whose single life hung the destinies of a country and the redemption of a race. It was always the same impression. Under the pleasantest light of his eyes, I divined a depth of melancholy unfathomable.

Yet I recognized then, almost as clearly as I do now, the "saving grace" of those gifts of imagination and humor, which gave him temporary "surcease from sorrow," and the soul-weariness of helpless pity, through poetry, the drama, and those droll "little stories," so often wisdom in homely disguise — parables of subtle significance. It takes nothing from my respect for him, as a hero and a Christian, to know that he kept on the stand by the side of his bed, volumes of his favorite humorists. When, in the dreary watches of the night, the bitter waters of his "sea of troubles" were rising to his lips, I doubt not he found the buoyant wit of "Pickwick" more potent to bear him up than the bat-wings of Young's "Night Thoughts." Doubtless there was for him more heart-lightenings in Artemus Ward than in Isaac Watts; and he may have found in the homely diet of Hosea Biglow more stimulating mental aliment than in all the philosophy of Athens or Concord. I believe that one good, hearty laugh did him more good than any number of those recitations of "O Why should the Spirit of Mortal be Proud?" he was addicted to in his low and sentimental moods.

Not till that woful time when a tidal wave of national mourning swept across the continent, did I look again on the face of Abraham Lincoln. It was at Philadelphia — one of the stations in the great funeral progress. He lay in state, in Independence Hall, where one could almost believe that he had a double guard of honor, one invisible to us — the august shades of men whose patriotic act made that chamber glorious forever.

Accorded a private view, I was able to remain as long as I could bear to stay beside the casket, gazing down on what seemed to me a dread *simulacrum* of the face of our great friend — so unlike was it, though so like. The color was not the pallor I remembered, but a sort of ashen gray; the mouth looked stern, and then, the total eclipse of those benignant eyes! People said the face was "peaceful"; but it was an awful peace, there remained such touching shadows of mortal sorrow, struggle and strain. It was as though the soul, sunk deep beyond deep in God's rest, had left in its garment of flesh the perfect mould of its mortal cares, its piteous yearnings, its unspeakable weariness.

I have always pitied those who have only such recollections of Abraham Lincoln, and have been fervently thankful that while he yet lived I looked on that now historic figure and found it heroic in its grand ungainliness; on that worn and rugged face, and found it both lovable and impressive; that my hand has been grasped, in greeting and farewell, by the hand that performed the grandest work of the century; that my eyes have gazed full into those sad, prophetic eyes, whose tired lids were pressed down at last by the long-prayed-for Angel of Peace.

And I am thankful that it was my privilege to know some of his greatest generals, and those splendid aids of his, the "war governors" of the North and West, and also the faithful statesmen and patriots, who here at the Capital "upheld his hands"—Stanton, Chase and Seward, Henry Wilson, Hannibal Hamlin, Thaddeus Stevens, Joseph Holt, all gone—the type gone!

> —"O, woe is me,
> To have seen what I have seen—see what I see!"

WASHINGTON, March 19th, 1895.

LINCOLN AS A STORY-TELLER.

BY GEN. EGBERT L. VIELE.

President Lincoln was sometimes criticised for the stories he used to tell. The broadness of these stories, it may be said, came from the atmosphere of the Western country, where it was necessary to give a little spice to an anecdote in order to attract attention. Mr. Lincoln always used with great effect any anecdote which he possessed for the purpose of enforcing and exemplifying a higher form of argument and impressing a fact upon the minds of his hearers.

Few people understand precisely the condition of Western life. They are crude and rude, though fast becoming otherwise. In Lincoln's time it was the life of the pioneer that is struggling with nature; and while people were working to obtain the food necessary for their absolute existence, there was little time for the cultivation of the graces and for the refinement of the intellect. So we must look at that country from the point of view of development.

In a broad sense American civilization is divided into three distinct lines. There is the civilization of the Atlantic coast, the earliest civilization, which was simply a reflex of European civilization. The tone and character of public affairs came from men who were familiar with public affairs in Europe, and had a knowledge of and an acquaintance with many of the statesmen of Europe.

The civilization of the valley of the Mississippi is distinct from this. It is purely an American civilization. The people of the valley of the Mississippi thought little and cared less for the settlers on the Atlantic or for the European nations. They lived in a world of their own, a vast, productive region, the most remarkable of its kind on this continent.

The civilization of the Pacific slope was that of adventurers of all kinds, tinged with the characteristics of the Mexican and the vices of the Mongolian who became mixed with it. So it will be seen that there are three distinct forms of life to be mingled together in the future of American civilization.

Abraham Lincoln was the product of the pure American civilization, just as Grant was, just as Sherman was. The valley of the Mississippi has given us a large number of great — marvellously great — men; great in intellect and great in stature. In fact, the State of Kentucky alone has furnished us with a large complement of great men capable of conducting the affairs of the country for a country if there were no other men competent to do so.

Kentucky is, physically, the Greece of America, just as the Hellenic Peninsula is the Greece of Europe; and from that State we have received already a vast amount of intellectual and physical development superior, in many respects, to that which has come from any other part of the country. During the Civil War there was a measurement made of the heads and bodies of the soldiers from the different sections of the country, and it was found that the Kentucky soldiers were larger in bone and brain, better, physically and mentally, than the soldiers from any other section of the country.

Abraham Lincoln was born in Kentucky, and he is of that breed.

My intimacy with him began on my arrival in Washington with the steamship "Daylight," and a body of armed volunteers that had answered the first call of the President for troops, and had opened the passage of the Potomac River to the Capital, being the first vessel, with troops, to arrive for the defence of the Capital by way of that river. Lincoln came down with Secretary Seward from the White House in a terrific downpour of rain and welcomed us on the wharf. Four of the men held a piece of tarpaulin over his head, one at each corner, and he held a reception there, shaking hands with every one, including the stokers from the engine-room, grasping their coal-black hands and exclaiming that they were as brave as any of us.

From that time until Mr. Lincoln's death I enjoyed the very closest intimacy with him. On one occasion he invited me to accompany him, the Secretary of War and the Secretary of the Treasury in a revenue cutter from Washington to Fortress Monroe. There was a small cabin in the boat divided by four partitions. During the period of eight or ten days we were together we never lost sight of each other. During the trip we were constantly engaged in conversation and discussion about war matters, much of the time being occupied in listening to Mr. Lincoln's wonderful fund of reminiscence and anecdote. If I had been a stenographer it seems to me that I could have filled a large volume made up of these remarkable stories, each and every one of them having aptness to the point under discussion. Of course I could not remember all of them. I remember many of them. Some of them it would hardly be right to print.

Some simple remark that some of the party might make would remind Mr. Lincoln of an apropos story. Mr. Chase happened to remark, "Oh, I am so sorry that I had to write a letter to Mr. So-and-So before I left home." Mr. Lincoln promptly responded: "Chase, never regret what you don't write; it is what you do write that you are often called upon to feel sorry for."

Here is another: Mr. Stanton said that just before he left Washington he had received a telegram from General Mitchell, in Alabama, asking instructions in regard to a certain emergency that had occurred. The secretary said that he did not precisely understand the emergency as explained by General Mitchell, but he had answered back, "All right; go ahead." "Now," he said, "Mr. President, if I have made an error in not understanding him correctly, I will have to get you to countermand the order." "Well," exclaimed Lincoln, "that is very much like the occasion of a certain horse sale I remember that took place at the cross roads down in Kentucky when I was a boy. A particularly fine horse was to be sold, and the people gathered together. They had a small boy to ride the horse up and down while the spectators examined the horse's points. At last one man whispered to the boy as he went by: 'Look here, boy, hain't that horse got the splints?' The boy replied: 'Mister, I don't know what the splints is; but if it is good for him he has got it, if it ain't good for him he ain't got it.' Now," said Mr. Lincoln, "if this was good for Mitchell it was all right: but if it was not I have got to countermand it."

I had the *entrée* to the White House. Though Senators,

Congressmen and diplomats were kept waiting, I was always admitted. On one occasion I had to go to the White House in company with a member of Congress to look after the interests of one of my old soldiers who was also a constitutent of this member of Congress. When we reached the Capitol the Congressman said: "You know that the President always admits Senators and Representatives before he admits others; therefore, I will put your name on my card and you will not be detained; you will have an opportunity of going right in." So we entered the Capitol and the Congressman got out his card, put my name on it above his own, and sent it in. In a moment or two the messenger came back and cried out (misapprehending my name), "General Weal." A bystander remarked, "The President has been listening to *General Woe* so long, it is no wonder he wants *General Weal* in a hurry." So I left the Congressman cooling his heels in the anteroom and went in. He said: "Well, Viele, what can I do for you?" I replied: "Mr. President, I came with Mr. Rudford of the House of Representatives, in behalf of a constituent of his and an old soldier of mine. Here is an application which"— He said: "Write it down on the outside." So I put the regular endorsement on the back of the application— the name, position, nature of the business, etc., and carried it back to the President. "Oh no!" he exclaimed, "what I want you to do is to write what you want me to sign." So I wrote: "The Adjutant-General will comply with the request of Captain Egan," etc., and the President signed " A. Lincoln." This simply illustrates the confidence he had in his friends.

On another occasion I had some very important paper to show him. As I entered the room Secretary Seward came in with some important dispatches and took his seat alongside the President just as I had handed him the paper I wanted him to look at. Secretary Seward, with an air of impatience, took it out of the President's hand and handed it back to me, saying, "Some other time; I have important business with the President." Mr. Lincoln said: "Not so fast, Seward," taking back the document from him; "I want to hear what Viele has to say about this matter."

I give these stories to illustrate the strong affection he had for his friends. He said to me once: "If I have got one vice it is not being able to say 'no.' And I consider it a vice. Thank God for not making me a woman. I presume if he had he would have made me just as ugly as I am and nobody would have ever tempted me."

Mr. Lincoln was a man of the highest degree of self-culture, in so far as regards a knowledge of the most beautiful and sublime writings in the English language. His memory was photographic in character. He could repeat from memory almost any passage after he had read it once, and nothing delighted him so much as to sit down of an evening among his immediate friends and repeat whole stanzas from Byron or Browning or the plays of Shakespeare. Most of the grand and sublime passages in literature were familiar to him.

And yet, so strong was his sense of humor that no ridiculous event or situation ever escaped his notice. One day on board ship I showed him in *Harper's Weekly* a funny little piece of rhyme which was amusing on account of the absurd use of words, such as "they sat side by side, and she sighed and he sighed," and so it went on in the same strain. This verse captured the President so completely that he sat down and sprawled himself out on the deck, and said: "Viele, lend me your penknife." I opened the knife and handed it to him, and he began to cut the piece from the paper. Just in the midst of this employment he looked up from his rather ungraceful attitude, and said: "Not a very dignified position for the President of the United States, but eminently convenient for the purpose!"

I have always protested against the constant assertion as to the early life of the President that he was a flat-boatman. He was not, by occupation. Everybody had more or less to do with flatboats on the Western rivers fifty years ago. But the flatboatman proper, engaged in it as an occupation, was generally a man of very low instincts. In this sense Lincoln was never a flatboatman, although on one or two occasions he may have had something to do with a trip on a flatboat; as, for instance, at the age of eighteen when a friend started with a boat-load of stores for New Orleans, and invited Lincoln to join him, an invitation which he accepted.

So, too, with regard to his rail-splitting. After his father had married his second wife, he removed to a spot on the north side of the Sangamon River, ten miles west of Decatur, Ill. On this occasion Abraham assisted in erecting a new home, and split the rails for the fence, an incident which was used in his canvass for the Presidency.

In this connection it should be remembered that Mr. Lincoln was a man of immense physique. During his lifetime he was probably as strong a man as you could find. The muscles of his body were like iron. He could take a heavy axe and, grasping it with his thumb and forefingers at the extreme end of the handle, hold it out on a horizontal line from his body. On board ship I have never seen a man who could perform this feat. Any man who will attempt to do it will see how difficult it is. He once said to me: "When I was eighteen years of age I could do this, and I have never seen the day since that I could not do it." He used to take great satisfaction in performing this feat before the strong sailors, and smile at their unsuccessful efforts to imitate it.

With Mr. Lincoln's great physical strength the labor of splitting rails was a mere amusement. It was not work; it was a kind of outlet for his surplus energy. Members of athletic associations devote a large portion of their time and spend considerable money simply for the purpose of keeping their muscles in shape. In the same way with Lincoln, rail-splitting was never gross labor to him, though it would have been to an ordinary man. He regarded it as little more than pastime to keep his muscles in play.

When I was Military Governor of Norfolk, Lincoln wrote his famous Proclamation of Emancipation. In that Proclamation he omitted all the loyal States, and all portions of other States that were occupied by United States troops and not under the dominion of the rebels.

On the first of January, the day set for the Proclamation to go into effect, I received a procession of five thousand Negroes in Norfolk who came to my home to wish me a happy New Year, and congratulate themselves on the fact that they had the rights of freedom. I did not dare tell them that the Proclamation did not apply to them, but I went to Washington and talked the matter over with Secretary Chase. He advised me to see the President, and, for fear the President might be engaged in some way, he asked me to take a note to him, and he would then see me at once. So I went over and saw him and told him of my experience with the five thousand Negroes. He said: "This is the difficulty; we want to keep all that we have of the border States — those that have not seceded and the portions of those which we have occupied. And, in order to do that, it is necessary to omit those areas I have mentioned from the effect of this Proclamation." The idea was to keep the border States where the War was going on for fear we might excite them by the thought of losing slavery, as we had not come to that issue yet.

Subsequently, I had occasion to complain to the President of what I thought was the injurious action of one of the Governors of the loyal States where I had a command. "Well, now," said Mr. Lincoln; "you remember what I told you about the border States. The same thing applies to the Governors of the loyal States. We cannot afford to quarrel with them about collateral issues. We want their soldiers."

One day I went to see Lincoln. He was being shaved. The Negro barber had just covered him with an immense coat of lather. He had sent word for me to come right in. He said: "I hope I don't scare you; I look frightful enough by nature without the addition of this lather."

On another occasion, sitting before his desk in his office, he quaintly remarked: "I wish George Washington or some of those old patriots were here in my place so that I could have a little rest."

NEW YORK CITY.

LINCOLN — AFTER THIRTY YEARS.

BY THEODORE L. CUYLER, D.D.

"When I have had to address a fagged and listless audience, I have found that nothing was so certain to arouse them as to introduce the name of Abraham Lincoln." So remarked Dr. Newman Hall, of London, to me last year; and I have had a similar experience with American audiences. No other name has such electric power on every true heart from Maine to Mexico. If Washington is the most revered, Lincoln is the *best-loved* man that ever trod this continent.

The thirtieth anniversary of his martyrdom stirs afresh the fount of memory and of tears in my own heart. On that fatal fourteenth of April, 1865, I was present at the glorious restoration of the old flag in Fort Sumter; and, after the halyard had passed through the hands of General Anderson, I was glad to get hold of it, in company with William Lloyd Garrison, George Thompson, of England, and several others, and help pull "Old Glory" up to the flagstaff peak. The next morning I addressed a thousand Negro children; and when I said to them, "Shall we invite your Father Abraham to come to Charleston and see the little folks he has made free?" a thousand black hands flew up with a shout. At that very moment the great, deep, melancholy eyes were sealed in death amid the weeping crowds at Washington! At Fortress Monroe, on our homeward voyage, the terrible tidings pierced us like a dagger. On the wharf near the Fortress poor Negro women had hung bits of coarse black muslin around their little huckster tables. One of the women said to me: "Yes, sah; Father Linkum's dead. They killed our best friend; but God be libin' yet. Dey can't kill him; I'se sure of dat." Her simple, childlike faith reached up to grasp the Everlasting Arm which had led Lincoln while leading her and her race out of the house of bondage.

Thirty years — the average term of one generation — have rolled away since that coffin, drenched with a nation's tears, was borne by the mightiest of modern funeral processions from Washington to Springfield. During that time many a famous reputation has waned, or has utterly disappeared; but Lincoln's looms larger every day. Since the time when a Corsican lieutenant of artillery presided over a congress of conquered kings at Tilsit, history has recorded no such startling elevation from obscurity. Napoleon's head grew dizzy; but Lincoln's grew more serene and clear and majestically poised the higher he rose. Let our American boys study and grave on their hearts the dozen or two lines that record the wonderful story. Here it is: Born in one of the rudest log cabins of Kentucky on the twelfth of February, 1809; his poverty-stricken boyhood spent in clearing away forests, and only one year spent in the rudimentary studies of a rustic school; at the age of nineteen a hired deckhand on a Mississippi flatboat; then a clerk in a country store in Illinois; next a student of law from a few books borrowed and studied by firelight; in 1834 a member of the State Legislature; in 1846 in Congress introducing a bill to abolish slavery in the District of Columbia; in 1858 waging the most protracted and brilliant debate with Douglas that our politics has ever known; in 1860 borne triumphantly into the Presidential chair by a popular voice "like the sound of many waters"; after four tempestuous years, and in the hour of victory, translated by a bloody martyrdom to his crown of glory, with four millions of broken fetters in his good right hand! What story is like unto that story? Thirty years have written and rewritten it in hundreds of forms, and it is not exhausted yet.

By this time we are all agreed that his lowly birth and early hardships were blessings in disguise; for one, I am thankful that he never rubbed his homespun back against the walls of a college. The "plain people," as he called them, were his university; the Bible and John Bunyan his earliest text-books. He felt the great throb of the "plain people's" hearts every hour that he was in the White House, and, next to God's leadings, they were his unerring guide. His plebeian simplicity of dress and manners, and his many humorous stories exposed him to the charge of clownishness and buffoonery; even Chief Justice Chase once aroused my ire by this unjust insinuation. His innumerable jests contained more wisdom than many a philosophic oration, and underneath his rustic manners this great child of nature possessed the most delicate instincts of the perfect gentleman. Lincoln often wore the saddest human face I ever saw; his occasional jokes were the safety valve to relieve his great, broken heart — broken by the nation's ceaseless agonies.

To what intellectual niche has the impartial verdict of thirty years assigned Abraham Lincoln? The only just scale by which to measure any man is the scale of actual *achievement;* and in Lincoln's case some of the tools most essential to success had to be fabricated by himself. The first count in the measurement is that with a calm, sublime reliance on God and the everlasting principles of Right he conducted an immense nation through the most tremendous civil war ever waged, and never committed a single serious mistake! The Illinois backwoodsman did not possess Hamilton's brilliant genius; yet Hamilton never read the future more sagaciously. He made no pretensions to Webster's massive and magnificent oratory; yet Webster never put more truth in portable form for the popular guidance. He possessed Benjamin Franklin's immense common sense and gift of terse proverbial speech, without Franklin's "fleshly lusts" and sceptical infirmities. In what may be styled civil literature Lincoln's position is unique; nearly all his productions are admirable, and a few of them are unequalled by any American pen. The immortal twenty-line address at Gettysburg is the high-water mark of sententious eloquence. With that speech should be placed the equally pathetic and equally perfect letter of condolence to Mrs. Bixby, of Boston, after her five sons had fallen in battle. With that speech, also, should be read that wonderful second Inaugural Address, which even the hostile London *Times* pronounced to be the most sublime state paper of this century. This second Address — his last great production — contains some of the best illustrations of his fondness for balanced antithesis and rhythmical measurement; there is one sentence which may be rendered into rhyme:

> "Fondly do we hope,
>   Fervently do we pray,
>   That this mighty scourge of war
>   May soon pass away."

Terrible as was the tragedy of that April night thirty years ago, yet it may be sadly true that Lincoln died at the right time for his own imperishable fame. It was fitting that his precious blood should be the last to be shed in the stupendous struggle. He had called over two hundred thousand heroes to lay down their lives, and then his own was laid down beside the humblest private soldier or drummer boy that fills the sacred mould of Gettysburg or Chickamauga. In an instant, as it were, his career crystallized into that pure white fame which belongs only to the martyr for justice, law and liberty.

For a whole generation his ashes have slumbered in his old, beloved home at Springfield. From that tomb his dust may be summoned on the last great Day of Judgment, when the millions of the liberated may gratefully say to their Liberator: "We were a-hungered, and thou gavest us the bread of mercy; we were thirsty for liberty, and thou gavest us to drink; we were strangers, and thou didst take us in; we were sick with two centuries of sorrow, and thou didst visit us; we were in the prison house of bondage, and thou camest unto us." And we may surely believe that the King will say unto him: "Inasmuch as thou hast done this unto the least of these my brethren, thou hast done it unto Me. Well done, good and faithful servant! Enter into the joy of thy Lord!"

BROOKLYN, N. Y.

LINCOLN'S MOST CONSPICUOUS VIRTUE.

FROM A CONFEDERATE GENERAL.

BY THE HON. JOHN T. MORGAN,

U. S. Senator from Alabama.

The character of Abraham Lincoln is not yet known to this generation, as it will be to those who shall live in later centuries. They will see, as we cannot yet perceive, the full maturity of his wisdom in its actual effects upon the destinies of two great races of men. Probably, he had an inadequate conception of his own work. Had he lived to full age, his guidance of the emancipation, that he decreed under military law, would have saved both races from many of the rough experiences that it has produced and will yet cause, by the effort to fuse the races into political harmony, against the mutual instinct that will keep them forever separated by race and social antagonisms.

The character of Mr. Lincoln was clearly displayed in his conduct of the War, but he was deprived of the opportunity for its full development in a period of peace and security. His most conspicuous virtue, as Commander-in-Chief of the Army and Navy, was the absence of a spirit of resentment, or oppression, toward the enemy, and the self-imposed restraint under which he exercised the really absolute powers within his grasp. For this all his countrymen revere his memory, rejoice in the excellence of his fame, and those who failed in the great struggle hold him in grateful esteem.

ABRAHAM LINCOLN AS SEEN BY A LIFE-LONG DEMOCRAT.

AFTER GOING THROUGH BALTIMORE.

BY COL. B. F. WATSON,

OF THE MASSACHUSETTS SIXTH REGIMENT.

My slight individual knowledge of Abraham Lincoln was during his first term as President, and was comprised in two interviews at the White House, one at the request of the officers of my regiment and the other at Mr. Lincoln's request, and to a brief correspondence of which I still retain two of his autograph letters, all, interviews and correspondence, having some connection with each other, although in dates separated by several months.

I first saw him on Sunday morning, April 21st, 1861, near the entrance to the Cabinet chamber in the White House. At the urgent request of the captains of the Sixth Regiment of Massachusetts Volunteers, I called upon Maj.-Gen. Winfield Scott, then commanding the United States Army. I was unattended. There is no special importance in the facts I am about to state unless it be remembered that this Sunday was but six days after the firing upon Sumter, and two days after the affair of Baltimore, that Washington and the whole country were surging under an excitement almost impossible to describe, and that I was the representative of a body of men who had been recently making history.

On the nineteenth of January, 1861, upon my motion, the commanders of its companies, Colonel Jones presiding, adopted a resolution tendering the services of the "Sixth" to the President. This first volunteering so impressed the authorities that the Sixth was first called by the President on the sixteenth day of April, 1861; it rallied from thirty cities and towns, fully armed and equipped, and travelled over 600 miles with such alacrity that it reached Washington in advance of all other organized and armed forces in the afternoon of the nineteenth of April, after a conflict in the streets of Baltimore in which it had four men killed, thirty-six wounded by gunshots, and many otherwise injured, all of its unarmed men being driven back. It left many dead and wounded rebels behind it.

By unfortunate circumstances which divided the troops into three separate detachments, I, then only second in command, was compelled to fight my way through Baltimore at the head of about fifty men of Company K, of Boston. This detachment both drew and shed the first blood in the great Rebellion, although the main conflict of the day took place soon after with the detachment following, commanded for the time by Captain Follansbee. Baltimore, with its 200,000 inhabitants, its prevailing Southern sympathies, and its notorious "Plug Ugly" element, was the strategic key by which the dis-unionists proposed to lock the loyal North out of the nation's Capital until its occupation in force from Baltimore and the South should compel the recognition of the Confederacy as the *de-facto* Government. A single regiment, untrained in war, exhibiting the pluck to break through this cordon of rebellion, could be hailed only with relief by the beleaguered Government and by that fraction of the residents of Washington who entertained positive sentiments of loyalty to the Union. Colonel Jones has testified that the President met the Sixth at the railroad station and said that if its arrival had been delayed a single day, Washington would have been in the hands of the rebels. It will appear later that the commanding general of the army entertained similar sentiments. Later on Congress recorded its tribute in a resolution tendering its thanks

"To the Sixth Regiment of Massachusetts Volunteers for the alacrity with which they responded to the call of the President, and the patriotism and bravery which they displayed on the nineteenth of April last in fighting their way through the City of Baltimore on their march to the defence of the Federal Capital."

The Sixth took possession of the Capital, and intrenched itself therein as though it had come to stay. It had not had a square meal since it left Philadelphia, the Thursday night before. Its experience had sharpened its appetite, for Baltimore had tendered no refreshments. Either by accident or by the design of some traitorous commissary, the presence of the "salt horse," as the boys familiarly called the meat which was offered them, could be detected by more of the senses than one, and was repulsive to all of them, and the large round crackers usually called "Hard-tack," the accompanying delicacy, were so adamantine from composition or antiquity as to withstand most assaults and, when conquered, to afford no sustenance. They were soon nicknamed "The regulars," from their supposed invincibility. Unless the veracity of veterans is to be questioned, certain retained specimens of these hard biscuit have since the Rebellion served as wheels to the play carts of two or three generations of veteran babies. My mission on that Sunday morning was to induce General Scott to order a change in this diet. The situation mitigated the presumption of such an application to an officer of such exalted rank. I found General Scott attending a meeting of the President and his Cabinet, convened to listen to the demands of the authorities of Maryland, including the Mayor of Baltimore, that no troops should pass over the sacred soil of Maryland in reaching Washington, and I thus accidentally became a participant in a meeting which has become historic, and of which, so far as I know, I am now the only survivor. Being summoned to the open door of the room, General Scott received my salute and my story. He drew himself up to the most impressive development of his magnificent proportions, and grandly announced: "The Sixth Regiment of Massachusetts, sir, shall have anything it wants; we depend upon the Sixth Regiment of Massachusetts to save the Capital of the country, sir." All fear of the "guard tent" for my presumption disappeared.

The General's statement was true, certainly upon that Sunday, and for four or five days thereafter, and until Gen. B. F. Butler, with the Seventh Regiment of New York and the Eighth of Massachusetts, arrived in Washington, by the way of Annapolis.

It seems to be the fact that the President and the Commanding General placed little reliance upon the semi-military and semi-political clubs, adorned with names of prominent politicians such as "Cassius M. Clay Invincibles," "Hannibal Hamlin Guards," or upon the three or four unarmed and uncombined companies of Pennsylvania militia who, in *post-bellum* times, have published themselves as "First defenders of the Capital."

While General Scott was speaking with me, President Lincoln came forward, and, after shaking hands, said he would like to introduce me to the Mayor of Baltimore and to learn if I could confirm the statements he had been making to the effect that he had personally exerted himself to protect the Sixth during its passage through Baltimore, and that he had marched much of the way through the city at its head. The Mayor and others, in the meantime, had gathered around and within hearing of the President's remarks. I fear my manner was not complimentary toward the Mayor. I am sure my speech was not. So recent had been my "baptism of fire" I doubtless bore my testimony with indiscreet zeal. I said, in effect, that under the circumstances it was unfortunate for the Mayor of Baltimore, as such, to appeal to me for a certificate of character; that we, as citizen soldiers, had endeavored to pass through Baltimore, not only in a peaceable and proper manner, but strictly in obedience to superior order, that insult and assault should be submitted to, and that wounds with firearms alone should justify retaliation; that at the beginning of our passage the police had threatened me that not a man of us would be allowed to go through the city alive; and that our graves had been already dug; that neither the police, nor other officials, in any instance to my knowledge, had attempted any protection; that prior to that moment I had never seen the Mayor; that I had been informed by one of the captains of one of the detachments that the Mayor did march about one hundred yards beside him, when he left saying that the position was too hot for him. So far as I was concerned, the interview was then ended by my withdrawing, the President having said that the rations should be made satisfactory.

Many times since I have recalled the scene. The Mayor's look of intense disgust, the astonishing dignity of the Commanding General, and the expression, half sad, half quizzical, on the face of the President at the evident infelicity of his introduction. If I did not leave that distinguished presence with my reputation for integrity unimpaired, the pressure of Abraham Lincoln's honest hand, as we parted, deceived me. My mission, at all events, was successful, and the rations improved.

While Washington remained isolated from the North, the Sixth, by General Scott's orders, daily marched in the streets and practised the street-firing drill, while the air was vocal with muttered curses; and more than one night the Regiment slept upon its arms in the Senate Chamber under orders to surround the White House at the first alarm, and defend the President from attack.

When I marched with the Sixth, I was a young lawyer, the owner and editor of a Democratic newspaper, and also Postmaster of Lawrence, Mass., which position I had held under the administrations of President Pierce and Buchanan. The Postmaster-General was the brother-in-law of the Assistant Secretary of the Navy, who in Lawrence had been my nearest neighbor and my friend. This brought me many kind attentions and courtesies, and also unsolicited assurances that my military services would insure my retention as Postmaster; but I persistently declined to associate officeholding with the simple duty I had rendered to my convictions as an American citizen. I now hold the proofs that even when the very existence of the Union was menaced efforts were being made to supplant me as Postmaster and also that, without my knowledge, counter efforts were being made by leading Republicans to have me retained. One of the aspirants to the place is now living in honorable old age to whom the President gave his assurance that I should be retained in office. Early in the month of May, when Washington was filling up with loyal troops, the Sixth was ordered to the Relay House, about eight miles from Baltimore, to guard the junction of the Washington branch with the main line of the railroad which led to Harper's Ferry, where the rebel forces under General Joseph Johnston were located and were receiving material aid from Baltimore. At this camp the Sixth spent the remainder of its original term of enlistment, and the short additional term volunteered by it on account of the insecurity felt by the Government after the first Bull Run disaster. The regiment elected me Lieutenant-Colonel soon after reaching the Relay House, and owing to Colonel Jones's promotion I thereafter commanded the Sixth. While stationed there I was informed that the United States Government would accept from me its first independent regiment. This was under a misapprehension of its authority as it was afterward defined. Some correspondence took place upon the subject, and I abandoned the idea for various reasons, mostly personal, and the Government apparently understood my determination. I certainly declined an invitation in writing dated July 13th, from one having authority, to visit Washington personally and confer with the Secretary of War upon the subject, and I dropped the matter out of mind.

About the first of August, the Sixth returned to Boston; being the first regiment to march; its career had excited great attention, and its reception along the homeward route was remarkable. Its every movement was chronicled in the press, and ovations, festivities, triumphal arches and oratory greeted it at every point. The famous War Governor, John A. Andrew, dismissed the regiment on Boston Common, in an Executive Order, saying of the Sixth :

"It was the first which went forward to the defence of the National Capital. It passed through Baltimore, despite the cowardly assault upon it, and was the first to reach Washington. Its gallant conduct has reflected new lustre upon the Commonwealth, and has given new historic interest to the nineteenth of April. It has returned after more than three months of action and responsible service. It will be received by our people with warm hearts and generous hands."

Within one week after my return my removal from the office of Postmaster was published. In reply to a telegraph inquiry if the rumor was true, the President, on the eighth day of August, wrote:

"If I signed a paper, in making a change in the office, it was among others, without my being conscious of this particular one."

He enclosed the Postmaster-General's memorandum, saying that the change had been made because the United States Government had tendered me the command of a regiment, and it was supposed that I was raising that regiment for service during the War. The President added :

"I shall talk fully with the Postmaster-General on the subject when I next see him."

This removal caused intense and widespread excitement. The exercise of political proscription, under the circumstances, and when the life of the nation hung in the balance, and the Government was believed to be doomed unless the services of the great body of the Northern

Democrats could be relied upon, caused apprehension in the minds of friends of the Union. Republicans and Democrats alike joined in denouncing the act. Letters came to me from men high in political and Federal office denouncing it, and I afterward learned that complaints were poured into the ears of the authorities at Washington. The newspapers of both parties in many parts of the North vied with each other in condemning the policy, and particularly its application to me, and I received more than my meed of praise. I heard nothing more from Washington. As the theme began to oppress me as too personal and possibly detrimental to the cause of the country, I wrote an editorial for my newspaper deprecating the agitation, which was widely copied but failed to stop the clamor. To show the spirit I quote a few words of it:

"The opposition to the removal comes perhaps not so much because of partiality to the present incumbent and his official conduct as from the unfortunate influence it may excite (limited, to be sure) upon the interests of the national cause at this critical juncture. . . . We have little diposition to criminate or rebel, especially when the Government needs a hearty support. Place and patronage are sweet, but the dear country and the flag have far superior claims. As heretofore, while differing in political sentiment on many subjects from the administration, we shall sustain with all our humble abilities all measures tending to vindicate the national honor and shall only sound the alarm when incompetency or unfaithfulness are apparent. Thus far we have endeavored to do the duty due from every citizen for the protection thrown around him by a good Government. The performance of that simple and natural duty entitles us to no special favors, *and none have been claimed.*"

After this I ceased to pay much attention to the affair, and departed for a much needed vacation. The clamor in the newspapers, it now appears, continued. A letter, dated the thirty-first of August, 1861, from a high official, informed me that the President was asking about my new regiment, and I was urged to take it to the front. I did not then appreciate the reason for the writing of that letter, and I did not reply to it, as I considered that the writer knew I had abandoned the project. Late in the month of September, 1861, while at the seashore, I received a telegram from the Postmaster-General that the President wanted to see me in Washington immediately. I reluctantly took the journey in response, and only because I believed the invitation was properly to be considered a command. When, on the first day of October, I asked an attendant at the White House to take my card to the President, saying that he had sent for me, to my amazement I was speedily conducted through the waiting throng which filled the corridors, and was introduced into the President's private office, the same room where I had formerly been introduced to President Pierce and President Buchanan. Mr. Lincoln was alone. He met me in the most cordial manner, and earnestly entered upon the statement of why I had been sent for. If I were at liberty and had the ability to do justice to his manner and language upon that occasion, the narrative could not fail to deepen the reader's conviction that Abraham Lincoln was not only patriotic, true and noble, but anxious to repair any fault he might have committed, and that his reputation for homely and forcible picturesqueness of speech had been fairly earned. His manner was kind and familiar. He immediately referred to my official decapitation by him, and condemned the act in as severe terms as those of any of his newspaper critics. He referred in enthusiastic and complimentary terms to the services the Sixth had rendered, and characterized my removal by him as specially unfortunate, when I had been ready to stake my life in his defence. He said he was unaware of what he was doing in my removal, as those who had induced it did not at the time inform him, and they afterward explained that I had accepted the tendered regiment and would not care to retain the post office, particularly when I knew what efforts politicians were making to succeed me. In very forcible language he said he would instantly reinstate me if he did not propose to place me in a much better position. I listened until he closed with the inquiry as to what position would be agreeable to me. I then said I was seeking no office and wanted none. In the most earnest manner he said that I must accept some appointment, so that it could be published that the administration had rectified its unintentional wrong; that the act was believed to be injuriously affecting enlistments. I said that I had not complained of my removal; that my military services had been performed from a sense of duty, and office had never in the least influenced me; that I recognized the right to appoint his political friends to office, and that I saw no occasion for exception in my case. He said that the same patriotism which had induced me to make the sacrifices I had made must prevail upon me to accept some place, in view of the injury to the cause which the clamor at my removal would effect. He said in substance that I should be appointed to any office that was agreeable to me or that I would accept. I told him that I would do all I could to stop the criticisms made on my behalf; that in time of war I could not accept any offer not connected with the military forces and that I had partially promised not to go again to the front. He then, jocosely I think, referred to the numerous appointments of brigadiers, and then said that a Paymastership of Volunteers was not only one of the most desirable positions in the army but one that might enable me to keep my promise. Without yielding my objection to office I admitted that his last suggestion offered the most plausible solution to the situation, but suggested that such a position in the regular army might more certainly insure my location near home. He said he would write to the Secretary and fix that. He wrote, read to me and then sealed the following letter, which I have never used, and the seal of which I never broke until after his assassination:

"EXECUTIVE MANSION, October 1st, 1861.
"HONORABLE SECRETARY OF WAR:

"*My dear Sir:*—The Postmaster-General and myself have special reasons for wishing to oblige Mr. Benjamin F. Watson, of Lawrence, Massachusetts. He has been appointed an Assistant Paymaster, or Paymaster of Volunteers, but he wishes the same post in the regular army. If there is any vacancy, not committed to any other person, let Mr. Watson have it. If there be no such vacancy, oblige him, as far as you can, by sending him to service at the place which suits him best. Yours truly,

"A. LINCOLN."

He then wrote on the envelope "Hon. Sec. of War," and added a memorandum most necessary in those days when the Government buildings were filled with crowds vainly seeking personal interviews with officials, "Please see Mr. Watson." No other justification existed for the statement in this letter, that I had been appointed, etc., than that I have herein narrated, excepting, probably, his determination to right that which he thought was a wrong, his desire to do nothing detrimental to the Union cause, his belief that he had hit upon that which I was bound patriotically to accept, and his decision that the appointment should be tendered whether accepted or not. I was gazetted Paymaster all over the country the next morning, but I did not for six weeks thereafter finally conclude to accept the office. After the President had read his letter and I was about to retire, Gen. B. F. Butler was announced. He was then in his zenith and all governmental doors were open to him. In his peculiar manner the General scanned me from head to foot and demanded what had brought me there. I replied that the Commander-in-Chief had sent for me. In reply the General, in his rough way, informed the President that we were friends and neighbors, whereupon the President narrated to him what had taken place between us and said that he had been trying to induce me to accept office. To this General Butler replied that he wanted me to be appointed Paymaster of the Gulf, with permission to employ all requisite clerks, and he added, "I will go on his bond." The President said it should be done accordingly. I said nothing. General Butler assumed that I was from that moment on his staff and made an appointment to call for me that evening at my hotel, and I left the President and the General together. That night I went with General Butler to visit the members of the Cabinet and heard the proposed expedition for the capture of New Orleans discussed in all its details. I subsequently accepted the office of Paymaster of Volunteers, and served until seriously disabled in the performance of duty, when, declining an appointment in the Veteran Reserve Corps, I resigned in October, 1864.

I never saw Abraham Lincoln again, but I shall carry through life the impression of his remarkable personality.

It need not be claimed that he was a perfect man; at times he may have exhibited weakness on the side of amiability; but if he was thereby led into error, his determination to be the fearless, upright man he was by nature, ultimately snapped asunder all of the cords woven by the influence of the strong and ambitious men who surrounded him — such men as Sumner, Seward, Chase, Ben Wade, Oliver Morton and others. His strength is shown by the fact that while bearing the burden of the leadership of a country disrupted by a great and bloody conflict, which in the beginning was of doubtful issue, he curbed and controlled the extraordinary men who, in a generation of intellectual conflict, dethroned King Cotton and destroyed the mighty institution of Slavery, before which the fathers of the Revolution were impotent.

Notwithstanding Abraham Lincoln's humor, his whimsical playfulness of expression and his keen appreciation of wit, which were always evident, the impression made by him at the time of which I write was of a man anxious, weary and heavy laden, earnestly laboring to perform the duties laid upon him. This impression was, of course, deepened and made permanent by the time and manner of his tragic death. In my opinion, he was the instrument chosen by Providence to effect the salvation of the Union and the triumph of the Flag.

NEW YORK CITY.

THE HOUR OF HIS THANKSGIVING.

"A THUNDERING OLD GLORY" — THE NEWS OF HIS ASSASSINATION — ANGRY CROWD AT THE SUB-TREASURY.

BY THE HON. L. E. CHITTENDEN,

Ex-Registrar of the Treasury.

The number of men whose acquaintance with Abraham Lincoln was intimate enough to enable them to form any just estimate of his character, is small and rapidly diminishing. If they are true to his memory, as they recall his voice and presence through the softening influences of thirty years, they will experience a sensation of regret that they did not better improve their opportunities and more fully appreciate his statesmanship and other great qualities. They are asking themselves how it could have happened that, when he was delivering his first inaugural address, writing his letter of August 22d, 1862, to Mr. Greeley, that of August 26th, 1863, to Mr. J. C. Conkling, and the address at Gettysburg, all which will be read and admired as the gems of our English speech while history endures, they did not recognize him as the greatest patriot, statesman and writer of his time? I suppose the reason must have been that our hopes and fears for the safety of the Union so engrossed all our thoughts that we had no time for other subjects, and as we knew that nothing but the success of our arms could save it, nothing greatly impressed us but victory on the field.

At last, after years of weary waiting, victory had come — not alone in one bloody battle, but all over the theatre of war. Around the seacoasts, up gulf, bayou and river, from the Ohio down through Nashville and Atlanta to the rice fields of the Savannah, up through Carolina pines and down through Virginia swamps, everywhere the eagles of victory were borne upon our standards. Lee, Gordon and other great war generals had sheathed their swords, and promised never again to draw them from their scabbards except under the Stars and Stripes. Grant had said to his prisoners, "Take your horses and goods to your homes, plough, sow and reap, and become good citizens." And all over the free North gray-haired sires, true-hearted wives and bright-faced children were making ready to welcome sons, husbands and fathers home from the War.

There was one form which it was grand to look upon in those days. Truly he wist not that his face shone like that of Moses when he came down from Sinai with the tables of the testimony in his hands. It was like a picture drawn by a great artist to express all the noble qualities of humanity — chiefly benevolence, kindness and charity; as grand a face as ever was given to man. I need scarcely be more specific. Such a face could belong only to Abraham Lincoln. In this hour of thanksgiving we were chiefly grateful for one mercy — I might well write above all others. It was that the trials of our Greatheart had come to an end. We had seen him when they began — when his face was smooth, genial and, on occasion, humorous. As his duties multiplied and his responsibilities were greater, we had seen them plough deep furrows in his face and make it so sad and sorrowful that it was painful to look upon. They were ended now. His faith had been justified. Worn and exhausted by four long years of strife, turmoil and perplexity, rest had come to him at last. He could rest in the peace of a restored Union, a saved Republic, for which he had wrought so faithfully, which he had so richly earned. Peace! Peace! North, South, and throughout the land! It was not unlike that other peace that passeth understanding.

Our Lincoln was never more noble in appearance than on Friday, April 14th, 1865. He had laid aside the burden of his cares; his heart was full of gratitude for a country saved, and overflowing with compassion for the conquered. At breakfast he had heard the story of Appomattox from the lips of his own son. All the day long he had been in consultation with members of his Cabinet and others over plans of reconstruction, in which there was no trace of cruelty or punishment. Toward evening he was intending to take his accustomed drive. As he was coming down the stairway a one-armed soldier said: "I would almost give my other hand if I could shake that of Abraham Lincoln." "You shall do that and it shall cost you nothing, my boy!" said the President. "He grasped my hand and held it," said the soldier, "while he asked my name and regiment and where I lost my arm; and said I was a brave soldier, and a lot of pleasant things." This man brushed something out of his eyes as he told the story, and ended it with: "I tell you, boys, Abe Lincoln is a thundering old glory!" I can say that never was a ruler so loved by his loyal people as Abraham Lincoln on that last day of his mortal life; but I should despair of describing more impressively than in these words of a private soldier.

I never read and I will not write about the remaining hours of this noble life. I prefer to think of him as he appeared to the soldier. Nor have I any words fit to describe the gloom of the next morning. Incidents of it I may recall.

The people seemed stunned by the shock. Then anger was fierce, silent, terrible. They were inclined to believe the crime that of the defeated Confederates. That belief was not true, and very dangerous, for a word would have turned them to vengeance against every one of doubtful loyalty. Without any call, and moved by impulse, they packed Wall Street from above the Sub-Treasury to a point below the Custom House — a silent, fierce, angry crowd. One man was struck to the pavement, and would have been torn in pieces if the police had not thrust him into a basement and guarded the door. He had spoken disrespectfully of Lincoln. "Here is one who will tell us about Lincoln!" shouted a well-known citizen. The person referred to was an officer of the Treasury. He was caught up and passed over the heads of the crowd to the ledge of an open window, whence he essayed to speak fitting memorial words of Lincoln. "He was murdered by a rebel spy!" exclaimed an angry voice. "Don't you believe it!" said the speaker. "The Confederates know the value to them of the kind heart of Lincoln; — they are not murderers! This assassin was either a fool or a madman!" "If he was we shall never know it, for he has escaped," said a voice. "He has not escaped!" said the speaker. "He might as well hope to escape death and the grave. The earth has no asylum for such an assassin, no cave in which he can hide. Every emancipated slave in the State to which he has fled will be a detective; every decent white man his betrayer. Do not forget that he is a madman; I repeat it, a madman. The South is responsible for many lives, but, thank the Almighty, not for this one. Let us set an example before the world, and, while we mourn our terrible calamity, cry with the Psalmist, 'O God, to whom vengeance belongeth, show thyself.'"

There was no outbreak; but a word of disrespect for Lincoln the people would not hear. A saloon proprietor tried it. His customers wrecked his saloon and beat him to insensibility. In a leading hotel the servants, from the chief clerk to the bootblacks, struck work until the housekeeper was put out of it. She had spoken contemptuously of "old Lincoln."

Abraham Lincoln was a man of the people. The people knew and loved him. That was a triumphal rather than a funeral procession which bore him from the Capital to his final rest, near his Springfield home. Since it passed there has been no hour in which he has not grown in the public esteem. We celebrate his birthday, and soon shall make it a national holiday, so that the Preserver shall have equal honors with the Father of his country. The time is not distant when the history of the life and times of Lincoln will be taught in our public schools.

NEW YORK CITY.

GOD IN LINCOLN.

LINCOLN IN NEW ORLEANS — ATTENDS A SLAVE AUCTION.

BY DAVID GREGG, D.D.,

Pastor of the Lafayette Avenue Presbyterian Church, Brooklyn.

God works through persons. This is his invariable law. He links a man or a woman to his purposes as a co-worker. Moses must superintend the Exodus. Deborah must lead his armies. Cyrus must issue the decree for the return of his captives. The twelve Apostles must act as the witnesses of his Son. Thus it is in the history inside the lids of the sacred Book, and thus it is in the history outside the lids of the sacred Book. Luther must be the head and front of the Reformation in Germany. John Knox must be soul of the Reformation in Scotland. Wesley must break the ecclesiastical shackles in England. Abraham Lincoln must pen the Emancipation Proclamation in the United States of America. If God's truth is to succeed, it must incarnate itself. If God's cause is to win a victory, it must embody himself in a person. There is no substitute for whole-souled consecrated persons. Without them liberty perishes from the earth, and abstract truth is simply principle on paper, a thing of cold type.

While God works through persons, yet something is requisite upon the part of those through whom God works. In order to success, it is requisite that those through God's works should be possessed by his purposes, and should be all on fire with his divine principles. Elijah, the Prophet of Fire, succeeded; but he succeeded because the whole man was in his mission. The half of Elijah would have failed. Abraham Lincoln succeeded; but everybody knows that his heart was with the slave. The Emancipation Proclamation was not a sudden growth. It was not an accident. It was evolved from the nature of the man. Some one has taken the Emancipation Proclamation and has deftly arranged its words so that they form an accurate profile of Abraham Lincoln's face. The picture is perfect, and not a letter of the Proclamation is wanting. This rightly represents things as they are. The man and the liberty which he proclaimed are one and inseparable. If we could see into the soul of the man, we should find that the Emancipation Proclamation was but a transcript of that which was deepest and most vital there.

Charles Carleton Coffin tells us in his history that when Abraham Lincoln was a young man, he built a raft for his employer and took a cargo of produce down the Mississippi River to the market of New Orleans. After he had sold the cargo, he and a fellow-boatman sauntered through the slave mart, where the Southern planters had gathered to buy and sell slaves. Black men and women and children were arranged in rows against the wall for inspection. The auctioneer proclaimed their good qualities as he would those of a horse or mule. Some of the blacks were Christians, and their Christianity was proclaimed as among their good qualities, which ought to command a higher figure in the market; it made them more conscientious and trustworthy as workers. Again and again the hammer of the auctioneer fell, and husbands and wives were separated forever, and children were, there and then, doomed never again to look into the faces of father and mother. That scene in the auction room set the blood of Lincoln on fire. His lips quivered and his voice choked in his throat, as he turned to his fellow-boatman, and said: "*If I ever get a chance to hit that thing, I will hit it hard, by the Eternal God.*" Who is he to hit the "*thing*" a blow? He is only a boatman, a splitter of rails, a teamster, a backwoodsman. Nothing more. His poverty is so deep that his clothes are in tatters. What position of influence or power is he likely to attain to enable him to strike a blow? The "*thing*" which he would like to hit is incorporated into the framework of society, and legalized in half the States composing the Republic. It is intrenched in Church and State alike. It is a political force, recognized in the Constitution, and it enters into the basis of representation. Is there the remotest probability that he will ever be able to smite such an institution? Why utter these words? Why raise the right hand toward Heaven and swear a solemn oath? Was it some dim vision of what might come to him through divine Providence in the unfolding years? Was it an illumination of the Spirit forecasting for the moment the impending conflict between right and wrong in which he was to take a conspicuous part? Was it a whisper by a divine messenger that he was to be the chosen one to wipe the "*thing*" from the earth, and give deliverance to millions of his fellow-men? Was it not rather the mind and heart and power of God planted deep in the depths of his very being, and abiding there with a holy impatience, waiting for the clock of destiny to strike? You may answer these questions as you please; but these are the facts of history. The hour of the nation came, and with it the golden moment for the slave. Then it was that the very same hand that was lifted in solemn oath before God in the New Orleans slave mart took up the God-inspired pen of liberty, and dashed off the Emancipation Proclamation which wrote out of existence the American slave, and the American slave mart, and the American slave master.

That was an act worthy of Jesus Christ. It was the act of Jesus Christ; for it was the spirit of Jesus Christ that filled the man with power and that found an outlet in American history through the personality and pen of Abraham Lincoln.

I remember that day well. It was the most thrilling day I have ever known. It was a day full of magnificent music. I shall never hear music more thrilling than the clink of the links of those four million of slave chains, as link struck link when the chains were snapped into a thousand parts beyond all hope of ever again being welded together. The harps of gold, struck by celestial hands, cannot make sweeter music.

LINCOLN'S KINDNESS OF HEART.

PLEADING FOR A DESERTER.

BY JOHN D. KERNAN, ESQ.

A STORY my father, the Hon. Francis Kernan, used to tell illustrates Lincoln's kindness of heart. When my father was a member of Congress, during the War, a woman came to him one day and said that her husband had been captured as a deserter and she wanted my father to go and see the President about the matter.

So the next morning he called on Mr. Lincoln. He found him very much occupied, but, sending in word that it was an urgent matter, the President saw him. My father gave the President the facts in the case. It seems that the man had been absent a year from his family and, without leave, had gone home to see them. On his way back to the army he was arrested as a deserter and sentenced to be shot. The sentence was to be carried out that very day. The wife had come on to intercede for her husband.

The President listened attentively, becoming more and more interested in the story. Finally he said: "Why, Kernan, of course this man wanted to see his family; and they oughtn't to shoot him for that." So he immediately rang his bell, called his secretary and gave him orders to send off telegrams suspending the sentence and ordering the record of the case to be sent to him. As he went on dictating to his secretary he became more and more anxious about the matter. He exclaimed: "For God's sake, get that off just as quick as you can, or they will shoot this man in spite of me!" The result was that the man got a pardon and took his place again in the army.

At the time my father was pleading for the man, Lincoln at first said: "I don't know, Kernan. It is very hard for me to interfere in these matters. Here is General So-and-So and General So-and-So, and they all insist that I am interfering with the discipline of the army, destroying its efficiency; but," said he, "I can't help it. Here is a man who just went home to see his wife and children and they caught him on his way back to the army. I don't think he ought to be shot for that, and I'm going to interfere." And, as I have just stated, he did.

NEW YORK CITY.

A TELEGRAPHER'S REMINISCENCE.

LINCOLN IN THE TELEGRAPH OFFICE—THE NOMINATION OF ANDREW JOHNSON—MR. LINCOLN'S FEARS.

BY CHARLES A. TINKER, ESQ.,

SUPERINTENDENT EASTERN DIVISION WESTERN UNION TELEGRAPH CO.

My acquaintance with the martyred President began thirty-eight years ago, in the spring of 1857, when I was a telegraph operator at Pekin, a small town in Illinois, ten miles south of Peoria. The telegraph office was located in the Tazewell House, the principal hotel of the place, and the favorite resort for lawyers and persons who had business in the court which was held in the town.

Even at that time Mr. Lincoln was familiarly known as "Old Abe," and was noticeable on account of his peculiar appearance and personal characteristics. He was then a practising lawyer, living in Springfield, the capital of the State. He was a great story-teller, and many a time, at the evening gatherings in the office, kept his small but appreciative audience in fits of laughter as he told a quaint anecdote to illustrate some point in an argument or some experience in daily life.

The first time he ever spoke to me was when, one afternoon, he came to my office in the corner of the room, and, looking over the tall railing, said: "Mr. Operator, I have always had a curiosity to see the telegraph work. You don't seem to be very busy, and as I have a half-hour or so to wait for dinner, I wonder if you would not explain it to me." I replied: "Certainly, sir, I should be pleased to do so"; and, inviting him inside the gate, I proceeded to show him the "working of the telegraph," explained the battery and its connection to the instruments, and the wires leading thence out of the window and away to the world without. I was encouraged by the readiness with which he comprehended it all. He seemed to grasp its intricacies, and remarked: "How simple it is when you know it all!"

In the fall of 1861, I entered the service of the United States Military Telegraph, and was assigned to the office in the War Department at Washington. Here I frequently saw the President passing in and out of the Department and on the streets, but was soon transferred to the field corps, and then only saw him as he occasionally visited the army. I have seen him riding with General McClellan and his staff at review, and it was a comical sight. On horseback his figure had the appearance of a huge clothespin on a line, his long legs dangling at the sides of the animal, and his pantaloons climbing to his knees; his silk hat on the back of his head, and his body doubled up and pounding the saddle in his frantic efforts to "keep up with the procession" and to maintain the dignity of the Chief Magistrate. Later on, however, he became, by experience, a better horseman, and it was a daily treat to see him ride by my house with his own body guard, as he passed to and fro between the White House and Soldiers' Home, his summer residence, sitting with ease and raising his hat to acquaintances whom he met.

In 1862, when I was a cipher operator in the War Department, Mr. Lincoln often visited the office and was always affable and courteous, sometimes even familiar, in his intercourse with the attachés of the office. He did not recognize me as the young telegraph operator he had met in the West, nor did I make my identity known until, on one occasion, when he was telling a story to a member of the Cabinet and some prominent army officers. He tried to recall the name of a certain man in Illinois whom I had known very well. It seemed to annoy him very much that he could not remember the name. With some trepidation I ventured to say: "Mr. President, permit me to suggest; was it not Judge Puterbough?" He turned upon me with a look of surprise, and shouted: "Why, yes! Did you know him?" Gaining confidence, I replied: "Yes, sir"; and he queried, "Where did you know him?" I responded again, more hopefully: "Down in Pekin, Illinois, where I had the honor of explaining to the present President of the United States the working of the telegraph, in the little office in the Tazewell House." He turned to his surprised audience, and exclaimed: "Well, isn't it funny that we should have met here?" and confirmed to them how he had first witnessed the working of the telegraph in the Tazewell House, at Pekin. Thus unceremoniously had his story been interrupted; but he soon gathered the threads and mended its fabric with "the missing link," Judge Puterbough, and I resumed my duty gathering news from the chaotic communications before me.

Mr. Lincoln not only had a vast fund of common sense, but often illustrated his opinions on some subject by a wise maxim. Once, when a trusted representative had been sent to perform some special service, and his report was not entirely satisfactory, I heard him remark: "When you want a thing done right, go do it yourself." At another time, I heard Mr. Seward say to him, jokingly: "Mr. President, I hear you turned out for a colored woman on a muddy crossing the other day." Mr. Lincoln laughingly remarked: "Did you? Well, I don't remember it; but I always make it a rule, if people don't turn out for me, I will for them. If I didn't there would be a collision." Another maxim, familiar to all, was: "Never stop to swap horses when crossing the stream."

His stories were always told upon the impulse of the moment, aroused by some remark or incident of conversation, or from what he had read in a message before him. He could not help their ready flow from his lips, and when told, and he had joined in the laughter which followed, he was as eager to listen to something new, if any of his listeners were fortunate enough to have a story he had not heard. But he was a restless listener, and it was not often that he gave way for others to talk.

Once he received a message from a zealous Irish soldier, with more courage than brains, or he would not have telegraphed direct to the President, who had been left behind in the retreat of the army across the Potomac before the advancing columns of Lee's army, with one gun of his battery on the bank of the river below Edward's Ferry. It read about thus: "I have the whole rebel army in my front. Send me another gun, and I assure your honor they shall not come over." This pleased the President greatly, and he sent him an encouraging reply, suggesting that he report his situation to his commanding officer. But I suppose the poor fellow didn't know where to look for him then, and had confidence that a message would reach the President, who was his Commander-in-Chief.

One Sunday morning as I was passing through the White House grounds toward the Department, I met the President coming from it. A little way off, scraping among the leaves under a tree, Major Johnson, the private secretary of Mr. Stanton, a man of perhaps thirty-five years, born and brought up in Washington, and, so far as I know, never having been outside the District of Columbia, also on his way to the Department, had stepped aside to gather a few horse-chestnuts, which abounded on the grounds. The President called to him: "Major, good-morning. What in the world are you doing there?" The Major turned quickly, doffed his hat, scraped and bowed. "Why, good-morning, Mr. President. I was just looking for a few horse-chestnuts." "Horse-chestnuts!" the President exclaimed. "Do you expect to find horse-chestnuts under a sycamore tree?" Sure enough, he didn't know the difference. The President laughed heartily, and nodded to me and passed by, while I escorted the novice in chestnutting to the Department, quite chagrined at the President's discovery of his ignorance.

At another time the President came into the office laughing, and remarked that he had just been reading a little book which some one had given his son, Tad. It was a story of a motherly hen, who was struggling to raise her brood and teach them to lead honest and useful lives; but in her efforts she was greatly annoyed by a mischievous fox, who made sad havoc with her offspring. She had given him numerous lectures on his wicked ways, and, said the President, "I thought I would turn over to the finis and see how it came out. This is what it said: 'And the fox became a good fox, and was appointed paymaster in the army.' I think it very funny that I should have appointed him a paymaster in the army. I wonder who he is?"

When Mr. Lincoln received the news of the nomination of Andrew Johnson to the Vice-Presidency, he was in his office. He read the message carefully, and soliloquized aloud: "Well, I thought possibly he might be the man. Perhaps he is the best man; but —" and rising from his chair passed out of the office, leaving me impressed with the significance of the unfinished sentence, which, in the light of the subsequent events, became a thrilling prophecy. In the discussion regarding Lincoln's preference for Hamlin or Johnson for the Vice-Presidency, I addressed a note to Mr. Charles A. Dana, reciting this incident. It was published in the *Sun*, and came to the notice of Major Johnson, formerly secretary to Mr. Stanton — the same who figured in the horse-chestnutting scene — and he referred to it in an interview upon the subject published in the Washington *Star*, in these words:

"Mr. Tinker was a telegraph operator in the room adjoining the office occupied by Secretary Stanton; and upon the occasion referred to, as soon as the President had gone, came into the Secretary's room and told me the entire story just as he has now told it in print."

Further on:

"Mr. Tinker's reminiscence is the most striking contribution to the literature of this controversy, and it would be, in my judgment, impossible to find a more convincing proof that Mr. Lincoln was neither the author nor the abettor of the Johnson nomination than that uncompleted sentence as it fell from his lips, drawn forth by the sudden news from Baltimore, 'Perhaps he is the best man; but —'"

Mr. Lincoln was a just man, but his great heart always leaned to the side of mercy. Many incidents are related of this phase of his character, but I will only mention one. I quote from a letter written by me to Maj.-Gen. George H. Thomas, of date May 23d, 1867:

"*General:* — I have had in my possession since the day it was written a telegram penned by our late loved President. Its history is this: Robert A. Maxwell, a quixotic individual, a resident of Philadelphia, has, during the War and since, humored a propensity for addressing numerous dictatorial and sensational dispatches to the President, his Cabinet and prominent officials of the Government. Those who are familiar with his character give no consideration to them."

On receipt of one of these dispatches, a copy of which I enclose, as follows:

"New York City, September 23d, 1863.
"His Excellency, A. Lincoln, President United States:
"Will Buell's testamentary executor, George Thomas, ever let Rosecrans succeed? Is Bragg dumb enough to punish Thomas severely and disgracingly?
"(Signed) Robert A. Maxwell."

President Lincoln came to the Department and handed me his reply, marked "Cipher," as follows:

"To Robert A. Maxwell, New York:
"I hasten to say that in the state of information we have here nothing could be more ungracious than to indulge any suspicion toward General Thomas. It is doubtful whether his heroism and skill exhibited last Sunday afternoon has ever been surpassed in the world. (Signed) A. Lincoln."

He lingered in the office while I was preparing it for transmission, and when nearly ready he remarked: "I guess, on the whole, Mr. Tinker, you need not send that. I will pay no more attention to the crazy fellow." I put it into my pocket, and have preserved it as a precious autograph. It is a priceless tribute to a noble hero, whose dauntless courage on that fatal day saved the Army of the Cumberland. My letter-press copy of the letter has this note:

"Delivered to him in person at Willard's Hotel, Monday evening, May 27th, 1867."

Mr. Lincoln was a plain, modest man, having little thought or care for the conventionalities of life. He would not wait an introduction if he had aught to say to his fellow-man. He was easily approached, and gave ready ear to any communication, but quickly manifested impatience if he found it was a subject without interest to him. He would frankly speak the truth and guide the applicant or supplicant, to the proper department, or dismiss him with words of wisdom, and resume his own path of duty. I hardly think there was any member of his Cabinet who enjoyed listening to his stories, although perhaps none of them would manifest impatience, except Mr. Stanton. He would never tell a story himself, and would not willingly spend his time listening to others. I have seen him abruptly leave the office for his own when Mr. Lincoln was reminded of a story and began to tell it. Mr. Lincoln paid no attention to the slight. On the contrary, treating it as a matter of fact — a personal trait of Mr. Stanton for which he was not responsible. He often called Mr. Stanton "Mars" and appeared to enjoy his discomfort at the fitting title.

Mr. Lincoln was an early riser, and often reached the office as early as any of the morning arrivals. His custom was to come over at least twice a day — morning, and evening after the Department hours — and when there was anything of importance transpiring about which he was especially anxious, he was frequently at the telegraph office till long after midnight. We took three copies of all the important dispatches addressed to the Secretary of War, Secretary of the Navy, General of the Army, or to the President. The hard copy for the official files, and two tissue copies, one for the Secretary of War, and one to be retained in the office. This retained copy was put in a little drawer on top of the cipher operators' desk, handy for reference, and accessible to the Secretary or President. Mr. Lincoln went direct to that drawer, took out all the copies and sat down at the desk and read the dispatches in order, laying them on one side, face down, till he had finished; and returned them to the drawer in the same order. If he came again the same day, he would go through the same operation until he had reached the previous pile, face down, when he would remark, "There, I have got down to the raisins," and replace them in the drawer. His reference to "the raisins" was illustrated by his story of the countryman who sat down to dinner at a city hotel, and undertook to get away with the entire bill of fare, and found relief when he reached the raisins.

The last time I saw Mr. Lincoln was on the afternoon of April 11th, three days prior to his assassination. He came to the office as usual that afternoon, and something reminded him of a story, and to illustrate the finale he gathered his coattails under his arms and, with about three long strides, crossed the room and passed out of the door with the last words of the story echoing from his lips. That evening I went home from the office ill with a slight fever which prevented my resuming duty until the early morning of April 15th, when I was aroused by loud voices in the street, from which I gathered that the President had been assassinated. I arose and dressed and hastily made my way to the office, passing crowds here and there in muffled debate; by Secretary Seward's house, where a sentinel was pacing to and fro; on to the War Department, where I learned the terrible truth of the ghastly events of the night just passed. My brief journal of that date contains their narrative, with this reference:

"Departments are closed and being draped in mourning. Our office feels most keenly the affliction which has thus been brought to the whole country in the death of Abraham Lincoln; for we had learned to look upon him in his daily visits there almost as a companion, while we venerated him for his goodness as a father. We had no heart to work; bitter tears flooded every eye, and grief choked utterance."

Thus ends my personal reminiscences of Abraham Lincoln. It is a blessing to have known him, and still a greater one to have enjoyed his almost daily companionship, as we of the War Department Telegraph Office did during his Presidential life.

NEW YORK CITY.

LINCOLN AND THE SLAVE TRADER GORDON.

REFUSING A REPRIEVE.

BY ETHAN ALLEN.

In 1861, E. Delafield Smith was United States District Attorney for the Southern District of New York, and I was his chief deputy. One of the first and most important trials in which I participated was the trial of William Gordon for slave trading. The trial was long and bitterly contested, and Gordon was convicted, the first conviction under the Slave Law that was ever had in the United States, either North or South.

Gordon was sentenced to be hanged by Judge Nelson, then the presiding Judge of the Supreme Court for this district. An effort was immediately made to have Mr. Lincoln pardon him, and the effort was very extraordinary and powerful in influence. Mr. Smith, the District Attorney, hearing of this fact, deemed it his duty (and he alone is responsible in the matter) to go to Washington and plead with Mr. Lincoln against clemency. When he met Mr. Lincoln, as he afterward reported to me on his return, Mr. Lincoln took out from his desk the reprieve already prepared and laid it before him. He picked up a pen, which he held in his hand while he listened to the argument of Mr. Smith on the imperative necessity of making an example of this man

Gordon, in order forever to terrorize those who were engaged in this business.

Mr. Lincoln listened to him very patiently and with a sort of wail of despair (as it was afterward described), flourishing the pen over the reprieve he said:

"Mr. Smith, you do not know how hard it is to have a human being die when you know that a stroke of your pen may save him."

He threw down the pen, however, and Gordon was executed in New York.

New York City.

A THEATRICAL MANAGER'S REMINISCENCES.

INTERVIEW WITH WILKES BOOTH — EFFECT UPON EDWIN BOOTH.

BY COL. WILLIAM E. SINN,

OF THE PARK THEATRE, BROOKLYN, N. Y.

THE year after the War broke out I was the proprietor of "Canterbury Hall," in Washington, where vaudeville entertainments were given. The same year I was associated with Mr. Leonard Grover in the management of the National Theatre. I remember that at the matinée performances at the "Canterbury" Mr. Lincoln's boys — particularly the young one, "Tad" — would often be sent down to see the performance. Mr. Lincoln himself was a frequent visitor at Grover & Sinn's National Theatre. He always gave us notice a day ahead, and we took care to have a private box reserved for him. From a business point of view, we were only too glad to have him visit the theatre, because it was a good advertisement, and we would have willingly given him complimentary tickets; but he would firmly decline them, invariably directing his secretary, or the messenger, to pay for the box.

One peculiar feature about Mr. Lincoln's theatre-going was that he never had the least desire (as many theatre-goers have) to go behind the scenes. He used to say that to do so would spoil the illusion surrounding the play.

When very prominent actors appeared, however, in whom he was specially interested, Mr. Lincoln would invite them into his private box between the acts, and have a chat with them. He was a great admirer of the drama, and was particularly fond of comedy. When a good strong comedian appeared at our house, male or female, you would always find Mr. Lincoln present at the performance, unless sickness or extremely important business prevented his attendance. He came to the "Canterbury" vaudeville performance only once or twice, but often sent his boys there to the matinées in charge of some grown person. He was very democratic in his ways, always had a pleasant word if he happened to meet me at the entrance to the theatre, which he generally did, as I had charge of the front of the house. On one occasion he glanced over the auditorium, the theatre was crowded. "Ah!" he exclaimed, "I guess *this* business will pay."

At the time the President was assassinated I (or rather the firm of Grover & Sinn) was running the Chestnut Street Theatre in Philadelphia. Three or four days before the assassination, Wilkes Booth was in Philadelphia on his way to Washington. I was very well acquainted with him. He told me he was going to Washington to play for a benefit. I think the benefit of Miss Susan Denin. Through some misunderstanding the benefit was postponed. After the tragedy at Ford's Theatre, it was thought that on the occasion of Miss Denin's benefit, when the President was almost certain to be present, Booth would have attempted to assassinate the Chief Magistrate.

The last time I saw Wilkes Booth was at the stage door of the Chestnut Street Theatre, Philadelphia, at about ten o'clock at night. He was going to take the train in an hour for Washington. On that same afternoon I had seen him and been with him for fully three-quarters of an hour, had walked down Chestnut Street with him, and left him to lunch with Miss Kate Pennoyer, an actress now retired from the stage. When I bade him good by he made a remark that I quickly recalled as soon as I heard of the assassination: "You will hear from me in Washington," he said. "I am going to make a hit." The term "hit" in theatrical parlance means a success. I said: "Good luck to you. You are a pretty good sort of an actor; I guess you will." The next thing I heard of Booth was the terrible news that he had killed President Lincoln.

Of course, after the assassination there was a close and careful examination as to Booth's antecedents and his movements just before the dreadful tragedy. It seems that during his few days' stay in Philadelphia he was seen a great deal in the company of Matt Canning (since deceased), at that time manager of Mme. Vestvali, who was playing then at Mrs. John Drew's Arch Street Theatre. He stopped over in Baltimore on his way to Washington, and there he was often seen in the company of John T. Ford, then the manager of the Halliday Street Theatre, Baltimore, and of Ford's Theatre, Washington, the scene of the assassination. After the assassination Mr. Ford was arrested on the belief that, having been seen with Booth so shortly before the event, he might know something about it. But the fact was that he knew no more about it than a child. But he was arrested and incarcerated in the Old Capitol prison, Washington. Matt Canning was also arrested in Philadelphia. I was very much scared myself, for I had been seen with Booth on Chestnut Street, Philadelphia, and had been in his company much of the time during his stay in the city. I escaped arrest, however, but I passed several sleepless nights and days of worriment thinking over the matter. In fact, I tried to persuade myself that I did not know Booth. When questioned in regard to the subject my memory was a blank. Mr. Ford and Mr. Canning were, of course, exonerated from any knowledge of the sad affair.

I was spending the evening with some friends on the night of the assassination — Good Friday night. As I was returning home about twelve o'clock, walking down Chestnut Street, I saw signs of great excitement; crowds were running along the street. I thought there was a big fire; but I soon learned the news, that Abraham Lincoln had been assassinated, killed by Wilkes Booth, the man I had been chatting with pleasantly but a few days, you might say a few hours, before.

Within three or four days there was a great hue and cry raised against not only the actor, but actors and theatrical people in general. "An actor had assassinated the President!" I can truly say that I do not know of any class of people in the community at that time who were more greatly shocked or more deeply grieved than the members of the theatrical profession. Whatever the faults of actors may be (and they have their faults like the rest of the human race), they are not given to deeds of violence. So far from being predisposed to such crimes, they are brought up to an art which views the events of history only on their pathetic or their scenic side. They are philosophers of life, endeavoring to portray it, rather than to take part in the political or social struggles of the age. Many well-meaning, but narrow-minded persons, however, after the assassination, could not say anything too bad about actors and the theatre. They were particularly severe in their allusions to Edwin Booth, the distinguished tragedian, brother of the assassin, who probably suffered more mental torture from the cruel act of his unnatural relative than did any one else in the country, outside of the President's own family. Edwin Booth was so overcome that he retired from the stage temporarily, and it was many months before he appeared in a theatre before an audience.

Edwin Booth never played in Washington City from the time of the assassination until his death. Theatrical managers offered him the most fabulous prices to go there, but he had made a resolution that he would never play at the Capital of the nation, so intimately associated with his brother's terrible crime; and he kept this resolution until the day of his death.

But the honors shown Edwin Booth in his later years, and the esteem in which he was held by all classes of the community, did something to atone for the cruel and thoughtless treatment he received at the hands of some prejudiced and ignorant persons soon after the tragedy.

Numerous rewards were promptly offered for the capture of Wilkes Booth. I added $500 to the reward that was offered in Philadelphia, and promptly did what I could to show that the members of the dramatic profession were not in sympathy with Wilkes Booth, and looked with horror upon his terrible crime.

The advertisement which I inserted in the Philadelphia newspapers was as follows:

"$500 REWARD. — The undersigned will add to the reward offered by the Government and municipal authorities the sum of FIVE HUNDRED DOLLARS for the arrest of JOHN WILKES BOOTH, the assassin of our late beloved President. I have no doubt but the sum of ten thousand dollars will be raised to further this really necessary object by the different Managers. In offering this reward I feel it my conscientious duty to aid to the utmost in bringing this atrocious murderer to justice. I feel convinced that every Manager in the land will second this object, and take the same view of the case. As this crime was committed in one of our principal theatres, we should endeavor to use our utmost ability in an object of so much importance to every American citizen.

"WILLIAM E. SINN, for GROVER & SINN."

It was not long before theatrical people in all parts of the country put themselves before the public in their proper light, condemning the crime, both in public and in private, both in the North and in the South, showing that, so far as the members of their profession were concerned, there had been no collusion in the matter, and that the crime had been committed by John Wilkes Booth in a false and cruel spirit of devotion to the South.

I think the assassination of President Lincoln was the severest blow the South could have had. Certainly the act was not endorsed by the thinking men in the South. So far from its being a benefit to the South, it put back reconstruction fully ten or fifteen years.

BROOKLYN, N. Y.

SOME TRAITS AND SAYINGS OF ABRAHAM LINCOLN.

HIS SELF-CONTROL; HIS FORESIGHT; HIS SYMPATHY.

BY WAYLAND HOYT, D.D.

CONSIDER the singular self-control of Abraham Lincoln. The scene is Washington. The time is a few days before Mr. Lincoln's first inauguration. Mr. Lincoln has been in Washington scarcely twenty-four hours. The night before he has eluded the desperate plot to assassinate him in Baltimore by passing through that city at an unexpected hour and in an unheralded way. Washington is throbbing and tumultuous with excitement. Rumors of all sorts are thick and clashing. Every hour is portentous with uncertainty. The ship is about to change captains, but amid the threatenings of a storm such as has never before growled and muttered and flashed in the horizon. The so-called Peace Congress is in session, helplessly seeking some way to still the storm. It is proposed, with very grumbling grace on the part of many of the members of it who have disloyal hearts and pro-slavery sympathies, to pay a visit on this evening to the President-elect. Though such members splutter and object, they cannot well refuse such evident proprieties of the moment. But with very different ceremony from that with which they had waited on President Buchanan a little time before — with reluctance, carelessness, in some cases with angry rudeness, they enter the parlor of the hotel in which Mr. Lincoln is quietly awaiting them. If any one wishes to study one of the most eminent instances of self-control in history, let him carefully read the description of this scene in Mr. Chittenden's "Recollections of President Lincoln and His Administration." It is too long to rehearse here, but there are few as fascinating pages in any literature.

Here is the gaunt, queer, homely, towering man, just escaped a dastardly attempt upon his life, standing amid utterly untried circumstances, confronted with problems such as had never massed themselves before an American statesman, in environment where an unguarded word might be a match to a magazine, an ill-considered gesture, even, the cause of an explosion, maligned and hated by multitudes, surrounded in this parlor by many men scowling with criticism, glad to trip him, hot with anger at his election, some determined already to band themselves into rebellion against him, soon to be the constitutional head of the Republic — and he, this plain man, Abraham Lincoln, with never a quiver in his voice, nor a touch of paleness on his gaunt cheek, nor the slightest cadence of irritation in his tone, the steady master of himself, these men, the whole occasion. Says Mr. Chittenden:

"It was reserved for the delegation from New York to call out from Mr. Lincoln his first expression touching the great controversy of the hour. He had exchanged remarks with ex-Governor King, Judge James, William Curtis Noyes and Francis Granger. William E. Dodge had stood awaiting his turn. As soon as his opportunity came, he raised his voice enough to be heard by all present, and, addressing Mr. Lincoln, declared that the whole country in great anxiety was awaiting his inaugural address, and then added: 'It is for you, sir, to say whether the whole nation shall be plunged into bankruptcy; whether the grass shall grow in the streets of our commercial cities.'

"'Then I say it shall not,' Mr. Lincoln answered, with a merry twinkle in his eye. 'If it depends upon me, the grass will not grow anywhere except in the fields and the meadows.'

"'Then you will yield to the just demands of the South. You will leave her to control her own institutions. You will admit slave States into the Union on the same conditions as free States. You will not go to war on account of slavery.'

"A sad but stern expression swept over Mr. Lincoln's face. 'I do not know that I understand your meaning, Mr. Dodge,' he said, without raising his voice; 'nor do I know what my acts or my opinions may be in the future, beyond this. If I shall ever come to the great office of the President of the United States, I shall take an oath. I shall swear that I will faithfully execute the office of President of the United States, of all the United States, and that I will, to the best of my ability, preserve, protect and defend the Constitution of the United States. This is a great and solemn duty. With the support of the people and the assistance of the Almighty I shall undertake to perform it. It is not the Constitution as I would like to have it, but as it *is*, that is to be defended. The Constitution will not be preserved and defended until it is enforced and obeyed in every part of every one of the United States. It must be so respected, obeyed, enforced and defended, let the grass grow where it may.'"

Silence fell. Dispute was impossible. No one could gainsay the weight and balanced justice of the words. They were entirely unpremeditated. But they fell and fitted as the light does. Mr. Lincoln's superb yet gracious self-control had won. And this self-control, so splendidly shining here, kept shining on through all the day of turmoil which had to follow. Ah, the strong and patient heart! Then shall the righteous shine forth as the sun, the Saviour promises. How the promise is already true for him, as, looking back upon the chaos and the darkness of those awful years, the hold of a tender but unremitting self-control glorifies the sad face of Abraham Lincoln.

Consider the strange prevision of Abraham Lincoln. How could he know so well and so much? It was Mr. Lincoln who believed in armored vessels like the "Monitor." It was because of his suggestion and insistence that the experiment of them was tried. While the battle was clashing between the "Merrimac" and the "Monitor" some one said: "Would it not be fortunate if the 'Monitor' should sink her?" "It would be nothing more than I have expected," calmly observed President Lincoln. "If she does not, something else will. Many providential things are happening in this war, and this may be one of them. The loss of two good ships is an expensive lesson, but it will teach us all the value of ironclads. I have not believed at any time during the last twenty-four hours that the 'Merrimac' would go right on destroying right and left without any obstruction. Since we knew that the 'Monitor' had got there, I have felt that she was the vessel we wanted." And she was the vessel wanted. The noteworthy thing is the prevision of this plain man who had never navigated anything himself beyond a Mississippi flatboat, that vessels of this sort were the ones to do the business. And this against the conviction of the Naval Department. How strangely he knew — this countryman from Springfield, Ill.! How his glances pierced! Well, I think if ever a man were divinely illumined and divinely guided Abraham Lincoln was.

Consider the sympathy of Abraham Lincoln. Do you know the story of William Scott, private? Mr. Chittenden gives the true version of it. He was a boy from a

Vermont farm. There had been a long march, and the night succeeding it he had stood on picket. The next day there had been another long march, and that night William Scott had volunteered to stand guard in the place of a sick comrade who had been drawn for the duty. It was too much for William Scott. He was too tired. He had been found sleeping on his beat. The army was at Chain Bridge. It was in a dangerous neighborhood. Discipline must be kept. William Scott is apprehended, tried by court-martial, sentenced to be shot. News of the case is carried to Mr. Lincoln. William Scott is prisoner in his tent, expecting to be shot next day. But the flaps of his tent are parted, and Mr. Lincoln stands before him. Scott said:

"The President was the kindest man I had ever seen; I knew him at once by a Lincoln medal I had long worn. I was scared at first, for I had never before talked with a great man; but Mr. Lincoln was so easy with me, so gentle, that I soon forgot my fright. He asked me all about the people at home, the neighbors, the farm, and where I went to school, and who my schoolmates were. Then he asked me about mother and how she looked; and I was glad I could take her photograph from my bosom and show it to him. He said how thankful I ought to be that my mother still lived, and how, if he were in my place, he would try to make her a proud mother, and never cause her a sorrow or a tear. I cannot remember it all, but every word was so kind.

"He had said nothing yet about that dreadful next morning; I thought it must be that he was so kind-hearted that he didn't like to speak of it. But why did he say so much about my mother, and my not causing her a sorrow or a tear, when I knew that I must die the next morning? But I supposed that was something that would have to go unexplained; and so I determined to brace up and tell him that I did not feel a bit guilty, and ask him wouldn't he fix it so that the firing party would not be from our regiment. That was going to be the hardest of all — to die by the hands of my comrades. Just as I was going to ask him this favor he stood up, and he says to me : 'My boy, stand up here and look me in the face.' I did as he bade me. 'My boy,' he said, 'you are not going to be shot to-morrow. I believe you when you tell me that you could not keep awake. I am going to trust you, and send you back to your regiment. But I have been put to a good deal of trouble on your account. I have had to come up here from Washington when I have got a great deal to do; and what I want to know is, how you are going to pay my bill.' There was a big lump in my throat; I could scarcely speak. I had expected to die, you see, and had kind of got used to thinking that way. To have it all changed in a minute! But I got it crowded down, and managed to say: 'I am grateful, Mr. Lincoln! I hope I am as grateful as ever a man can be to you for saving my life. But it comes upon me sudden and unexpected like. I didn't lay out for it at all; but there is some way to pay you, and I will find it after a little. There is the bounty in the savings bank; I guess we could borrow some money on the mortgage of the farm. There was my pay was something, and if he would wait until pay-day I was sure the boys would help; so I thought we could make it up if it wasn't more than five or six hundred dollars.' 'But it is a great deal more than that,' he said. Then I said I didn't just see how, but I was sure I would find some way — if I lived.

"Then Mr. Lincoln put his hands on my shoulders, and looked into my face as if he was sorry, and said: 'My boy, my bill is a very large one. Your friends cannot pay it, nor your bounty, nor the farm, nor all your comrades! There is only one man in all the world who can pay it, and his name is William Scott! If from this day William Scott does his duty, so that, if I was there when he comes to die, he can look me in the face as he does now, and say, I have kept my promise, and I have done my duty as a soldier, then my debt will be paid. Will you make that promise and try to keep it?'"

The promise was given. It is too long a story to tell of the effect of this sympathizing kindness on private William Scott. Thenceforward there never was such a soldier as William Scott. This is the record of the end. It was after one of the awful battles of the Peninsula. He was shot all to pieces. He said:

"Boys, I shall never see another battle. I supposed this would be my last. I haven't much to say. You all know what you can tell them at home about me. I have *tried* to do the right thing! If any of you ever have the chance, I wish you would tell President Lincoln that I have never forgotten the kind words he said to me at the Chain Bridge — that I have tried to be a good soldier and true to the flag — that I should have paid my whole debt to him if I had lived; and that, now, when I know that I am dying, I think of his kind face, and thank him again, because he gave me the chance to fall like a soldier in battle, and not like a coward by the hands of my comrades."

Was there ever a more exquisite story? Space forbids the half telling it. But the heart of Abraham Lincoln — how wide it was, how beautiful and particular in its sympathies. Who can doubt a gracious providence, when at such a crisis such a wise, strong, tender hand was set to grasp the helm of things? What wonder that Secretary Stanton said of him, as he gazed upon the tall form and kindly face as he lay there, smitten down by the assassin's bullet: "There lies the most perfect ruler of men who ever lived."

MINNEAPOLIS, MINN.

LINCOLN IN HARTFORD.

THE YEOMAN ORATOR—DISCUSSES HIS SECRETARY OF THE NAVY—REFUSES WINE—NAMES THE REPUBLICAN CLUBS.

BY DANIEL D. BIDWELL,

Editor of the Hartford "Evening Post."

It was on a train that was two hours late that Mr. Lincoln came to the Charter Oak City in the early evening of March 5th, 1860. A meeting at which he was to deliver the main speech was due to open in a scanty fifteen minutes. Without a thought of solace for the inner man the hardy railsplitter stepped into one of the crazy "public carriages" of the Hartford of 1860 and bade the Jehu to sprint for the old city hall, in which the meeting was to be held.

A large crowd had collected in the building. In it was a larger infusion of young men than was usually the case in *ante-bellum* political assemblies. The president of the meeting was but twenty-nine, but he combined with natural coolness solid qualities which are possessed by few men who have the experience of twice twenty-nine years. He was George G. Sill, since then Lieutenant-Governor of Connecticut. In introducing the gaunt ex-frontiersman Mr. Sill referred to him as "one who has done yeoman service for the young party," with a slight emphasis on the word "yeoman," sufficient to remind his auditors of the democratic birth and unpretentious appearance of Tom Lincoln's son. This happy stroke, made as it were with the delicacy of the rapier rather than with the emphasis of the bludgeon, caught the fancy of the crowd. It was probably with it in mind that Mr. Lincoln in a few words preliminary to his address, after explaining the cause of his delay styled himself a "dirty shirt" exponent of Republicanism. His gaunt, homely figure, unpretending manner, conversational air, careless clothing and dry humor made him at once a favorite with the audience, who felt that he was indeed a man of the people.

Mr. Lincoln's speech was meaty, logical, convincing. It dealt largely with the question of slavery. The Hartford *Times* in its account the following day referred to Lincoln as an Abolitionist, but the reference may have been due to the fact that the *Times* was the leading Democratic paper in Connecticut.

After the meeting was over Mr. Lincoln, escorted by Mr. Sill, entered an open carriage. Several hundred young men closed in around the vehicle, and, forming spontaneously in military ranks, accompanied the vehicle in progress to the house of Mayor Timothy M. Allyn. They saluted their favorite with storm after storm of enthusiastic cheers.

Turning to Mr. Sill, Mr. Lincoln said, humorously: "The boys are wide awake. Suppose we call them the Wide-awakes."

His suggestion was followed. A few days later a marching Republican club was formed, and its originators gave to it simply the name "The Wide-awakes." Other marching clubs followed fast and thick in its wake. To each one, as it was christened, was given the name "Wide-awake"; and from Stonington to Salisbury, Conn., was fairly speckled with "Wide-awake Clubs."

At Mayor Allyn's fine old colonial mansion a baker's dozen sat down to dine. Champagne was served at the meal; but Mr. Lincoln, with one of his humorous smiles, politely declined to indulge.

The following morning was raw and gusty; but bad atmospheric conditions had no effect on Lincoln, who early in the forenoon took a long stroll through the city. On his return he stepped into the bookstore of Brown & Gross, on the corner of Main and Asylum Streets. The little establishment was one of the oldest as well as one of the best in New England outside of Boston. In it Mr. Lincoln met for the first time his future Secretary of the Navy. The two spent two hours in exchanging political and economic views. This interview may fairly be said to have led to the offer of the navy portfolio, some eight or nine months later, to Mr. Wells. Testimony to this effect was given, shortly after his inauguration, by President Lincoln.

ABRAHAM LINCOLN'S BIRTHDAY.

SENATOR HOAR'S COMPARISON — A NEGRO'S TRIBUTE TO LINCOLN.

BY R. R. WRIGHT,

President of the Georgia State Industrial College.

As the American Missionary Association has selected the birthday of Abraham Lincoln as the day on which to commemorate the act of liberating four million of American slaves, the writer thought that perhaps the accompanying letter [printed on p. 1] from the late George W. Curtis, on Lincoln, would prove interesting. In a sense Lincoln and that Association are intimately connected in work for the American Negro. The one secured, the other has done much to preserve, his liberty for him. Neither could perhaps have been of true service to the Negro without the other.

Mr. Lincoln was, in truth, a great and good man; the man not only for his time, but for the colored people. It has occurred to a distinguished correspondent of mine, Senator Hoar, that Mr. Lincoln had many traits for which the colored people are noted. Among these traits were a sweetness of disposition, great patience of the wrong; he had no memory for injustice; was forgiving; was ready to wait for the slow processes by which God accomplishes great and permanent blessings for mankind.

Like the Negro, Mr. Lincoln was born in a hovel. He had to labor incessantly for his daily bread. His educational advantages were the poorest. He had scarcely a year's schooling. He was deprived of books. The Bible, "Pilgrim's Progress," "Life of Washington," "Robinson Crusoe" and "Æsop's Fables" were the books to which he owed most. His early narrow escapes showed that he was a providential man. With all this, Mr. Lincoln's religious sense was deep and pervading. The very biography of Mr. Lincoln's struggles for bread, for clothes, for money and for "a little learning" reads so much like the story of some Negro battling against adversity. Had Mr. Lincoln been a member of the Negro race it is doubtful if he would have outstripped Frederick Douglass in the race of life. May it not be stated that the two typical Americans are Abraham Lincoln and Frederick Douglass?

Mr. Lincoln was noted for his great common sense and for his political sagacity. Senator Hoar thinks that with all his great and grand qualities, Mr. Lincoln was a born politician and was even a perpetual wire-puller; that it was by his great shrewdness that he secured the adoption of the Thirteenth Amendment, kept the border States from going out of the Union, and held back the anti-slavery sentiment of the North until the time was ripe to strike the blow for his Emancipation Proclamation. There is no doubt of the fact that Mr. Lincoln had great political sagacity and an abundance of common sense. He knew what to do next and when to do it. Some people believe or affect to believe that Mr. Lincoln was not ardently earnest and sincere in the desire to free the slaves. Indeed, they seem to believe that he was indifferent upon this point; that his only desire was to save the Union. I cannot think so. As a great statesman and "student of the slow processes of the great mills of God," he abided God's time with the profoundest and most reverent faith. As he had expressed his belief that this nation could not long exist half slave and half free, with this conviction, he undoubtedly felt that in the course of events the great Ruler in the affairs of nations would accomplish the freedom of the American slaves.

PERSONAL RECOLLECTIONS OF ABRAHAM LINCOLN.

BY HENRY W. KNIGHT.

My first recollection of Mr. Lincoln was at the review of the Army of the Potomac in the spring of 1863, just preceding the battle of Chancellorsville. This noble army had been in winter quarters since the fatal affair under Burnside at Fredericksburg, and Gen. Joseph Hooker was now Commander-in-Chief. Our forces were never in better condition than at this time. Three corps of the army — the Sixth, commanded by Gen. John Sedgwick of Connecticut, "Uncle John," as he was familiarly called by his corps; the Third, commanded by General Sickles; and the Second, under command of General Hancock — were drawn up in one grand line, and numbered fully 5000 men.

I had the honor of belonging to the Sixth Corps. As Mr. Lincoln approached to review our corps I had a fine opportunity of seeing him. He rode, in a very awkward manner, a magnificent black horse, was dressed in a suit of plain black clothes, with a much-worn black silk hat. His pale, sad face, in strong contrast to his dark apparel, certainly looked singularly out of place by the side of bluff Joe Hooker, whose florid countenance, splendid uniform and beautiful white horse, fairly glittered by the side of the plain man who rode at his right hand.

In the campaign of 1864 I became disabled, and was transferred to the Veteran Reserve Corps. This body of men was composed of wounded and disabled soldiers — too much disabled to stand active service, and yet good for garrison and guard duty. I was assigned to duty at Washington. I was placed in charge of the guard at the War Department, and here it was that I frequently saw Mr. Lincoln. His favorite time for visiting the War Department was between eleven and twelve at night, and when there was no one in the building but the telegraph operator and his two or three messengers and the guard in charge of the building. We were all quite sure of one thing — the harder it rained or the fiercer the winds blew, the more certainly would he come; for he seemed to love to go out in the elements, and to commune with Nature in her wildest moods.

I seem to see him now, as — his tall, ungainly form wrapped in an old gray shawl, wearing usually a "shockingly bad hat," and carrying a worse umbrella — he came up the steps into the building. Secretary Stanton, who knew Mr. Lincoln's midnight habits, gave a standing order that, although Mr. Lincoln might come from the White House alone (and he seldom came in any other way), he should never be permitted to return alone, but should be escorted by a file of four soldiers and a non-commissioned officer. I was on duty every other night. When Mr. Lincoln was ready to return we would take up a position near him, and accompany him safely to the White House. I presume I performed this duty fifty times. On the way to the White House, Mr. Lincoln would converse with us on various topics. I remember one night when it was raining very hard that he came over, and about one o'clock he started back. As he saw us at the door, ready to escort him, he addressed us in these words: "Don't come out in this storm with me to-night, boys; I have my umbrella, and can get home safely without you." "But," I replied, "Mr. President, we have positive orders from Mr. Stanton not to allow you to return alone; and you know we dare not disobey his orders." "No," replied Mr. Lincoln, "I suppose not; for if Stanton should learn that you had let me return alone, he would have you court-martialed and shot inside of twenty-four hours." I recollect another very pleasing incident that took place in the same building. Those who may have been in the old War Department may remember that there were two short flights of stairs which had to be ascended in order to reach the second floor. At the head of the first flight was a platform or landing, and here the non-commissioned officer in charge of the guard had a desk and chair. Mr. Lincoln had to pass me whenever he came up these stairs, and as he did so I always arose, and, taking off my hat, remained standing till he passed. The taking-off of the hat was a mark of personal respect simply, for no soldier on duty, under any circumstances, is required to raise his hat. On one occasion, Mr. Lincoln, who always had a pleasant "Good-evening," and sometimes stopped to pass a word or two, hesitated on this landing, and, looking at the wall, where hung a pair of axes to be used in case of fire, asked what they were there for. I replied that they were to be used in case of fire. "Well, now," said he, "I wonder if I could lift one of those axes up by the end of the handle?" and, suiting the action to the word, he took one down, and, laying the heavy end on the floor, he commenced raising it till he held it out at arm's length, and kept it there several seconds. "I thought I could do it," he said, as he put it down. "You try it." I did try it, and failed. Mr. Lincoln laughed, and as he passed on he said: "When I used to split rails, thirty years ago in Illinois, I could lift two axes that way; and I believe I could do it now, and I will try it some other time."

Soon after this circumstance General Grant took command of the Army of the Potomac, and in order to have all the available forces at command he ordered every able-bodied soldier to the front, and this included a detachment of cavalry which, for a long time, had been President Lincoln's body guard to and from the Soldiers' Home. I was detailed on one occasion to escort the President to the Home. While on our way we had to pass Carver Hospital. As we approached the front gate, I noticed what seemed to be a young man groping his way, as if he were blind, across the road. Hearing the carriage and horses approaching, he became frightened, and walked in the direction of the approaching danger. Mr. Lincoln quickly observed this and shouted to the coachman to rein in his horses, which he did as they were about to run over the unfortunate youth. I shall never forget the expression of Mr. Lincoln's face on this occasion. Standing beside the carriage was the young man, dressed in the uniform of a private soldier. He had been shot through the left side of the upper part of the face, and the ball, passing from one side to the other, had put out both of his eyes. He could not have been over sixteen or seventeen years of age, and, aside from his blindness, he had a very beautiful face. Mr. Lincoln extended his hand to him, and while he held it he asked him, with a voice trembling with emotion, his name, his regiment and where he lived. The young man answered these questions, and stated that he lived in Michigan; and then Mr. Lincoln made himself known to the blind soldier, and with a look that was a benediction in itself spoke to him a few words of sympathy and bade him good-by. A few days after this incident, an old "chum" from my own regiment wrote me that he was at Carver Hospital, and asked me to come and see him. I went, and while there I asked after the blind soldier who had lost his eyes. I then learned that the following day, after his interview with the President he received a commission as a First Lieutenant in the Regular Army of the United States, accompanied by an order of retirement upon full pay; and if he is living to-day, he is doubtless drawing the salary of a First Lieutenant in the United States Army on the retired list.

I never shall forget that dark hour in our nation's history, the fourteenth of April, 1865. I was on duty at the War Department. Everything seemed peaceful, and nothing was heard but the quiet tread of the sentinel as he paced his beat. Suddenly a great commotion was heard outside, and in a moment the soldier on duty at the Pennsylvania Avenue front came rushing in, and, with a face pale as death, broke to us the tidings of the most accursed crime in modern history. The excitement, the madness and the sorrow that filled our souls on that occasion was simply indescribable. I wanted to run down to the theatre, but I dared not leave my post. While waiting, amid the most intense anxiety, Colonel Pelouze, one of the Adjutant-Generals at the War Department, rushed into the building and ordered me to take my men as fast as I could to the front door of Ford's Theatre. In less time than it takes to tell it, we started on the "double quick" for the theatre. As we turned the corner of Pennsylvania Avenue we encountered an immense crowd gathered about the building. We quickly reversed our muskets, and, using the butts of them, freely forced our way to the door of the theatre, where we met Major Hay, then the private secretary of President Lincoln. He requested me to make a passage through the crowd, so that the President might be carried across the street to a Mr. Peterson's house, where he died the next morning. This we quickly accomplished, and soon the bleeding form of Abraham Lincoln was carried past us, and while the tears rolled down our cheeks, there was not one of our number but would have willingly shed his own blood could it but have saved the life of him we all loved so well. So ended the career of Abraham Lincoln, and from all civilized nations on the face of the earth rose a cry of sympathy and horror; sympathy for his death and horror for the dark crime that caused it!

NEW YORK CITY.

LINCOLN AS A RHETORICAL ARTIST.

HOW HE LEARNED TO DEMONSTRATE.

BY. AMOS W. PEARSON,

EDITOR OF THE NORWICH, CONN., "BULLETIN."

THE visit of Abraham Lincoln to Norwich on March 9th, 1860, is one of the memorable events of the century. It was subsequent to his great political debate with Douglas, and just prior to his nomination for the Presidency. The irrepressible conflict, which soon culminated in the Civil War, was at its height, and as a free-State champion against the extension of slavery to the Territories, Lincoln was admired and respected. The announcement that he was to make a campaign address in Norwich was a signal for one of the greatest and most enthusiastic public gatherings ever held in this place. The old town hall was packed, and concerning that speech, the Rev. John Gulliver, D.D., said: "I learned more of the art of public speaking in listening to Mr. Lincoln's address than I could have learned from a whole course of lectures on rhetoric."

The late Rev. Dr. Gulliver was so interested in Lincoln and his masterly address that he ventured to ask him where he was educated, and it was then that he replied:

"Well, as to education, the newspapers are correct. I

never went to school more than six months in my life. I can say this: That among my earliest recollections I remember how, when a mere child, I used to get irritated when anybody talked to me in a way I could not understand. I do not think I ever got angry at anything else in my life; but that always disturbed my temper, and has ever since. I can remember going to my little bedroom, after hearing the neighbors talk of an evening with my father, and spending no small part of the night walking up and down and trying to make out what was the exact meaning of some of their, to me, dark sayings.

"I could not sleep, although I tried to, when I got on such a hunt for an idea until I had caught it; and when I thought I had got it, I was not satisfied until I had repeated it over and over; until I had put it in language plain enough, as I thought, for any boy I knew to comprehend. This was a kind of passion with me, and it has stuck by me; for I am never easy now, when I am handling a thought, till I have bounded it north and bounded it south, and bounded it east and bounded it west.

"But your question reminds me of a bit of education which I am bound in honesty to mention. In the course of my law reading I constantly came upon the word *demonstrate* — I thought, at first, that I understood its meaning, but soon became satisfied that I did not. I said to myself, 'What do I mean when I demonstrate, more than when I reason or prove?' I consulted Webster's Dictionary. That told of 'certain proof,' 'proof beyond the probability of doubt'; but I could form no sort of idea what sort of proof that was. I thought a great many things were proved beyond the possibility of a doubt, without recourse to any such reasoning as I understood demonstration to be.

"I consulted all the dictionaries and books of reference I could find, but with no better results. You might as well have defined blue to a blind man. At last I said, 'Lincoln, you can never make a lawyer if you do not understand what demonstrate means'; and I left my situation in Springfield, went home to my father's house, and stayed there until I could give any proposition in the six books of Euclid at sight. I then found out what demonstrate meant, and went back to my law studies."

This bit of autobiography opens to view one quality of Lincoln which answers for his strong self-training, his growth and the simplicity of style which gave him power.

It was this visit to "the Rose of New England" which introduced "Honest Old Abe" to our people, and created an abiding interest in his welfare and a love for him that has never waned.

TYPE OF THE AMERICAN PEOPLE.

THE DESTROYER OF SLAVERY — ABRAHAM LINCOLN,
1865–1895.

BY F. B. SANBORN,

AUTHOR OF "LIFE OF JOHN BROWN."

THE flight of time, which in thirty years effaces flourishing reputations of American dignitaries, has only enlarged our view and increased our admiration of Lincoln the Emancipator. Nature warns us against those eager reformers and devotees of their own fame who "run before they are sent"; but no such imputation rests upon the sad magnanimity of our martyred President of 1865. Under the guidance of Heaven, and, as it were, against his own hardly won consent, he became the destroyer of that atrocious evil — American slavery. In vain might he wish to lighten the stroke; it fell but the more fatal from his delay. Yet, in its death agony, the monster had strength to slay its most generous foe.

In his early career of laborious obscurity, as well as in his conspicuous station, Lincoln was the type of the American people. In what other land could he have risen so high without betraying or ignoring the institutions that enabled him to rise? But power in his hands was wielded with a magnanimity unequalled, and wellnigh without personal aims. "This way of thinking," says Raleigh, "is what gave men the glorious appellation of deliverers and fathers of their country; this made mankind incapable of bearing their very appearance without applauding it as a benefit."

Yet the powers of Lincoln's mind were of no mean order. They could not be gauged by the common standard, to which his modesty referred them. His sagacity was not that of the average man; rather was it the aggregate wisdom of the multitude, slowly aroused, and seldom at fault. His logic was as peculiar as his candor; he would state the arguments of his adversary more clearly than his own, and seldom did he urge his own with so much force as when they had ceased to convince him. His masterly use of language was the unstudied dialect of the people, shaped in the mould of an orator, crammed with the homeliest figures and suffused with the broadest humor.

Never was a public man so amiable, so accessible, so patient, so forgiving. If it was sometimes feared that this virtuous softness might be of detriment to his country, yet how winning is the light in which it leaves his gracious memory! Toward that long-suffering race which looks up to Lincoln as its deliverer his heart was warm when his judgment might be something cold. To them "the glance of his eyes gave gladness, and his every sentence had the force of a bounty." To us he might have seemed to neglect their cause, but they had no voice of censure; their gratitude while he lived, and their desolate sorrow at his death, are his highest eulogy.

In the universal lamentation of thirty years ago, mine found expression in a few verses which still seem appropriate, after so long a time:

Though forts are stormed and cities won,
  And banded Treason melts away,
As sullen mists that hate the sun
  Flee at the bright assault of Day —
  Our heavy hearts will not be gay.

For thee we mourn, in victory's hour,
  Whose courage no defeat could shake ;
Who held'st the State's resistless power
  In trust but for thy people's sake :
  For thee thy people mourning make.

For He that sways the world with love
  (Though War and Wrath His angels are)
Throned thee all earthly kings above,
  On threatened Freedom's flaming car,
  To frighten tyrants, near and far.

His purpose high thy course impelled
  O'er war's red height and smoldering plain ;
When awe, when pity thee withheld,
  He gave thy chafing steeds the rein,
  Till at thy feet lay Slavery slain.

Then ceased thy task — another hand
  Takes up the burden thou lay'st down ;
Sorrowing and glad, the rescued land
  Twofold awards thy just renown —
  The Victor's and the Martyr's crown.

CONCORD, MASS.

RECOLLECTIONS OF ONE WHO STUDIED LAW WITH LINCOLN.

BY JOHN H. LITTLEFIELD,

Author of Lecture, "Personal Recollections of Abraham Lincoln."

I BECAME acquainted with Mr. Lincoln through my brother, General Littlefield, who was present at one of the famous debates in Illinois, between Lincoln and Douglas, in 1858. At Ottawa, in that State, at the conclusion of Lincoln's speech, Douglas was carried by his admirers to his hotel. Then my brother, who was sitting up in a tree, acting as reporter for one of the St. Louis newspapers, seeing how Douglas was carried to his hotel, dropped from the tree and, with several friends, proceeded to carry Lincoln to his hotel in true Southwestern style. Lincoln protested — "Don't, don't. This is ridiculous"; but they carried him to his lodgings.

In this way my brother made the acquaintance of Mr. Lincoln. One day he said to him: "I have a brother [myself] in Grand Rapids, Mich., studying law. I would like to have him read law with you." "Send him along," said Mr. Lincoln; "we will try and do what we can for him." So, after some correspondence in February, 1859, I entered the law office of Lincoln & Herndon, and remained there until Mr. Lincoln was elected to the Presidency.

In February, before he was nominated, I wrote out a speech, having freely consulted books in the State Library and in Lincoln & Herndon's library. One day I said to Mr. Lincoln: "It is important that I get this speech correct, because I think you are going to be the candidate." I told him I would like to read him the speech. He consented, sitting down in one corner of the room, with his feet on a chair in front of him. "Now," said he, in his hearty way, "fire away, John; I think I can stand it." As I proceeded he became quite enthusiastic, exclaiming: "You are hitting the nail on the head there!" He broke out several times in this way, finally saying: "That is going to go."

The lamented Ellsworth borrowed that speech of me on one occasion for the purpose of delivering it and, I am sorry to say, he failed to return it. This I have always regretted because the speech was composed under Mr. Lincoln's immediate eye.

Mr. Lincoln used to come to the office at odd times, having no particular hours. He did a good deal of work at home. He was a very industrious man. Whenever he had anything of interest on hand he was a hard worker. One of the secrets of his success was his ability to " bone down" to hard work. Whenever he had an important case on hand he would withdraw himself more or less from society, and would devote himself with great care to the case. At such times he would display wonderful power of concentration. He used to go about in a sort of brown study. Sometimes he would take his young son Tad and, throwing him over his shoulder, would go out on the prairie. The boy being on his shoulder would seemingly give him the necessary ballast so that he could, in nautical parlance, go to windward well. By the time he returned to the house he would have a clear conception of the case and have the knotty points unravelled.

While in the office considering some important case I have frequenly known him to put the book down, and all at once break out: "Do you know what this case makes me think of?" and then he would tell a story. In this way humor would enliven jurisprudence.

One day he came to the office and had scarcely opened the door when he exclaimed: "John, did I ever tell you that rat story?" Then he told, with great earnestness, about a man who stammered, and who tried to cure himself of the habit by whistling.

He was very democratic and approachable. Frequently in going along the street he would meet some old friend and start in: "By the way, I am just reminded of a story," and he would stop in the street and tell the yarn. There was no postponement on account of the weather.

It must not be understood, however, that Mr. Lincoln was not a very serious man; in fact, he was one of the most serious men I have ever known. You might say that his seriousness was a species of melancholy. He was much of the time a sad, serious man, and a good deal of his humor was evidently for the purpose of counteracting these moods and throwing you off your guard; because when he got into these moods he was too serious for comfort.

But it was surprising to see what a fund of anecdote he had. No story could be told but he could match it, and "go one better." He had a remarkable memory. He remembered faces well, and could, on the instant, recall where he had seen people and how he had made their acquaintance.

All his life he was an extreme temperance man. At

one time he belonged to the "Sons of Temperance" in Springfield, and in his early manhood frequently made temperance speeches. In his habits he was a strict temperance man.

And he was a remarkably clean man in his conversation. He endured some *risqué* stories on account of their wit. Once a young man came to the office, and he undertook to tell a broad story that had no wit in it. He told it simply because it was broad. Lincoln took him by the nape of his neck and ordered him out of the office, saying: "Young man, never come here with such a story. If there had been any real wit in it you might have been pardoned."

Lincoln did not seem to have any pleasures common to men of the world. He was not a great eater nor a drinker. The nearest approach I ever knew him to make toward entertainment or pleasure was after he was nominated at Chicago. He used to play barn ball there nearly every day — throwing a ball up against a brick building and trying to catch it. I often used to play with him. That is the nearest approach to pleasure I ever saw him make.

In literature he seemed to prefer Shakespeare and Burns. He could recite whole passages from Shakespeare, notably from "Hamlet," with wonderful effect. He was very fond of the drama. In "Hamlet," he claimed that the passage commencing: "Oh! my offence is rank," etc., was better than the soliloquy. He said that the great beauty of Shakespeare was the power and majesty of the lines, and argued that even an indifferent actor could hold an audience by the power of the text itself.

Lincoln was what you would call an odd, a singular man. A large part of his time was spent in study and thought. He was a very deep and close thinker, and a genuine logician.

In regard to religious matters he did not talk to Herndon on those subjects. Herndon one day intimated to me that he did not know what Lincoln believed. All the talk in Herndon's book about Lincoln's religious belief is clap-trap. Whatever he may have believed in early days, he did not talk with Herndon on the subject of religion during the time I was there. He rarely attended church; he spent Sunday at home, quietly. Mrs. Lincoln attended the Presbyterian church, and the children were brought up in that faith.

This is what Mr. Lincoln said to me on the subject of religion, the nearest approach he ever made to talking on the subject: One day he stopped his work and said to me, suddenly, "John, it depends a great deal on how you state a case. When Daniel Webster stated a case, it was half argument. Now," said he, "you take the subject of predestination; you state it one way, and you cannot make much of it; you state it another, and it seems quite reasonable."

Lincoln always manifested interest in everybody with whom he associated. When you first met him and studied him he impressed you with being a very sad man and a very kind man. He struck you as being a man who would go out of his way to serve you. There was about him a sense of self-abnegation. Lincoln impressed me as a man who had arrived at a point in Christianity without going to church that others struggle to attain, but do not reach, by going. I never in all my life associated with a man who seemed so ready to serve another. He was a very modest man in his demeanor, and yet gave you an impression of strong individuality. In his freedom of intercourse with people he would seem to put himself on par with everybody; and yet there was within him a sort of reserved power, a quiet dignity which prevented people from presuming on him, notwithstanding he had thrown down the social bars. A person of less individuality would have been trifled with.

In money matters he was economical and thrifty, because he did not seem to have much desire to spend money on himself. He did not smoke, chew or drink; and a suit of clothes would last him a long time because he was not restless in his manner.

In regard to his attire I used to wonder why he did not appear to be "dressed up"; for when I looked at him a second time I would see that he was as well dressed as the average lawyer, wearing a plain broadcloth suit, a high hat, and fine boots. But his angularity and individuality were so pronounced that the clothes seemed to lose their character, as it were.

Lincoln displayed great eagerness to learn on all subjects from everybody. When he was introduced to persons his general method was to entertain them by telling them a story, or else cross-question them along the line of their work, and soon draw from them about all the information they had.

As a lawyer, in his opening speech before the jury, he would cut all the "dead wood" out of the case. The client would sometimes become alarmed, thinking that Lincoln had given away so much of the case that he would not have anything left. After he had shuffled off the unnecessary surplusage he would get down to "hard pan," and state the case so clearly that it would soon be apparent he had enough left to win the case with. In making such concessions he would so establish his position in fairness and honesty that the lawyer on the opposite side would scarcely have the heart to oppose what he contended for.

He would not undertake a case unless it was a good one. If it was a poor case he would almost invariably advise the client to settle it the best way he could. When a case had been misrepresented to him and he afterward discovered the fact in court, he would throw it up then and there. One of the great secrets of his success was the reputation he had of being a thoroughly honest lawyer. Long before he became President he was known by the *sobriquet* of "Honest Old Abe." He had become such a synonym for honesty that everybody was willing to yield assent to nearly every proposition he advanced, either in or out of court.

Lincoln's manner of speaking was very deliberate. His voice was frequently pitched on a high key. His argument was logical, and his emphasis was in harmony with the points he made.

In regard to the assassination, it is a singular fact that the President when Booth fired at him, and Booth when he was shot by Corbett, were both wounded in the same place, over the right ear. But while in Lincoln the nerve of sensation was affected and he was unconscious, in Booth the nerve of motion was affected but the nerve of sensation was not; while the President was unconscious and suffered no pain, in the case of the assassin he suffered excruciating agony up to the time of his death. It seemed to be a case of poetical justice.

BROOKLYN, N. Y.

MR. LINCOLN AT THE COOPER INSTITUTE.

A CRITICAL VIEW.

BY HENRY M. FIELD, D.D.,

EDITOR OF THE "EVANGELIST."

I NEVER saw Abraham Lincoln but two or three times in my life. But I *did* see him on his first appearance before an Eastern audience, when he gave an address which was lauded to the skies *afterward*, though it produced no great impression at the time. It was not till his debates with Douglas that Lincoln was heard of in the East. He had been in Congress once, but did not make a ripple; nor was he very widely known even in the West. From 1842 to 1847 I lived in St. Louis (perhaps a hundred miles from Springfield), and I never heard his name. But Douglas had a national reputation, and a man who could stand up before the Little Giant, and give him blow for blow, was no ordinary antagonist, and the people of the East were curious to know what manner of man he might be.

To gratify this curiosity he was invited to New York to give a lecture in Cooper Institute on the political questions before the country. It was a dark and rainy night, and the hall was but half filled. The late Maunsell B. Field was on the platform, and beckoned me to join him, apparently in fear that there would be a beggarly appearance of those who wished to do honor to "the orator of the evening," to use the grand phrase with which a lecturer was sometimes presented to empty seats.

The great hall was not then arranged as it is now, with the platform at the side. It was then at the extreme end. Presently the door behind us opened, and half a dozen persons walked slowly in, conducting a figure such as I had never seen before — tall, lank, homely in every feature, and awkward in every gesture. As I sat in a chair beside him, I could not but observe him closely. He spoke in a high-pitched voice, in which there was not a trace of the smooth-tongued orator; and yet, as he went on, something caught the ear, and as he unfolded link after link in the iron chain of his argument, he compelled attention and respect. When he would emphasize a point, he would stretch out his long arms, and his clinched hand came down as if he were a blacksmith striking on his anvil, and the final impression was one of great natural, but untrained power.

When he was through, those who sat round him came up to shake his hand and pay him the usual compliments to a stranger. Horace Greeley, who had come in late and sat at some distance, shuffled up to say a few patronizing words, which I doubt not were sincere, for he said to me as he passed, that "*it had some good points in it.*" Imagine my surprise, to read some years afterward in one of our reviews or magazines, an article from his pen in which he spoke of this very address as a masterpiece of political wisdom; indeed almost as if it had been one of the greatest productions of the human intellect!

Ah, Horace! Horace! Hadst thou become like one of us, to change thy judgment with the changing time? Was that very simple occasion magnified as it vanished into the distance? It is a weakness that is common to us all. Nor would I recall it against you that, in the dark days of the War you murmured at its "snail's progress," speaking bitterly and even savagely, as when you told me with a vehemence that caused you to mix your metaphors, that Lincoln was "the slowest piece of lead that ever crawled!" But you made full reparation at the last, when all was over and you saw that one who was in the centre of operations could judge better than those at a distance, and that there might be a moral greatness in mere patience and endurance.

And now, as I recall that dark night at the Cooper Institute, when I first saw Abraham Lincoln, his unique appearance ceases to be a matter of criticism and becomes almost sublime; for its very defects, its want of outward grace, its plainness almost to homeliness, with the simplicity of manner and of speech, brought him nearer to the hearts of the people. It is out of such materials that the Almighty chooses the instruments to carry out his designs, taking one of the people to be a leader of the people. He who took David from the sheepfold to be the King of Israel took Abraham Lincoln from the humble surroundings of his early life to lead a nation through the most awful crisis of its history.

NEW YORK CITY.

P

WHAT GENERAL SHERMAN THOUGHT OF LINCOLN.

THE NOBLEST OF MEN—NATURE'S ORATOR.

BY THE REV. GEORGE W. PEPPER,

CAPTAIN AND CHAPLAIN OF THE EIGHTIETH OHIO VOLUNTEERS.

IN a book which I had written upon General Sherman's campaigns and of which he spoke kindly, there was a reference to a visit which I made to General Lee, who spoke kindly of Grant's terms. In referring to this, General Sherman said: "General Lee always seemed to me to be a man of solid sense, fully alive to the responsibilities of the important station he occupies, sincerely devoted to the interests of the people over whom he wields such vast influence, and is indefatigable in ways and means for their physical, mental and moral elevation. And there is not one of the leaders in the South to-day who possesses the confidence of the people as General Lee. But how such a man, with revolutionary blood in his veins, educated by the Government, could take up the sword against the Union consecrated by a hundred years of unexampled prosperity, is a mystery I cannot understand."

I mentioned to him that when at Savannah General Howard gave me a letter to a Methodist pastor, asking the use of his church for me to preach in to the Union soldiers. "Yes," said Sherman, "Howard is a Christian; he possesses a combination of personal courage and purity of character and Christian manhood seldom witnessed in war. In the darkest and most trying hours I always found him hopeful, cheerful and ready."

Contrary to my expectations, he spoke in the highest terms of Logan, remarking that General Logan's oratory was not his only attractive quality. "I always liked him for his patriotism, for his eloquence. That one sentence of his at the breaking out of the War, 'The men of the Northwest will hew their way to the Gulf with their swords,' added thousands of soldiers to the ranks. He was not formed of the stuff of which parasites are made."

But it was for Lincoln that he had words of warmest praise. Lincoln was "the purest, the most generous, the most magnanimous of men. He will hold a place in the world's history loftier than that of any king or conqueror. It is no wonder that the parliaments of Europe, that the people throughout the civilized world should everywhere speak of him with reverence; for his work was one of the greatest labors a human intellect ever sustained."

I asked him his opinion of Lincoln's eloquence. His answer was: "I have seen and heard many of the famous orators of our country, but Lincoln's unstudied speeches surpassed all that I ever heard. I have never seen them equalled, or even imitated. It was not scholarship; it was not rhetoric; it was not elocution; it was the unaffected and spontaneous eloquence of the heart. There was nothing of the mountain torrent in his manner — it was rather the calm flow of the river."

During this conversation Sherman was full of enthusiastic admiration for the old soldiers. He was proud to be the commander of such men. He told with what a thrill of admiration the friends at home would speak in the years to come of their sieges, their battles and their victories, and quoted Sir John Moore's dying words after Corunna: "I hope they will do me justice at home."

I told him that his soldiers were equally attached to their old General, and I gave him the following incident as one proof: At Raleigh, N. C., when his treaty with Johnston had been rejected, some of the professed religious journals of the North had written extremely bitter and untruthful articles as to Sherman's motives in accepting the surrender of Johnston, going so far as to say that the terms were inspired by Roman Catholic influences. These religious Cassandras scattered these papers all over the country; all the venerable old women believed that the country was ruined. Bundles of these newspapers were sent to the army; the soldiers at Raleigh were so enraged that they collected the obnoxious sheets in a pile and set fire to them to the song of

"John Brown's body lies a-mouldering in the grave,
But his soul goes marching on."

This was the only opportunity I ever enjoyed of a long conversation with General Sherman, and my remembrance of him is as vivid and fresh at this hour as when it took place. He was a soldier cast in the mould of Roman firmness, the very ideal of such a warrior as might have commanded the Tenth Legion. He combined with qualities renowned in war others not less heroic; for no heart was more distinguished for kindly and generous affections. Under that singular, wiry exterior nature had implanted a spirit of fire and an irresistible energy which reminds one of the Italian exploits of Lannes or the victorious intrepidity of Nelson.

"Free as he was in act and mind,
He leaves no braver heart behind."

CLEVELAND, OHIO.

AS LINCOLN APPEARED IN THE WAR DEPARTMENT.

BY ALBERT B. CHANDLER,

PRESIDENT AND GENERAL MANAGER POSTAL TELEGRAPH CO.

DURING the War it fell to my lot to be assigned to duty in the Military Telegraph Office, in the War Department at Washington. An important part of my duty was to translate "received" cipher messages and prepare "sent" messages for transmission in cipher, for the President, Secretary of War, General-in-Chief and other principal officers of the Government. It was Mr. Lincoln's habit to visit this office almost daily, and sometimes oftener; and he probably spent more hours there, from the beginning of 1863 to the end of his life, than in any other one place, except the White House.

On the evening of August 7th, 1863, while I was alone in the office, Mr. Lincoln came in bringing a long message which he had written with his own hand, addressed to Governor Seymour, of New York. He sat down at a desk and carefully revised it, and then called me to sit by him while he read it, so that I might understand it, and see that it was properly transmitted. He explained to me something of the occasion of it, a special messenger having come over from New York with a long message from Governor Seymour, urging, among other things, that the draft should be suspended until the

United States Supreme Court had decided as to the constitutionality of the draft law.

He told me a funny story about a Boston minister who had been drafted, and the criticism that he made upon that method of recruiting the army, the point of which I failed to note, and cannot now recall. The message to Governor Seymour was, in part, as follows:

"Your communication of the 3d instant has been received and attentively considered.

"I cannot consent to suspend the draft in New York, as you request, because, among other reasons, time is too important.

"I shall direct the draft to proceed in all the districts, drawing, however, at first from each of the four districts, to wit: the 2d, 4th, 6th and 8th, only 2200, being the average quota of the other class. After this drawing these four districts, and also the 17th and 29th, shall be carefully re-enrolled, and, if you please, agents of yours may witness every step of the process. Any deficiency which may appear by the new enrolment will be supplied by a special draft for that object, allowing due credit for volunteers who may be obtained from these districts respectively during the interval. And at all points, so far as consistent with practical convenience, due credit will be given for volunteers. And your Excellency shall be notified of the time fixed for commencing a draft in each district.

"I do not object to abide a decision of the United States Supreme Court, or of the judges thereof, on the constitutionality of the draft law. In fact, I should be willing to facilitate the obtaining of it; but I cannot consent to lose the time while it is being obtained. We are contending with an enemy who, as I understand, drives every able-bodied man he can reach into his ranks very much as a butcher drives bullocks into a slaughter pen. No time is wasted, no argument is used. This produces an army which will soon turn upon our now victorious soldiers already in the field, if they shall not be sustained by recruits as they should be. It produces an army with a rapidity not to be matched on our side, if we first waste time to re-experiment with the volunteer system, already deemed by Congress, and palpably, in fact, so far exhausted as to be inadequate. And then more time to obtain a court decision as to whether a law is constitutional which requires a part of those not now in the service to go to the aid of those who are already in it; and still more time to determine, with absolute certainty, that we get those who are to go in the precisely legal proportion to those who are not to go.

"My purpose is to be in my action just and constitutional, and yet practical in performing the important duty with which I am charged, of maintaining the unity and the free principles of our common country."

Mr. Lincoln's kindness of heart was often exhibited. On several occasions he came to the office near midnight with a message written with his own hand, and acting as his own messenger, in order that there should be no mistake or delay in bringing respite to a condemned soldier. I think he never failed to interpose his power to prevent the execution of a soldier for sleeping on his post, or any other offence than a wilful and malicious act; and even in such cases when brought to his attention, he made the most careful review of the facts, and always seemed more anxious to find the offender innocent than guilty; and when guilty, he was disposed to take into consideration, as far as possible, any extenuating circumstances, in favor of the wrongdoer.

On New Year's morning, 1864, as I entered the upper hall of the War Department, Mr. Lincoln was about opening the door of the Military Telegraph Office. A woman stood in the hall crying. Mr. Lincoln had observed this, and as soon as he was seated he said to Major Eckert: "What is that woman crying about just outside your door?" The Major replied that he did not know. "I wish you would go and see," said Mr. Lincoln. So the Major went out and learned that the woman had come to Washington expecting to be able to go to the army and see her soldier husband, which was not altogether unusual for ladies to do, while the army was in winter quarters; but very strict orders had recently been issued prohibiting women from visiting the army, and she found herself, with her child, in Washington, incurring much more expense than she supposed would be necessary, with very little money, and in great grief. This being explained to the President, he said, in his frank, off-hand way, "Come now, let's send her down; what do you say?" The Major explained the strict orders that the department had lately issued, the propriety of which Mr. Lincoln recognized, but he was still unwilling to yield his purpose. Finally the Major suggested that a leave of absence to come to Washington might be given the woman's husband. The President quickly adopted the suggestion, and directed that Colonel Hardie, an assistant Adjutant-General on duty in an adjoining room, should make an official order permitting the man to come to Washington. After reading over the messages which had been received since his last previous visit to the office, he returned to the White House, having lightened the burden of one sad heart just one year after sending forth his immortal Emancipation Proclamation.

A sister of mine, who had married in Southern Georgia before the War, was anxious to visit her Northern home in the spring of 1864. After long delays I received information of her purpose, and of the supposed fact that it would be practicable for her to pass through the Confederate lines. Being uncertain whether she could best accomplish this at Savannah or at Richmond, I explained the circumstances to Mr. Lincoln, when he at once wrote permission for her to pass through the Federal lines, first taking the oath of allegiance and another of like import, the one to be sent to the headquarters of the Army of the James, in front of Richmond, General Butler; and the other to the headquarters of the Department of the South, General Gilmore. But after making the long and, at that time, exceedingly tedious journey to Richmond, she found it impossible to overcome the objections of Confederate officers, so that she was compelled to return to her Southern home without reaching ground whereon Mr. Lincoln's authority would have afforded her ample protection.

His fondness for story-telling and the extent to which he indulged it is well known, and has not, I think, been overstated. His sense of the ridiculous was exceedingly keen, his memory surprising, and his power of illustration, and even of mimicry, was often demonstrated in the use of very simple, sometimes funny, and sometimes undignified stories. One of the first I remember happened in this wise: He had just seated himself at a desk, with the latest messages before him, when he heard a newsboy on the street crying, "Here's yer *Philadelphia Inquiry.*" He mimicked the peculiar pronunciation and tone of the boy, and then said: "Did I ever tell you the joke the Chicago newsboys had on me?" Replying negatively, he related: "A short time before my nomination I was at Chicago attending a lawsuit. A photographer of that city asked me to sit for a picture, and I did so. This coarse, rough hair of mine was in a particularly bad tousle at the time, and the picture presented me in all its fright. After my nomination, this being about the only picture of me there was, copies were struck to show those who had never seen me how I looked. The newsboys carried them around to sell, and had for their cry, "Here's yer Old Abe; 'll look better when he gets his hair combed"; and he laughed heartily as he finished the relation.

It had so happened for several days that Major Eckert had been out whenever the President came into the office. Coming in one day and finding the Major counting money at his desk, Mr. Lincoln remarked that he believed the Major never came to the office any more except when he had money to count. The Major declared that his being out when the President happened to come in was simply a coincidence, and this reminded him, the Major, of a story: "A certain tailor in Mansfield, Ohio, was very stylish in dress and airy in manner. Passing a shopkeeper's door one day the shopkeeper puffed himself up, and gave a long blow expressive of the inflation of the conceited tailor, who indignantly turned and said: 'I'll learn you not to blow when I'm passing,' to which the shopkeeper instantly replied: 'And I'll teach you not to pass while I'm blowing.'" The President said that was very good — very like a story which he had heard of a man who was driving through the country in an open buggy, and was caught at night in a pouring shower of rain. He was hurrying forward toward shelter as fast as possible; passing a farmhouse, a man, apparently struggling with the effects of bad whisky, thrust his head out of the window and shouted loudly, "Hullo! hullo!" The traveller stopped and asked what was wanted. "Nothing of you," was the reply. "Well, what in the d—— do you shout hullo for when people are passing?" angrily asked the traveller. "Well, what in the d—— are you passing for when people are shouting hullo?" replied the inebriate.

The Major then asked Mr. Lincoln if the story of his interview with complainants against General Grant was true, viz., that he had inquired solicitously where the General got his liquor, and on being told that the information could not be given, the President replied that he would very much like to find out, so that he might get enough to send a barrel to each one of his generals. Mr. Lincoln said that he had heard the story before, and that it would have been very good if he had said it, but that he didn't. He supposed it was "charged to him, to give it currency." He then said the original of the story was in King George's time. Bitter complaints were made to the King against his General Wolfe in which it was charged that he was mad. The King replied angrily: "I wish he would bite some of my other generals then." He then mentioned a bright saying which he had recently heard during the riots in New York in which the Irish figured most conspicuously: "It is said that General Kilpatrick is going to New York to quell the riot; but his name has nothing to do with it."

On one occasion we had received news of a series of raids into rebel territory. Stoneman had just returned from an expedition into East Tennessee and Southwestern Virginia. Sherman had divided the Confederacy and safely reached Savannah. Grierson and Wilson had each been heard from in Alabama and Mississippi, and no State seemed free from our incursions. The President said it put him in mind of a weary traveller in one of the Western States, who, after journeying all day, came at night to a small log cabin. He went in and asked the occupants if he could be accommodated with food and lodging. He was told they could provide him with a place to sleep, but that there was not a "bite of victuals" in the house. The traveller gladly accepted the pallet of straw, and soon fell asleep; but was awakened in a short time by whispers which disclosed that there was a cake baking in the ashes, and the woman and her husband were congratulating themselves on the way in which they had kept their food and deceived the hungry traveller. Feeling angry that they should have told him they had nothing to eat when it was not true, and that they were now "chuckling" over it, he determined to spoil their game. He began to move restlessly, and finally got up and complained of feeling very badly. The woman asked him what was the matter. He told her he was much distressed in mind and could not sleep, and went on to say that his father when he died had left him a large farm, but that he had no sooner taken possession than mortgages began to appear, and, taking the fire poker, he said: "My farm was situated like this," illustrating by drawing the poker through the ashes, so as to entirely surround the ash cake with the lines. "First one man got so much of it off on this side; then another brought in a mortgage and took off another piece there; then another there, and another there, and there and there," drawing the poker through the ashes each time to explain locations, "until," said he, "there was nothing of the farm left to me at all, which I presume is the case with your cake." "And I reckon," said Mr. Lincoln, "that the prospect is now very good for soon having the Rebellion as completely cut up as that ash cake was."

When he had finished reading telegrams announcing Sheridan's last fight with Early, in the Shenandoah Valley, he said he thought Early's army was in about the same condition as a dog he once heard a man say he had killed by filling a piece of punk with powder, and, setting it on fire, he clapped it inside of a biscuit, and, as the dog rushed at him as usual, tossed the biscuit to him; in an instant the dog snapped it up and swallowed it. Presently the fire touched the powder and away went the dog, his head in one place, a leg here and another there, and the different parts of him scattered about. "But," said the man, "as for the dog, *as a dog*, I was never able to find him"; "and this," he said, "was very much the condition of Early's army, *as an army*."

Mr. Stanton came one evening from his room and stood in the doorway of the telegraph office, without coming in. Mr. Lincoln did not notice him at first; as he looked up from his writing and perceived him standing there, he bowed low and said, with much gravity: "Good-evening, Mars."

The only occasion on which I knew him to use a profane word was on receipt of a telegram from General Burnside, then in Greenville, East Tennessee, announcing that he expected a portion of his command to be at Jonesboro at a certain time. Eagerly looking over the map to see the position of the force under Burnside's command, it seemed to him that the portion referred to was marching away from instead of to the rescue of General Rosecrans, as ordered. Mr. Lincoln reread the dispatch, thinking there must be some mistake, and repeated to himself: "Jonesboro? Jonesboro? D—— Jonesboro!" and he immediately addressed a telegram to Burnside, saying:

"If you are to do any good to Rosecrans it will not do to waste time at Jonesboro. It is already too late to do the most good that might have been done; but I hope it is not too late to do some good. Please do not lose a moment."

During my knowledge of him Mr. Lincoln always dressed in plain black, his clothes sometimes "showing wear." I think I never saw him wear an overcoat; instead of that he wore an ample, plain but peculiarly figured gray shawl, and his usual way of disposing of it as he entered the office was to hang it across the top of the inner door, which was nearly always standing open, and so high as to be out of the reach of a man of ordinary height. When sitting at a desk writing briefly he sometimes assumed a half-kneeling, half-sitting posture, with one knee on the carpet. When composing at some length it was his habit to look out of the window and, apparently unconsciously, scratch his head, particularly his temples, often moving his lips in whispers, until he had his sentence framed, when he would put it on paper. He wrote rather slowly but quite legibly, taking care to punctuate accurately. His spelling was faultless, which is not true of all great men, even those of education; and yet on two or three occasions he asked me, while writing, as to the use of one or two "l's" or two "t's." He rarely erased or interlined; and his diction, so peculiar to himself, always seemed to me the perfection of plain, simple English. He sometimes read aloud, and on one occasion I remember his reading to me at some length, rather slowly and thoughtfully, and purposely mispronouncing certain words, placing the accent on the wrong syllable and the like. He was at this time sitting opposite me beside the large table on which I was writing, his chair leaned back against the wall, his legs crossed, one foot resting upon the round of his chair and the other suspended in space. During this reading he stopped occasionally to remark upon the subject of his reading — a detailed description of a battle — and one of his remarks, I remember, was upon the meagreness of adjectives in the language to express the different degrees of feeling and action.

NEW YORK CITY.

LINCOLN AND THE ABOLITIONIST RIOTS.

TO PREVENT HIS INAUGURATION.

BY AARON M. POWELL.

Though one of the early Abolitionists and editor of their organ, the *Anti-Slavery Standard*, I was not personally acquainted with Mr. Lincoln. I can recall two or three things of interest in connection with him, however; for instance, his speech at the Cooper Institute, in 1859, which undoubtedly opened the way for his becoming President. After his election there was a systematic attempt made to prevent his inauguration. The Knights of the Golden Circle, whose headquarters were in the South, had their allies and coworkers among the Democrats of the North. About the time of Lincoln's inauguration we antislavery workers were holding a series of conventions in New York and other cities. The persons just referred to used the occasion of these meetings for a series of mobs, extending from New York to Utica, Syracuse, Rochester, Buffalo, etc. Wherever we appeared we were confronted with a disorderly crowd seemingly organized by the same general hand. In Utica the mob had taken possession of the hall before we could organize our convention, and we had to hold our meeting in a private house. In connection with these mobs they circulated reports in the newspapers that the North repudiated the Abolitionists and Lincoln. In Utica we learned that the evening before we were mobbed a group of men had gathered in a lawyer's office. They prepared resolutions which were sent out the next day repudiating the Abolitionists and Lincoln. The central figure of that group, as we learned afterward upon investigation, was none other than Horatio Seymour. The purpose of these riots and mobs was to give the impression to the South, and the country generally, that the North, as well as the South, was inimical to Lincoln's inauguration.

At Syracuse we were driven from our hall, and a free speech meeting was organized, at which the Rev. M. E. Strieby, now one of the secretaries of the American Missionary Association, presided. I attempted to speak, but being recognized as one of the Abolitionists who were to have addressed the convention, there was a great howl from the disorderly element present. In the rear of the hall, directing the movements of the mob, was Col. John A. Green, one of Horatio Seymour's lieutenants. Susan B. Anthony, Charles L. Redmond, a colored man, the Rev. Samuel J. May and the Rev. Beriah Green were present as speakers on this occasion. Just as we left the platform the mob, largely composed of men from the Salt Works, led by Colonel Green, opened on us a shower of eggs. At a meeting in Auburn, which we were allowed to hold, they put pepper on the stoves, nearly suffocating speakers and audience, especially the former, who could not reach the windows handily. In Rochester we were again confronted by the mob. In Boston George W. Smalley, now of the New York *Tribune*, and some other young men slept in the house of Wendell Phillips as his body guard.

All these riotous proceedings were carried on, as we were assured, to create a sentiment against Lincoln and to prevent his inauguration. The reader will recall how he had to change his plans about going through Baltimore to the Capital, which he had to reach in a sort of clandestine manner.

New York City.

LINCOLN AND CHARLES A. DANA.

BY DAVID HOMER BATES,
General Manager Bradstreet's Agency, New York.

"With malice toward none, and charity for all"—"The judgments of the Lord are true and righteous altogether." The above, taken from Lincoln's second inaugural, March 4th, 1865, so well illustrates his loving nature and his trust in God, that I am led to speak of them, and to add my humble tribute to his memory.

The writer, then a mere youth, first met Abraham Lincoln in the month of April, 1861, only ten days after Sumter had been fired upon. With three other telegraph operators, namely, David Strouse and Samuel Brown, both since deceased, and Richard O'Brien, now Superintendent of the Western Union Telegraph Company at Scranton, Penn., I started from Altoona, Penn., under orders from Col. Thomas A. Scott, General Manager Military Railroads and Telegraphs, to report to Simon Cameron, Secretary of War. The rebel Gilmor, from Baltimore, having destroyed the bridges over the Bush and Gunpowder Rivers, we were forced to go by water from Havre de Grace to Annapolis. We sailed on the "Maryland," which was afterward burned in New York harbor, and since reconstructed for service between Mott Haven and Jersey City. On the boat was Ormsby M. Mitchell, celebrated astronomer and soldier.

Arriving at Annapolis, we reported to General Butler, who had just established his headquarters at the Naval Academy, after the brief and exciting outbreak of the Baltimore mob.

From Annapolis we travelled to Washington by rail, and there reported at the War Department for orders. The Secretary's office was in the southeast room, on the second floor of that historical building. The telegraph instruments were in the adjoining room, and as we were ushered in, Mr. Lincoln appeared with Secretary Simon Cameron, Gen. Winfield Scott, and one or two others. Cameron was by no means small of stature, while General Scott was massive, as well as tall. At the moment, the latter was the chief object of our curiosity, although the kindly face of Mr. Lincoln was very attractive. It was my lot during the succeeding four years, until the very night of his taking off by the bullet of Booth, to see him nearly every day, as he generally came to the telegraph room early in the morning, and also in the evening, so that he might receive the latest telegrams from the various military headquarters.

These telegrams were mostly in cipher, and it was sometimes a task to decipher a difficult message because of telegraphic errors. His interest and anxiety at such periods were very great, especially when the dispatches referred to a battle. Charles A. Dana, now editor of the New York *Sun*, had been assigned to the duty of visiting Grant's headquarters in Mississippi, and afterward in Tennessee, and his telegraphic reports were generally full, and always of great interest. Mr. Lincoln looked forward eagerly to Mr. Dana's accounts of the various engagements with the enemy. The latter's strong virile manner of expressing himself on important questions is well known; and as they were audibly read by Mr. Lincoln, possibly merited criticisms were softened in the reading by side remarks. It was his habit to read aloud, and to bring his listeners into the current of his thoughts by question or suggestion.

In our cipher code there were several words, each translated "Jefferson Davis." Other words stood for "Robert E. Lee," and so on. Whenever Mr. Lincoln came to these words, he would shorten or transform them into something else, for instance, "Jeffy D.," "Bobby Lee," etc., so that there seemed to go out from him at such times, and indeed on many other occasions, a gentle, kindly influence. He seemed to be thinking of the leaders of the Rebellion as wayward sons rather than as traitorous brethren.

Once, not more than sixty days before his death, he came into the telegraph office with a photograph of himself, which had been addressed to his wife, and sent through the mail. The sender had added to the picture a rope, which passed around the neck, and then upward, tautly drawn, as indicating his hellish desire. Mr. Lincoln remarked that it had caused Mrs. Lincoln some anxiety, which he did not share, although he added some words of sorrow, that any human being could be so devoid of feeling as thus to wound an innocent woman. As for himself, he received many similar missives, and had come to look upon them with nothing more than a passing thought.

As above indicated, Mr. Lincoln made his accustomed call at the War Department Telegraph Office on the afternoon of Friday, April 14th, 1865, the day of his assassination. He came earlier than usual, however, because, as was afterward learned, of his expected visit to the theatre.

Although I was on duty at the time, I have no distinct remembrance of the occasion, for what occurred a few hours later was so appalling that memory retained nothing clearly, except that which took place after the awful news was received. First came word that the President was shot; then, horror following fast upon horror, the savage attack upon Secretary Seward, the frustrated efforts to reach and kill Secretary Stanton, Vice-President Johnson and other members of the Government; and as the successive accounts crystallized, a fearful dread filled every soul lest it should be found that the entire Cabinet had been murdered. An hour or more of this awful suspense, and we received a message from Major Eckert, who had gone quickly with Secretary Stanton to the house on Tenth Street, to which the President had been carried. This news simply assured us of the present safety of Stanton, while confirming our worst fears concerning the President.

A relay of messengers was established between Major Eckert and the War Department, and all night long they carried their portentous news in the form of bulletins, in the handwriting of Secretary Stanton, addressed to Gen. John A. Dix, Commanding General, New York City, and which were distributed to the press throughout the country. As these bulletins were spelled out in the Morse telegraph characters over the wires leading North, it seemed to those of us (as I remember, Albert Chandler, Charley Tinker, and two or three others) whose fingers manipulated the keys, that never were sadder signals formed. Our hearts were at once stunned and on fire.

The awfulness of the scenes transpiring before us hushed us into silence, except for an occasional outburst of sorrow and amazement; and tears, of which none of us were ashamed, were freely shed. As the hours slowly passed, hope revived as to the President's life being spared; but at last, about 7.30 A.M., the tension broke and we knew for a certainty that he was dead. Then we looked out upon the light of day, which before we had not observed, or at least with consciousness; and the force of the blow seemed to be increased by recalling the previous day when we had last seen the President. We thought of his daily visits, and most of all, in the close presence of our great sorrow, did we think of his loving heart, and the many evidences he had given us of the entire absence from that heart of anger or resentment toward his country's enemies.

Let me close this cursory reference by a short quotation from a midnight speech made by Mr. Lincoln on the night of November 10th, 1864, as he was leaving the War Department after the welcome news of his re-election to the Presidency:

"So long as I have been here I have not willingly planted a thorn in any man's bosom. While I am deeply sensible of the high compliment of re-election, and duly grateful, as I trust to Almighty God, for having directed my countrymen to a right conclusion, as I think for their own good, it adds nothing to my satisfaction that any other man may be disappointed or pained by the result. May I ask those who have not differed from me to join with me in this same spirit toward those that have?"

LINCOLN'S FAREWELL TO SPRINGFIELD.

TRUST IN DIVINE GUIDANCE.

BY GEORGE W. F. BIRCH, D.D.

Mr. Lincoln was a member of the congregation of the First Presbyterian Church of Springfield, Ill. His pastors were Drs. John G. Bergen, James Smith and John H. Brown, all of whom are dead.

I went to Springfield a licentiate in February, 1861, and became the pastor of the Third Presbyterian Church of that city, remaining in charge until September, 1869. Several households of Mr. Lincoln's family connections were members of my congregation.

Of course I was in touch with many of Mr. Lincoln's intimate companions for eight years and more, and am quite familiar with his personal history; yet my peculiar interest in him arises from the fact that at a turning-point of my life I met him at one of the turning-points of his grand career. The first three days of my ministry in Springfield were his last three days at his old home, so that I have but one personal reminiscence of Mr. Lincoln. It was an event of probably not more than fifteen or twenty minutes. There was but time for a handshake and to hear him say good by to his old friends and neighbors of Springfield. As I stretch my vision across the thirty-four years which have rolled away since the rainy morning of February 11th, 1861, I count that brief experience one of the great privileges of my life. The lapse of time only deepens the impression of the long, gaunt form with its thoughtful face, as in the true simplicity of his real greatness Abraham Lincoln lingers on the rear platform of the car to take his last look at the old home and to say the last word to his townsmen. It was as if he would carry them away in his big heart when he said:

"My friends: No one not in my position can realize the sadness I feel at this parting. To this people I owe all that I am. Here I have lived more than a quarter of a century. Here my children were born, and here one of them lies buried. I know not how soon I shall see you again. I go to assume a task more difficult than that which has devolved upon any other man since the days of Washington. He never would have succeeded except for the aid of Divine Providence, upon which he at all times relied. I feel that I cannot succeed without the same Divine blessing which sustained him; and on the same Almighty Being I place my reliance for support. And I hope you, my friends, will all pray that I may receive that Divine assistance, without which I cannot succeed, but with which success is certain. Again, I bid you an affectionate farewell."

It seems to the writer that the man who could say such a "good by" could not do otherwise than write the Emancipation Proclamation and the Gettysburg Oration. The Springfield Address is the declaration of the purpose of a conscientious statesman.

If my life has any inspirations my glimpse of Abraham Lincoln is one of them.

NEW YORK CITY.

A SIDE-LIGHT AND AN INCIDENT.

LINCOLN'S DESCRIPTION OF SHERIDAN.

BY CHARLES HAMLIN,

Late Adjutant-General United States Volunteers.

No estimate of Abraham Lincoln as a leader and ruler would be complete that fails to notice and take into account his ready ability to dispatch with ease matters arising for daily decision during the Presidency. Many hours of every day were consumed in receiving and listening to callers, and it is to his lasting credit that he turned no one away unheard. Besides his industry and orderly method of transacting business, evident to all, he had a reserved power, inherent and inborn, of which he must have been conscious early in life. This reserved power, akin to repose in character, or, to use his own words, "the courage to follow to the end the right as God gave him to see the right," will serve to explain his mastership in great crises. The most original, self-possessed man of the time, he refused to abandon after that celebrated midnight conference with his friends and advisers, in the historical campaign of 1858, the great principle contained in his "house-divided-against-itself" speech. Other examples will occur to the reader — his determination to preserve the whole Union, and his patience in abiding the time when he could issue the Emancipation Proclamation.

In speaking of his easy dispatch of business, I recall an incident, of which I was a witness, illustrating Mr. Lincoln's thorough knowledge of legislative details and his power of gently refusing to grant requests when obliged to do so.

Major B. Weller Hoxsey, of the Excelsior Brigade, with whom I was well acquainted, and who had been brevetted for gallantry in action, found his commission expired and himself mustered out of the service one morning at the head of his regiment, in front of Petersburg, in the summer of 1864. Having become previously wounded, so that he could no longer march on foot with his regiment, he had acted as ordnance staff officer for Generals Berry, Carr, Humphreys and Prince, commanding the second division of the Third Army Corps — the famous Joe Hooker division — from Fredericksburg to the Wilderness, after much hard fighting on the Peninsula, next under Pope, and at Gettysburg. Being thus incapacitated by reason of his wounds to accept a commission in the regular army, and desiring to remain in the service until the close of the War, he came from Virginia to Washington to obtain an appointment on the volunteer staff. He accordingly sought an interview with President Lincoln, who at once received him and heard his application and modest request to be returned to active duty as a staff officer. He presented testimonials of his high service tendered by many prominent officers, and I added my own evidence of his fine standing and ability. The President having invited us to sit, pulling up some chairs for the purpose, turned to a shelf near his right hand and took down a large volume of the Laws of Congress. He opened to the page and section of the Act; put his finger on the line, and read aloud the words which authorized him to make staff appointments only on the request of the general commanding a brigade, division or corps. The Major admitted that he had not brought with him such an application, for he had not thought it necessary. "It cannot be done," said President Lincoln, "without such a request. I have no more power to appoint you, in the absence of such request, than I would have to marry a woman to any man she might desire for her husband without his consent. Bring me such an application and I will make it at once, for I see you deserve it."

He could easily avoid a direct answer when he thought it was impolitic to make known his opinions, and evade inquisitive visitors who asked questions simply to gratify their curiosity. His reply to one of the latter, who wanted to know his opinion of Sheridan at the time he had just come from the West to take command of the cavalry under Grant, is too good to be lost. Turning to his inquirer, he asked: "Have you seen Sheridan?" "No," was the answer. "Then," said Mr. Lincoln, "I will tell you just what kind of a chap he is. He is one of those long-armed fellows with short legs, that can scratch his shins without having to stoop over to do it."

BANGOR, ME.

REMINISCENCES OF LINCOLN AS A LAWYER.

INCIDENTS OF HIS PRACTICE IN ILLINOIS — INTERESTING CASES — A NOTABLE ADDRESS TO A JURY.

BY JUDGE LAWRENCE WELDON,

OF THE UNITED STATES COURT OF CLAIMS.

(FROM AN INTERVIEW.)

[Judge Lawrence Weldon, of the United States Court of Claims, is one of the very few men in the legal profession, now living, who knew Abraham Lincoln well, as a lawyer. The acquaintance, which ripened into warm personal friendship, began in the early day of Illinois, when no sign foretold the future of the greatest American produced by America. Judge Weldon was a young man just turned twenty-four and admitted to the bar, who removed from Ohio to Illinois, hung out his shingle in Clinton, a village of less than one thousand population; and two months after, in September, 1854, met Mr. Lincoln for the first time. Mr. Weldon, as a young law student in Ohio, had heard more or less of Mr. Lincoln, when the latter was a member of Congress, a few years before. Now that he had cast his fortunes in the same State, but a dozen miles from Mr. Lincoln's home, and that his professional duties would bring him on the same circuit, naturally increased the young lawyer's interest in the man he already knew a good deal of by hearsay — an interest still further weighted when he found that by the retirement of Judge Logan, a then prominent lawyer, from active practice, Mr. Lincoln was regarded as the leader of the bar throughout the State. Mr. Lincoln was at that time scarcely forty-five years of age, but was alluded to in popular parlance as "old Mr. Lincoln," and frequently would be pointed out by boys of the town with the exclamation, "There — there goes old Mr. Lincoln!" — a term meaning no disrespect, but, on the contrary, rather friendly curiosity and admiration. A man of forty-five is much too young to be sensitive about his age, and Mr. Lincoln seemed always amused. When asked how long they had been calling him old, he replied: "Oh, they commenced that trick before I was thirty."

— JANET JENNINGS.]

It was at Bloomington, during the fall term of Court, that I first saw Mr. Lincoln, whose appearance made a strong impression on me.

I can see Mr. Lincoln now, through the fading memories of forty years, as clearly as if it were yesterday. He was always clean shaven, wearing no beard, neatly dressed, but extremely plain, and apparently more indifferent to fashion than others of our profession out there, even in that day. I was young, and probably noticed Mr. Lincoln's clothes more particularly, because I expected a man who had been in Congress to dress a little more fashionably. Mr. Lincoln came over from the courthouse to the hotel where the lawyers put up, as we used to say, while attending court. Stephen A. Douglas, who was then making a campaign in defence of the Kansas Nebraska bill, was at the hotel. Judge Douglas presented me to Mr. Lincoln, and said: "Mr. Weldon is a young lawyer from Ohio who has come to make his home in Illinois." Mr. Lincoln was very cordial, and, shaking hands with me, replied: "Well, I hope he will find he has made a good trade from Ohio to Illinois."

I remember when we were introduced that Mr. Lincoln at once impressed me by his unaffected, sincere manner and precise, accurate mode in which he stated his thoughts even when talking about commonplace things. We were in Judge Douglas's rooms, where they talked about old times very pleasantly, and during the conversation Mr. Douglas broadened the hospitalities by asking Mr. Lincoln to drink something, following the custom which then generally prevailed of keeping liquors in his rooms. Mr. Lincoln declined, and Mr. Douglas, in a tone of surprise, said: "Why, do you belong to the temperance society?"

Mr. Lincoln replied: "I do *not* in theory, but I do in fact belong to the temperance society in this, to wit — that I do not drink anything, and have not done so for very many years."

The conversation then drifted to other channels, and shortly after Mr. Lincoln went out, J. W. Fell, then and now a leading citizen of Illinois, came in and said there was a strong desire among the citizens to have a discussion by Mr. Douglas and Mr. Lincoln, and that this would afford the crowds then in town, the luxury of hearing the acknowledged champions on both sides. It was plain to see that the proposition irritated Judge Douglas, and he asked, with considerable majesty of manner: "Whom does Mr. Lincoln represent in this campaign — Abolitionist or Old Line Whig?" Mr. Fell said Mr. Lincoln was an Old Line Whig. Douglas retorted:

"Oh yes, I am now in the region of the Old Line Whig. When I am in Northern Illinois I am assailed by an Abolitionist, when I get to the centre I am attacked by an Old Line Whig, when I go to Southern Illinois I am beset by an Anti-Nebraska Democrat. It looks to me like dodging a man all over the State. If Mr. Lincoln wants to make a speech he had better get a crowd of his own, for I most respectfully decline to hold a discussion with him."

Of course, Mr. Lincoln had nothing to do with the proposed discussion except, perhaps, to say he was willing to speak. He was not aggressive in the defence of his doctrines or enunciation of his opinions, but he was brave and fearless in the protection of what he believed to be right. In 1854 and down to the commencement of the War, the circuit practice in Illinois was still in vogue, and the itinerant lawyer was as sure to come as the trees to bud or leaves to fall. Among these Mr. Lincoln was the star. He stood above and beyond them all. He travelled the circuit, attending the courts in the district of Judge David Davis, afterward a Justice of the Supreme Court, this district extending from the centre to the eastern boundary of the State, right on, spring and fall, until nominated for the Presidency. Mr. Lincoln liked the atmosphere of a courthouse, and seemed contented and happy when Judge Davis was on the bench, and there were before him the "twelve good and lawful men" constituting the jury. He was among friends and acquaintances in every county, and always knew the leading men on the jury. He could broadly be called an industrious lawyer, and when his adversary presented a reasonably good affidavit for continuance, Mr. Lincoln was willing that the case should go over until the next term. No condition could arise in a case beyond his capacity to furnish an illustration with an appropriate anecdote or story. Judge Davis was always willing that Mr. Lincoln should tell a story in court, even if it disturbed the gravity of the situation, and no one enjoyed these occasions of mirth more than his Honor on the bench, Judge Davis himself. At the same time Mr. Lincoln was always respectful and deferential toward the court, and never forgot the professional amenities of the bar. He was a lawyer who dealt with the deep philosophy of the law, always knew the cases which might be quoted as absolute authority, but beyond that contented himself in the application and discussion of general principles. He moved cautiously, and never examined or cross-examined a witness to the detriment of his side. If the witness told the truth he was safe; but woe betide the unlucky and dishonest individual who suppressed or colored the truth against Mr. Lincoln's side. Mr. Lincoln's speeches to the jury were most effective specimens of forensic oratory. He talked the vocabulary of the people, and the jury understood every point he made and every thought he uttered. He never made display for mere display, but his imagination was simple and pure in the richest gems of true eloquence. He constructed short sentences of small words, and never wearied the mind with mazes of elaboration. Mr. Lincoln was particularly kind to young lawyers, and I remember with what confidence I always went to him, because I was certain he knew all about the matter and would cheerfully tell me. I went to him one day with a paper I did not understand. How long ago it seems!—but I see him now, standing in the corner of the old courtroom, and as I approached him he said: "Wait till I fix this plug for my 'gallus,' and I will pitch into it like a dog at a root."

I then saw that he was trying to connect his suspender with his trousers by making a "plug" act the part of a button. Mr. Lincoln probably, like other people of that day and section, had been taught to say "gallows," and he never adopted the modern word "suspenders." He used old-fashioned words whenever they could be sustained as proper, and homely phrase, but was never ungrammatical. Indeed, he was singularly correct and grammatical. He could not perhaps be called a great lawyer, measured by the extent of his acquirement of legal knowledge. He was not an encyclopedia of cases, but in the text-books of the profession and in the clear perception of legal principles, with natural capacity to apply them, he had very great ability.

One of the most interesting incidents in my early acquaintance with Mr. Lincoln was a lawsuit in which Mr. Lincoln was counsel for the plaintiff and I was counsel for the defendant. Even then, in a trial that was the sensation of an obscure village on the prairies, Mr. Lincoln showed that supreme sense of justice to God and his fellow-men, which but a few years later made him the friend of the oppressed and liberator of the slave.

This lawsuit was in the spring of 1856, two years after I had made my "trade from Ohio to Illinois," and the case was tried where the parties lived — in the little village of Clinton.

It was a family quarrel between two brothers-in-law, Jack Dungee and Joe Spencer. Dungee was a Portuguese who came up from a Portuguese settlement in Tennessee to make his home in Illinois. He was extremely dark-complexioned, but not a bad-looking fellow; and, after a time, he married Spencer's sister, with the approval of the Spencer family, as shown at the trial. The Spencers were called well-to-do people; and Joe Spencer, who was worth probably five or six thousand dollars, was regarded as well off for that early day in the West. I don't remember the origin of the quarrel, but it became bitter; and the last straw was laid on when Spencer called Dungee a "nigger," and followed it up, they said, by adding "a nigger married to a white woman." The statute of Illinois made it a crime for a Negro to marry a white woman, and, because of that, the words were slanderous. I could not believe Joe Spencer, though a rough, ignorant fellow, would be such a fool as to involve his sister by this charge against his brother-in-law. He did not deny calling Dungee a "nigger," but denied the words which made the complaint in the declaration, on which Dungee, through Mr. Lincoln, brought the suit for slander, claiming, I think, two thousand dollars damages. C. H. Moore, a well-known lawyer of Illinois, was associated with me as counsel for Spencer. Judge David Davis was on the bench, and the suit was brought in the De Witt Circuit Court. When the case came up, Mr. Moore and myself appeared for the defence and demurred to the declaration, which, to the annoyance of Mr. Lincoln, the court sustained. Whatever interest Mr. Lincoln took in the case before that time, his professional pride was now aroused by the fact that the court had decided that his papers were deficient. Looking across the trial table at Moore and myself and shaking his long, bony finger, he said: "Now, by Jing, I will beat you boys!"

"By Jing" was the extent of his expletives, and beyond that he did not go in the expression of surprise or indignation. At the next term of the court Mr. Lincoln appeared with his papers amended, and fully determined to make good his promise to "beat you boys"; and we thought his chances pretty good to do it, too. We knew our man was a fool not to have settled it; but still we were bound to defend and clear him, if we could. Though it was nearly forty years ago, I shall never forget Mr. Lincoln's looks as he rose to state his case to the jury. He was not excited, but manifested a great earnestness, not only because of his client, but he also wanted to redeem himself from the implication arising from the fact that he had been, as the lawyers say, "demurred out of court." I recall some of his opening sentences when he said:

"Gentlemen of the Jury: I do not believe that the best way to build up and maintain a good reputation is to go to law about it, and during my practice at the bar it has been my uniform policy to discourage slander suits. But, gentlemen, in this case, forbearance had ceased to be a virtue, and this courtroom, dedicated to the sacred cause of justice, is the only place where my client can seek protection and vindication. If the malice of the defendant had rested satisfied with speaking the words once or twice, or even thrice, my client would have borne it in silence. But when he went from house to house, *gabbling*, yes, *gabbling* about it, then it was that my client determined to bring this suit."

It would be impossible to describe the force of the word "gabbling," as emphasized by Mr. Lincoln. It was as splendid in its dramatic effect as the word "fail" in Richelieu, when uttered by Booth or Barrett. Another equally dramatic and powerful stroke, was his direct reference to Spencer's accusation that Dungee was a "nigger." It had a curious touch of the ludicrous, by Mr. Lincoln's pronunciation of a word, which instead of detracting seemed to add to the effect. I hear him now, as he said:

"Gentlemen of the Jury: My client is not a Negro, though it is no crime to be a Negro — no crime to be born with a black skin. But my client is not a Negro. His skin may not be as white as ours, but I say he is not a Negro, though he may be a Moore."

"Mr. Lincoln," interrupted Judge Davis, scarcely able to restrain a smile, "you mean a Moor, not Moore."

"Well, your Honor, Moor, not C. H. Moore," replied Mr. Lincoln, with a sweep of his long arm toward the table where Moore and I sat. "I say my client may be a Moor, but he is not a Negro."

In the argument of the case on the testimony Mr. Lincoln made a most powerful and remarkable speech, abounding in wit, logic and eloquence of the highest order. His thoughts were clothed in the simplest garb of expression, and in words understood by every juror in the box. After the instructions were given by the court the jury retired, and in a few moments returned with a judgment for the plaintiff, in a sum which was a large amount for those days, though I do not recall the exact figures. Of course it was going to break up our man, who, strange to say, could not realize the situation, but wanted to carry the case to the Supreme Court. Mr. Lincoln had said his client did not want to make money out of the suit, so we told Spencer the best thing he could do would be to get Dungee to remit some of the damage and be thankful. He finally accepted this advice, and we went to Mr. Lincoln and said:

"Mr. Lincoln, you have beaten us, as you said you would. We want now to ground the weapons of our unequal warfare, and as you said your client did not want to make money out of the suit we thought you might get him to remit some of the judgment. We know Spencer has acted the fool, but this judgment will break him up."

Said Mr. Lincoln:

"Well, I will cheerfully advise my client to remit on the most favorable terms. The defendant *is* a fool. But he has one virtue. He is industrious and has worked hard for what he has, so I am not disposed to hold him responsible. If every fool was to be dealt with by being held responsible in money for his folly, the poorhouses of the country would have to be enlarged very much beyond their present capacity."

Well, the result of Mr. Lincoln's advice to his client was that Dungee agreed to remit the whole judgment, by

Spencer paying the costs of the suit and Mr. Lincoln's fee. Mr. Lincoln then proposed to leave the amount of his fee to Moore and myself. We protested against this, and insisted that Mr. Lincoln should fix the amount of his own fee. After a few moments' thought he said: "Well, gentlemen, don't you think I have honestly earned twenty-five dollars?" We were astonished, and had he said one hundred dollars it would have been what we expected. The judgment was a large one for those days; he had attended the case at two terms of court, had been engaged for two days in a hotly-contested suit, and his client's adversary was going to pay the bill. The simplicity of Mr. Lincoln's character in money matters is well illustrated by the fact, that for all this he charged twenty-five dollars.

The first time I ever heard Mr. Lincoln's favorite verses, "Oh, why should the Spirit of Mortal be Proud," he repeated them. It was during a term of court, in the same year, at Lincoln, a little town named for Mr. Lincoln. We were all stopping at the hotel, which had a very big room with four beds, called the "lawyers' room." Some of us thin fellows doubled up; but I remember that Judge Davis, who was as large then as he was afterward, when a justice on the Supreme Bench, always had a bed to himself. Mr. Lincoln was an early riser, and one morning, when up early as usual and dressed, he sat before the big, old-fashioned fireplace and repeated aloud from memory that whole hymn. Somebody asked him for the name of the author; but he said he had never been able to learn who wrote it, but wished he knew. Nobody in the room could tell; but I know that I, and I will venture to say that all the rest, soon after looked it up, so impressed were we by its beauty when Mr. Lincoln repeated it that morning. But I always felt that it would not have been quite the same had anybody but Mr. Lincoln repeated it. The hymn seemed to fit the man. I remember there were a great many guesses, and some said Shakespeare must have written it. But Mr. Lincoln, who was better read in Shakespeare than any of us, said they were not Shakespeare's words. I made a persistent hunt for the author, and years after found the hymn was written by an Englishman, William Knox, who was born in 1789, and died in 1825.

It was in the campaign of 1858 that Mr. Lincoln made a great speech at Springfield, on the seventeenth of June. That speech was one of the most remarkable he ever delivered. It was the one in which he used the expression, "A house divided against itself cannot stand." In the latter part of July, Douglas began his regular campaign in De Witt County, which was a strong Buchanan county. We wrote Mr. Lincoln he had better come and hear Douglas speak at Clinton, which he did. There was an immense crowd for a country town, and on the way to the grove where the speaking took place, Mr. Lincoln said to me: "Weldon, I have challenged Judge Douglas for a discussion. What do you think of it?" I replied, "I approve your judgment in whatever you do."

We went over a little to one side of the crowd and sat down on one of the boards, laid on logs for seats. Douglas spoke over three hours to an immense audience, and made one of the most forcible political speeches I ever heard. As he went on he referred to Lincoln's Springfield speech, and became very personal, and I said to Mr. Lincoln:

"Do you suppose Douglas knows you are here?"

"Well," he replied, "I don't know whether he does or

not; he has not looked in this direction. But I reckon some of the boys have told him I am here."

When Douglas finished there was a tremendous shout for "Lincoln," which kept on with no let-up. Mr. Lincoln said: "What shall I do? I can't speak here."

"You will have to say something," I replied. "Suppose you get up and say you will speak this evening at the courthouse yard."

Mr. Lincoln mounted the board seat, and as the crowd got sight of his tall form the shouts and cheers were wild. As soon as he could make himself heard he said:

"This is Judge Douglas's meeting. I have no right, therefore, no disposition to interfere. But if you ladies and gentlemen desire to hear what I have to say on these questions, and will meet me this evening at the courthouse yard, east side, *I will try* to answer the gentleman."

Douglas had taken off his cravat, for it was extremely warm, and he was now putting it on as he turned in the direction of Mr. Lincoln. Both became posed in a tableau of majestic power. The scene was a meeting of giants, a contest of great men; and the situation was dramatic in the extreme. Lincoln made a speech that evening which in volume did not equal the speech of Douglas, but for sound and cogent argument was the superior. Douglas had charged Mr. Lincoln with being in favor of Negro equality, which was then the bugbear of politics. In his speech that evening Mr. Lincoln said:

"Judge Douglas charges me with being in favor of Negro equality, and to the extent that he charges I am not guilty. *I am guilty* of hating servitude and loving freedom; and while I would not carry the equality of the races to the extent charged by my adversary, I am happy to confess before you that in some things the black man is the equal of the white man. In the right to eat the bread his own hands have earned, he is the equal of Judge Douglas or any other living man."

When Lincoln spoke the last sentence he had lifted himself to his full height, and as he reached his hands toward the stars of that still night, then and there fell from his lips one of the most sublime expressions of American statesmanship. The effect was grand, the cheers tremendous. After the meeting his friends congratulated him on the beauty of the thought, and Mr. Lincoln said:

"Do you think that is fine?" When assured it was, he laughingly added: "Well, if you think so, I will get that off again."

It was in 1859, while attorney for the Illinois Central Railroad, that in connection with C. H. Moore, Mr. Lincoln attended to the litigation of the company. He appeared in one case which the company did not want to try at that term, and Mr. Lincoln remarked to the court: "We are not ready for trial."

Judge Davis asked: "Why is not the company ready to go to trial?"

Mr. Lincoln replied: "We are embarrassed by the absence, or rather want of information from Captain McClellan."

"Who is Captain McClellan, and why is he not here?" asked Judge Davis.

Mr. Lincoln said: "All I know of him is that he is the engineer of the railroad, and why he is not here deponent saith not."

In consequence of Captain McClellan's absence the case was continued. Lincoln and McClellan had never met up to that time, and the most they knew of each other was that one was the attorney and the other the engineer of the Illinois Central Railroad. In little more than two years from that time the fame of both had spread as wide as civilization, and each held in his grasp the fate of a nation. The lawyer was directing councils and cabinets, and the engineer, subordinate to the lawyer as Commander-in-Chief, was directing armies greater than the combined forces of Wellington and Napoleon at Waterloo.

It was in 1860 at a State Convention held at Decatur, Ill., to appoint delegates to Chicago, that Governor Oglesby started the rail *furore*. Mr. Lincoln had lived in that county and had worked on a farm with John Hanks, making rails, but of course many years before. Oglesby arranged that Hanks himself should march into the convention at the proper moment with a rail on his shoulder, and if possible, one of the identical rails. When Mr. Lincoln rose to speak his attention was called to the rail, and with his usual readiness he said:

"Fellow-citizens: It is true that many years ago John Hanks and I made rails down on the Sangamon. We made good, big, honest rails; but whether that is one of the rails I am not, at this distant period of time, able to say."

Mr. Lincoln closed his reference to the rails with a eulogy on free labor, embracing the finest thoughts of his theory on that subject. And thus was inaugurated the rail movement.

A few weeks after Mr. Lincoln went into the White House he appointed me United States Attorney, with, of course, my duties in Illinois. But I always went to see him when I came to Washington, and, on one occasion, he revived a story about a mutual friend in Illinois, Robert Lewis, which we had often enjoyed together out there with Mr. Lewis himself. I was stopping at Willard's, where, just at that time, there were parties interested in cotton which it was difficult to bring up from certain insurrectionary districts, because of the contest between the civil and military authorities, as to the policy of bringing cotton out of the seceded States, permits being issued by the Treasury Department, which were nullified by the military. The gentlemen at Willard's were anxious to learn from the President, if possible, what would be the probable result of the contest, and requested me to broach the subject, on my visit to the White House. After talking with Mr. Lincoln for some time on other matters, I referred to the cotton subject, and said these gentlemen had requested me to ask him how it would be likely to turn out. The moment I made the inquiry, a smile, amused and bright, lighted up Mr. Lincoln's face, and he said:

"By the way, what has become of our friend, Robert Lewis?"

I replied that Mr. Lewis was still in his old home, and clerk of the court, as he had been for many years.

"Well," said Mr. Lincoln, "do you remember a story Bob used to tell us about going to Missouri to look up some Mormon lands belonging to his father?"

I replied: "Mr. President, I've forgotten the details of the story. I wish you would tell it."

Lewis was a warm personal friend of Mr. Lincoln, and he told the story that evening, with much enjoyment, and as he only could tell it. The story was in substance as follows:

When Bob Lewis became of age he found among his father's papers some warrants and patents for lands in

Northeastern Missouri, where attempts at Mormon settlement had been made. He thought the best thing he could do would be to look up these lands, see if they were worth anything, and establish his title. It was long before the day of railroads, and Bob started on horseback, equipped with a pair of old saddlebags, in one side of which he packed his papers, and in the other some necessary articles of the toilet, but which Bob himself had said, made less bulk than his title papers. He travelled a long way round, but finally got into that part of Missouri where he thought he could locate his section of land, and, bringing up before a solitary cabin, hitched his horse, took his saddlebags, and knocked at the door. A gruff and not hospitable voice bade him enter. I am sorry I cannot give in Bob's own words the description of the interior, as Mr. Lincoln repeated it. The conspicuous objects, however, perhaps one might say ornaments, were the proprietor, a lean, lanky-looking man, who looked to Bob about eleven feet long, stretched before a big fireplace, "necking" bullets, and above the fireplace hung on a couple of buck's horns a rifle which also looked about eleven feet long. The man looked up as Bob entered, but made no pause in his busy occupation of preparing bullets. Bob said he was the first to pass the time of day, and then he inquired about the section of land on which the cabin was located. The proprietor knew nothing about that section, or any other in Missouri, and apparently was indifferent to his visitor's desire for information. Finally Bob got out his papers, looked them over, and said:

"Stranger, I am looking up some lands belonging to my father. I've got the titles all right here in these papers," and he proceeded to prove it by reading the papers aloud. When he had finished, he said: "Now that is my title to this section. What is yours?"

The proprietor of the cabin by this time showed a slight interest, stopped his work a moment, raised himself on his elbow and pointing to the rifle, said:

"Young man, do you see that gun?" Mr. Lewis admitted he did, very frankly.

"Well," said the pioneer, "that is my title, and if you don't get out of here pretty quick you will feel the force of it."

Bob hurriedly put his papers in his saddlebags, dashed out of the cabin, mounted his pony and galloped down the road, though he declared the proprietor of the cabin snapped his gun twice at him before he turned the corner. But he never went back to disturb that man's title. Now, the military authorities have the same title against the civil authorities that closed out Bob's title to his Mormon lands in Missouri. The military have the guns. The gentlemen themselves may judge what the result is likely to be.

When I returned to Willard's, and told the anxious cotton speculators, they laughed heartily over the story; but they understood what would be the policy of the administration as well as if a proclamation had been issued.

Mr. Lincoln was not a story-teller, but he had the happy faculty of always being ready with a story or anecdote which relieved him in the discharge of duties, from the humblest walks of life to the complicated responsibilities of President of the United States.

Here is one where he relieved the embarrassment of his situation as President by a master-stroke of wit. It was related to me by Judge David Davis, who, while on the Supreme Bench, went to the White House with the gentlemen in question, and presented them to the President. In 1862, the people of New York City feared bombardment by Confederate cruisers, and public meetings were held to express the gravity of the situation. Finally a delegation of fifty gentlemen representing in their own right $100,000,000 was selected to go to Washington and see the President about the propriety of detailing a gunboat to protect New York City. The interview was arranged with the President, but Mr. Lincoln was puzzled to know what to say or do when the New York men appeared. He said beforehand he had no gunboats that could be spared from active service, but as they had come over for that purpose he would have to see them. The delegation went up to the White House and were presented by Judge Davis. The chairman made an appeal to the President for protection, and said they represented the wealth of the city of New York — "one hundred millions" in their own right. Mr. Lincoln heard them attentively, much impressed, apparently, by the "hundred millions." When they had concluded, he said:

"Gentlemen, I am, by the Constitution, Commander-in-Chief of the Army and Navy of the United States, and as a matter of law I can order anything done that is practicable to be done; but as a matter of fact, I am not in command of the gunboats or ships of war — as a matter of fact, I do not know exactly where they are, but presume they are actively engaged. It is impossible for me, in the condition of things, to furnish you a gunboat, the credit of the Government is at a very low ebb, greenbacks are not worth more than forty or fifty cents on the dollar, and in this condition of things, if I was worth half as much as you gentlemen are represented to be, and as badly frightened as you seem to be, I would build a gunboat and give it to the Government."

Judge Davis said he never saw one hundred millions sink to such insignificant proportions as it did when that delegation left the White House, sadder but wiser men. They had learned that money as well as muscle was a factor of war.

WASHINGTON, D. C.

INCIDENTS RECALLED IN WASHINGTON.

RECOLLECTIONS OF EX-SECRETARY McCULLOCH AND MRS. McCULLOCH AND JUDGE SHELLABARGER.

BY JANET JENNINGS.

Ex-Secretary McCulloch, now eighty-six years old, but still in good health, delights in reminiscences of Abraham Lincoln. Mr. McCulloch was president of the Bank of Indiana, with his home at Indianapolis, when called to Washington by Mr. Lincoln to organize the Bureau of the Comptroller of the Currency. It was a work of great responsibility, incessant labor, untiring zeal, watchfulness and patriotic devotion to the Government. History records how ably and loyally Mr. McCulloch served at the head of this Bureau for two years, when with his second administration President Lincoln appointed him Secretary of the Treasury. It was at the darkest hour of the War, just before the light of victory which brought peace to the country. He was very loth to accept the position even after his name had gone to the Senate. Speaking of it the other day, and of the tremendous strain he was under while organizing and carrying on the affairs of the Currency Bureau, the Ex-Secretary said: "But I could not help myself. Mr. Lincoln sent for me, and when I went into his room, he looked at me with his sad, weary eyes, and throwing his arm over my shoulder said: 'You *must;* the country *needs* you.'"

Many of Mr. Lincoln's stories are parables. But he was not more ready with their appropriate application, than he was with quotations from the Bible, for the same purpose, as the following related by the Ex-Secretary will show:

"It was in the darkest days, when the credit of the Government was at low ebb, and we were trying to dispose of the ten-forty bonds. Jay Cooke had come forward and taken a large amount of the bonds — the only banker, apparently, who at the moment had the patriotism and courage to do it. Cooke, in my opinion, has never received the credit he deserved for that act, at once so noble and brave. The bonds proved valuable, and it was soon a fact, that it was no risk to take them. Then it was, that other bankers felt reassured, and a delegation of bankers, from New York and other parts of the country, came to Washington, to see the President about the bonds. They first came to me at the Treasury, stated they were actuated by patriotic motives to save the credit of the Government, and desired an interview with Mr. Lincoln. My nephew, Albin Man, now a lawyer in New York, was in my office, where he had come broken in health by duty at the front. I sent him over to the White House to ask the President for the interview — and, by the way, my nephew was here a few days ago, and recalled the incident. The President said he would see the gentlemen, and shortly after we went over, and were shown into Mr. Lincoln's room. He looked very tired and worn — sat with his feet stretched out, resting them on the table he used for his desk. He arose at once, stepped forward, and I presented the bankers, Mr. Lincoln shaking hands with each as I introduced them by name. Then I said, by way of explaining their business:

"'Mr. President, these gentlemen have come to Washington from patriotic motives — to help us save the credit of the Government. They want to buy our bonds; they will put money in the treasury; and, Mr. President, you know "where the treasure is, there will the heart be also."'

"I am a big man, but Mr. Lincoln drew himself up, standing

head and shoulders above all, and, with a peculiar smile on his face, replied:

"'Yes, Mr. Secretary; but there is another passage of Holy Writ which you may remember — "Where the carcass is, there will the eagles be gathered together."'"

Mrs. McCulloch, who at that time largely shared in her husband's anxieties and cares, spoke of two little incidents illustrating Mr. Lincoln's nature, so quick to forgive and condone. She said:

"I went to the White House, one Saturday afternoon, to Mrs. Lincoln's reception, accompanied by Mrs. Wm. P. Dole, whose husband was Commissioner of Indian Affairs. There were crowds in and out of the White House, and during the reception Mr. Lincoln slipped quietly into the room, and stood back alone, looking on as the people passed through. I suggested to Mrs. Dole that we should go over and speak to the President, which we did. Mr. Lincoln said, laughingly: 'I am always glad to see you, ladies, for I know you don't want anything.'

"I replied: 'But, Mr. President, I do want something; I want you to do something very much.'

"'Well, what is it?' he asked, adding, 'I hope it isn't anything I can't do.'

"'I want you to suppress the Chicago *Times*, because it does nothing but abuse the administration,' I replied.

"'Oh, tut, tut! We must not abridge the liberties of the press or the people. But never mind the Chicago *Times*. The administration can stand it if the *Times* can.'

"I went over to the White House one evening. It was the last time Mr. Lincoln spoke in public. The news of the surrender had come; the city was excited, bonfires burning everywhere, and before the White House a crowd so dense that I and the friends with me went around to the basement door and were let in there, then made our way upstairs to the window where the President stood speaking to the people outside packed about the portico. Mr. Lincoln had written out some remarks on about half a dozen pages. Tad sat at a little table by the window; and when his father finished the sheets he took them and placed them carefully on the table, one by one, until Mr. Lincoln had ended. I remember well that all through Mr. Lincoln's speech there was uppermost kindly feeling for the South and dissuasion for the excited crowd outside from all bitterness and hard feeling. Mr. Lincoln was followed by Mr. Harlan, Secretary of the Interior, who, however, did not follow Mr. Lincoln's line of thought and words; and when Mr. Harlan said, 'What shall we do with the rebels? what shall we do with them?' the hoarse voices outside shouted up: 'Hang them!' Tad Lincoln looked at his father and said, quickly: 'No, papa; not hang them, but hang on to them.'

"Mr. Lincoln replied: 'Tad has got it. We must hang on to them.'

"The following night Mr. Lincoln was assassinated. My husband had gone early in the evening to ask about Secretary Seward, who had been injured by a carriage accident a few days before; then on his return from Mr. Seward's he had retired early, being very tired. About twelve o'clock we were roused by the news of the assassination. My husband started at once for Ford's Theatre, walking down alone, though I begged him to take a man with him. But he would not, and went off alone to the house on Tenth Street where Mr. Lincoln had been taken; and there, with the other members of the Cabinet, he remained till morning."

Judge Shellabarger, of Ohio, whose Congressional service covered President Lincoln's years in the White House, speaks of a visit to Mr. Lincoln, giving this incident:

"I, like many other members of Congress, did not see Mr. Lincoln often, because we felt that he was overwhelmed with the burdens of the hour, and people giving him no rest. But a young man in the army, Ben Tappan, wanted a transfer from the volunteer service to the regular service, retaining his rank of lieutenant, and with staff duty. There was some regulation against such transfer; but Tappan's stepfather, Frank Wright, of Ohio, thought it could be done. He had been to Secretary Stanton, who was an uncle of young Tappan by marriage, and, on account of this so-called relationship the Secretary declined to act in the matter. Wright and I therefore went up to the White House to see the President about it. After talking it over Mr. Lincoln told a story, the application of which was that the army was getting to be all staff and no army, there was such a rush for staff duty by young officers. However, he looked over Lieutenant Tappan's paper, heard what Secretary Stanton had told us about his delicacy in transferring Lieutenant Tappan against the regulation because of the relationship by marriage. Then Mr. Lincoln wrote across the application something like the following endorsement:

"'Lieutenant Tappan, of —— Regiment, Volunteers, desires transfer to —— Regiment, Regular service, and assigned to staff duty with present rank. If the only objection to this transfer is Lieutenant Tappan's relationship to the Secretary of War, that objection is overruled.

"'A. LINCOLN.'

"This, of course, threw the responsibility of breaking the regulation on Secretary Stanton. We never heard anything more about the transfer."

WASHINGTON, D. C.

MR. LINCOLN IN NEW YORK.

HIS ADDRESSES IN NEW ENGLAND — "RIGHT MAKES MIGHT."

COMPILED FROM CORRESPONDENCE.

MR. LINCOLN's speeches in New York and in New England introduced him so favorably to the East that its delegations in the nominating conventions were not surprised that he should be a favorite candidate for the Presidency, nor were they unfavorably inclined to him. How he happened to be invited to speak in New York is told on pages 27 and 28 by Mr. Henry C. Bowen.

Until Mr. Lincoln reached New York he was under the impression that he was to speak in Brooklyn; and when on the evening of February 27th, 1860, he stood before his audience in Cooper Institute, he saw before him a crowded assemblage of listeners, among whom were many from whom, in his modest judgment of himself, he would have been inclined rather to ask advice than to give them instruction. William Cullen Bryant presided and David Dudley Field escorted the speaker to the platform. "Since the days of Clay and Webster," said the *Tribune* the next morning, "no one has spoken to a larger assemblage of the intellect and mental culture of our city." For two years his name had been one of the most prominent before the people, coming rapidly up in public esteem to rank with those of Seward and Douglas; and yet he was utterly unknown in person except in the West. The representative men of New York were naturally eager to see and hear one whose force and wit had attracted so large a share of the public attention. Perhaps it was the nature of his audience and the larger responsibility which he felt in speaking on such an occasion that called out all the strength and dignity of the man, and somewhat restrained his rollicking humor. It is remarkable that there was not a story in his speech from beginning to end. In the first half of it there was not a word to call forth a smile; it was only in the last part of the address that by occasional flashes he suggested the possession of powers which he could not quite conceal. His address was a magnificent success, and he instantly took rank with the masters of the platform. He took for his text, a phrase just uttered by Senator Douglas:

"Our fathers, when they framed the Government under which we live, understood this question just as well and even better than we do now."

This question was, Slavery in the Territories; and Mr. Lincoln immediately proceeded to give a historical analysis of what the fathers who formed the Constitution thought on this subject. There were thirty-nine of them, and he gave evidence to prove that twenty-one had left on record their opinion that the Federal Government had the right to regulate or control slavery in the Territories. They were mentioned one by one, and it was proved that of those who had left no record by their votes on this point, most were presumably of the same opinion. It was a very careful and thorough study, worthy of an expert in our early history. Yet he declared that even if such were not their view, it should not estop us from doing what we now see to be wise and right. He then addressed himself to the South, showing its inconsistency, proving that where it claimed conservatism it was going back on the record of Washington, who signed an act of Congress enforcing the prohibition of slavery in the Northwestern Territories, and of Jefferson and the other Federal heroes. He ridiculed the doctrine of that sort of popular sovereignty which means letting everybody carry slavery wherever he pleases. He denied that Republicanism was responsible for John Brown's raid and declared that there were insurrections in the South before Republicanism was thought of. He exclaimed:

"But you will not abide the election of a Republican President! In that supposed event, you say, you will destroy the Union; and then, you say, the great crime of having destroyed it will be upon us! That is cool. A highwayman holds a pistol to my ear, and mutters through his teeth, 'Stand and deliver, or I shall kill you, and then you will be a murderer!'"

What the South wanted, he said, was that the North should cease to call slavery wrong and call it right; that Senator Douglas's new sedition law must be enacted and enforced, suppressing all declarations that slavery is wrong, whether made in politics, in presses, in pulpits or in private; that fugitive slaves must be arrested and returned with greedy pleasure; the free-State constitutions must be pulled down and the whole atmosphere must be disinfected from all taint of opposition to slavery. This he declared the North would not do. The North did not intend to interfere with slavery in the slave States; but it would never allow slavery to be extended to the Territories. The smiles, the laughter, the outbursts of applause which greeted the speaker's telling points showed that Mr. Lincoln's arguments had met ready acceptance. The speech was printed in full next morning in the daily papers, and he was declared to be one of nature's orators. He was invited, during his brief visit East, to speak in Connecticut and Rhode Island. It was substantially the same address, but with great variety of utterance and with more freedom of illustration, that he gave in Hartford, New Haven, Norwich and Providence. Referring to the way that the Democrats were charging all sorts of crimes upon the Republicans, he said, at Hartford: "Let them go on with their howling. They will succeed when by slandering women you get them to love you, or by slandering men you get them to vote for you."

He laughed at Senator Mason, of Virginia, who, on account of this "sectional warfare," was dressing in homespun in order to avoid goods manufactured in the North. Said he: "To carry out his idea he ought to go barefoot. If that's the plan, they should begin at the foundation, and adopt the well-known 'Georgia costume' of a shirt collar and a pair of spurs."

The next night, March 6th, he addressed the citizens of New Haven at length and with even more vigor and raciness. He contrasted the two theories that slavery is right and that slavery is wrong, and defended Seward's use of the expression, "an irrepressible conflict." He denounced the utter indifference of those who said they did not care whether slavery was going up or down, that it was merely a matter of dollars and cents; that a Negro is inferior to a white man, just as a crocodile is inferior to a Negro. Said he:

"I am not ashamed to confess that twenty-five years ago I was a hired laborer, mauling rails, at work on a flatboat — just what might happen to any poor man's son. I want every man to have a chance, and I believe a black man is entitled to it, to better his condition! that he may be a hired laborer this year, and the next work for himself, and finally hire men to work for him. Up here in New England you have a soil that scarcely sprouts black-eyed beans, and yet where will you find wealthy men so wealthy, and poverty so rarely in extremity? There is not another such place on earth!"

On February 28th, Abraham Lincoln spoke to a Republican meeting in Railroad Hall, Providence, opening the campaign. Governor Hoppin presided, and the Hon. Thomas A. Jenckes acted as president of the meeting, and Mr. John Eddy as secretary. Mr. Lincoln began by alluding good-naturedly to some remarks in the *Press* and the *Post*, which he had read on his way thither in the cars, and after having humorously commented upon the words in the *Press*, he proposed to take as the main subject of his speech, topics suggested by the quotation which the *Post* made from one of his former speeches. His point was that the country cannot permanently endure half-slave and half-free. He made a striking and permanent impression as of a man possessed of thorough honesty and of sincere, earnest belief in all that he said. His address abounded in good humor, keen satire and witty thrusts that cut like a master's blade. But these were only the flashes upon a plain, simple, cogent reasoning which made his position impregnable, and carried his audience with him. Mr. John Eddy is still living in Providence, and recalls the occasion vividly. Mr. Lincoln stopped at his house.

Mr. Lincoln also spoke in Norwich, Conn. Col. Hugh H. Osgood, of Norwich, was in New York the day after Mr. Lincoln had spoken in Cooper Institute, and an intimate friend told him of the wonderful eloquence of Mr. Lincoln, and besought him to get him to come to Norwich, as he was so sure he would be a wonderful success in speaking to the people. Accordingly, Colonel Osgood got his friend, Gen. Henry N. Birge, a nephew of Governor Buckingham, to go to Hartford, where Lincoln was to speak that night and secure him. This he did, and created the same impression that he had made elsewhere. The Hon. Amos W. Prentice presided, and Daniel P. Tyler, of Brooklyn, who had made the Western circuit with Mr. Lincoln, spoke at the public meeting, and also Mr. John F. Trumbull, of Stonington. After the meeting there was quite a reception at the Wauregan House, and these gentlemen sat together and told stories with Mr. Lincoln till late at night. Mr. Trumbull was a famous story-teller, and about one o'clock, after Mr. Lincoln had gone to his room, another story had come to Mr. Trumbull, and he went to Mr. Lincoln's door and said: "Mr. Lincoln, I have just thought of another story I want to tell you." Mr. Lincoln said, "Come in." He was sitting down half undressed, and there they sat exchanging stories until after three o'clock. The late Prof. John P. Gulliver, in an unpublished letter, says:

"I remember that, in introducing Mr. Lincoln that evening, Mr. Prentice said: 'I trust that after the next Presidential election we shall see the orator of the evening presiding in the Senate over his old opponent, Stephen Arnold Douglas,' when some one said: 'Hurrah for Abraham Lincoln for Vice-President!' and we all laughed and shouted, thinking it a capital joke. How little we realized what pathos and tragedy, what suffering and glory, our careless compliments were calling down upon the long, ungainly, rollicking man who was laughing with us, and as heartily as any of us. But when he rose to speak, his expression and attitude created an instant hush. His first sentence, 'My fellow-citizens, there is, in fact, but one political question before the people of this country, and that is, *Is slavery right, or is it wrong?*' impressed us as the proclamation of a great captain on the battle-field, much as the words of Napoleon may have awed the army of Egypt — 'Soldiers! from the summit of those pyramids forty centuries are looking down upon you!'"

His closing sentence rose to the climax of moral sublimity, and it seemed that an old Hebrew prophet had come back to earth when, with profound emotion, he rolled forth the majestic words:

"Men of America! history through the centuries has been teaching us that might makes right. Let it be our mission in this nineteenth century to reverse the maxim, and to declare that right makes might!"

ANECDOTES OF LINCOLN.

STORIES ABOUT HIM—CHOICE STORIES BY HIM—SOME OF HIS APT ILLUSTRATIONS—HIS EPIGRAMMATIC SAYINGS.

WE have gathered the following stories told of Lincoln and by Lincoln from various sources, including Nicolay and Hay's voluminous work,* Carpenter's "Six Months in the White House," Raymond's, Thompson's and other lives of Lincoln. We have included none which are not believed to be genuine.

A Specimen of Ridicule.

In the campaign of 1848 Mr. Lincoln made a number of speeches. Referring to the attempt to glorify General Cass for his services on the frontier in the war with Great Britain, he thus humorously referred to his own military experiences in the Black Hawk War:

"Did you know, Mr. Speaker, I am a military hero? In the days of the Black Hawk War I fought, bled and came away. I was not at Stillman's defeat, but I was about as near it as General Cass was to Hull's surrender; and, like him, I saw the place very soon afterward. It is quite certain I did not break my sword, for I had none

---

* Abraham Lincoln: A History; by John G. Nicolay and John Hay. In ten volumes. New York, The Century Co., 1890. The extracts are quoted from it by permission of the authors.

to break; but I bent my musket pretty badly on one occasion. If General Cass went in advance of me picking whortleberries, I guess I surpassed him in charges on the wild onions. If he saw any live fighting Indians, it was more than I did, but I had a good many bloody struggles with the mosquitoes; and although I never fainted from loss of blood, I can truly say I was often very hungry. If ever I should conclude to doff whatever our Democratic friends may suppose there is of black-cockade Federalism about me, and thereupon they shall take me up as their candidate for the Presidency, I protest that they shall not make fun of me, as they have of General Cass, by attempting to write me into a military hero."

A Gentle Official Reprimand.

The President was called upon to deliver a reprimand to an officer who had been tried by court-martial for quarrelling. It was probably the "gentlest," say his biographers, Nicolay and Hay, ever recorded "in the annals of penal discourses." It was as follows:

"The advice of a father to his son, 'Beware of entrance to a quarrel, but, being in, bear it that the opposed may beware of thee!' is good, but not the best. Quarrel not at all. No man resolved to make the most of himself can spare time for personal contention. Still less can he afford to take all the consequences, including the vitiating of his temper and the loss of self-control. Yield larger things to which you can show no more than equal right; and yield lesser ones though clearly your own. Better give your path to a dog than be bitten by him in contesting for the right. Even killing the dog would not cure the bite."

Lincoln as a Lawyer.

As a lawyer, according to Messrs. Nicolay and Hay, Mr. Lincoln, notwithstanding "all his stories and jests, his frank, companionable humor, his gift of easy accessibility and welcome, was, even while he travelled the Eighth Circuit, a man of grave and serious temper, and of an unusual innate dignity and reserve. He had few or no special intimates, and there was a line beyond which no one ever thought of passing." They thus describe him in the courtroom:

"He seemed absolutely at home in the court room; his great stature did not encumber him there; it seemed like a natural symbol of superiority. His bearing and gesticulation had no awkwardness about them; they were simply striking and original. He assumed at the start a frank and friendly relation with the jury which was extremely effective. He usually began, as the phrase ran, by 'giving away his case'; by allowing to the opposite side every possible advantage that they could honestly and justly claim. Then he would present his own side of the case, with a clearness, a candor, an adroitness of statement which at once flattered and convinced the jury, and made even the bystanders his partisans. Sometimes he disturbed the court with laughter by his humorous or apt illustrations; sometimes he excited the audience by that florid and exuberant rhetoric which he knew well enough how and when to indulge in; but his more usual and more successful manner was to rely upon a clear, strong, lucid statement, keeping details in proper subordination and bringing forward, in a way which fastened the attention of court and jury alike, the essential point on which he claimed a decision. 'Indeed,' says one of his colleagues, 'his statement often rendered argument unnecessary, and often the court would stop him and say: "If that is the case, we will hear the other side."'"

Judge David Davis said of him:

"The framework of his mental and moral being was honesty, and a wrong cause was poorly defended by him."

Advice to a Client.

To a man who once offered him a case, the merits of which he did not appreciate, he made, according to his partner, Mr. Herndon, the following response:

"Yes, there is no reasonable doubt but that I can gain your case for you. I can set a whole neighborhood at loggerheads; I can distress a widowed mother and her six fatherless children, and thereby get for you six hundred dollars, which rightfully belongs, it appears to me, as much to them as it does to you. I shall not take your case, but I will give a little advice for nothing. You seem a sprightly, energetic man. I would advise you to try your hand at making six hundred dollars in some other way."

The King who lost his Head.

Early in 1865 Mr. Lincoln and Mr. Seward received three commissioners from the Confederacy, Messrs. Stephens, Hunter and Campbell, with reference to peace negotiations. They wanted Mr. Lincoln to recognize the President of the Southern Confederacy as the head of a government. This Mr. Lincoln refused to do. Mr. Hunter urged this very strongly, declaring that the recognition of Mr. Davis's power to make a treaty was the first and indispensable step to peace, and referred to the correspondence between King Charles I and his Parliament as a trustworthy precedent for a constitutional ruler dealing with rebels. When Mr. Hunter made this point Mr. Lincoln's face is said to have assumed the peculiar look which always preceded a hard hit, and he responded:

"Upon questions of history I must refer you to Mr. Seward, for he is posted in such things and I do not profess to be; but my only distinct recollection of the matter is that Charles lost his head."

An Apt Illustration.

Shortly after he was inaugurated, when office seekers were besieging him and important news of the outbreak in the South was coming to him hourly, he said:

"I am like a man so busy in letting rooms in one end of his house, that he cannot stop to put out the fire that is burning the other."

The Uses of a Chin-fly.

When a friend brought to his attention the fact that a member of his Cabinet was seeking for the nomination while Mr. Lincoln was a candidate for renomination, the President accepted the announcement with the utmost good humor, and said:

"My brother and I were once ploughing corn on a Kentucky farm, I driving the horse and he holding plough. The horse was lazy, but on one occasion rushed across the field so that I, with my long legs, could hardly keep pace with him. On reaching the end of the furrow, I found an enormous *chin-fly* fastened upon him, and knocked him off. My brother asked me what I did that for. I told him I didn't want the old horse bitten in that way. 'Why,' said my brother, '*that's all that made him go.*' If Mr. —— has a Presidential *chin-fly* biting him, I'm not going to knock him off, if it will only make his department *go.*"

A Negro's Idea of Mr. Lincoln.

Everybody knows that the colored people regarded Mr. Lincoln almost as a superhuman being. Colonel McKaye tells of a meeting of colored people in North Carolina who had heard of Mr. Lincoln and who tried to give utterance to their impressions as to what kind of a being he was. In the midst of their discussion a white-headed leader arose and said:

"Brederin, you don't know nosen' what you'se talkin' 'bout. Now, you just listen to me. Massa Linkum, he eberywhar. He know eberyting. He walk de earf like de Lord!"

His Kindness of Heart to the Distressed.

Mr. Lincoln's kindness of heart was known to everybody. Vice-President Colfax says that his doorkeepers had "standing orders from him that, no matter how great might be the public throng, if either Senators or Representatives had to wait or to be turned away without audience, he must see before the day closed every messenger who came to him with a petition for the saving of life."

Accounts of many such cases are given. A woman carrying a baby waited three days at the White House to see Mr. Lincoln. Her husband, who had sent a substitute, had enlisted subsequently himself when intoxicated, and had deserted from the army, and had been caught and sentenced to be shot. On his way through the anteroom Mr. Lincoln heard the baby cry. "He instantly went back to his office and rang the bell. 'Daniel,' said he, 'is there a woman with a baby in the anteroom?' I said there was, and, if he would allow me to say it, I thought it was a case he ought to see; for it was a matter of life and death. Said he: 'Send her to me at once.' She went in, told her story, and the President pardoned her husband. As the woman came out from his presence her eyes were lifted and her lips moving in prayer, the tears streaming down her cheeks." Said Daniel: "I went up to her and, pulling her shawl, said: 'Madam, it was the baby that did it!'"

Hearing a Mother's Plea.

The following incident is said to have occurred the same week:

"One day the Hon. Thaddeus Stevens called with an elderly lady in great trouble, whose son had been in the army, but for some offence had been court-martialed, and sentenced either to death or imprisonment at hard labor for a long term, I do not recollect which. There were some extenuating circumstances, and after a full hearing the President turned to the Representative and said: 'Mr. Stevens, do you think this is a case which will warrant my interference?' 'With my knowledge of the facts and the parties,' was the reply, 'I should have no hesitation in granting a pardon.' 'Then,' returned Mr. Lincoln, 'I will pardon him'; and he proceeded forthwith to execute the paper. The gratitude of the mother was too deep for expression, save by her tears, and not a word was said between her and Mr. Stevens until they were halfway down the stairs on their passage out, when she suddenly broke forth, in an excited manner, with the words: 'I knew it was a Copperhead lie!' 'What do you refer to, madam?' asked Mr. Stevens. 'Why, they told me he was an ugly-looking man,' she replied, with vehemence. 'He is the handsomest man I ever saw in my life.'"

A Midnight Pardon.

A Congressman who heard that a friend of his in the army had been court-martialed and sentenced to be shot, failing to move Secretary Stanton to grant a pardon, rushed to the White House late at night, after the President had retired, and forced his way to the President's bedroom, and earnestly besought his interference, exclaiming, earnestly, "This man must not be shot, Mr. Lincoln. I cannot allow him to be shot!" "Well," said the President in reply, "I do not believe shooting will do him any good. Give me that pen." And so the pardon was granted.

His Own Defence of his Clemency.

Speaking of the large number of cases he had dealt with in this way, Mr. Lincoln on one occasion said:

"Some of our generals complain that I impair discipline and subordination in the army by my pardons and respites; but it makes me rested, after a hard day's work, if I can find some good cause for saving a man's life, and I go to bed happy, as I think how joyous the signing of my name will make him and his family and his friends."

And with a happy smile beaming over that care-furrowed face, he signed that name that saved that life. His idea was that "when a man is sincerely penitent for his misdeeds and gives satisfactory evidence of the same, he can safely be pardoned; and there is no exception to the rule."

The Long and Short of It.

On the occasion of a serenade at the White House Mr. and Mrs. Lincoln, who was below the medium height, were called for. They appeared at the window together, and the President said: "Here I am, and here is Mrs. Lincoln. That's the long and short of it."

Too Many Pegs.

Referring once to his difficulty in finding commands for all those who wished to be appointed generals, he said: "The fact is I have more pegs than I have holes to put them in."

His Answer to Troublesome Critics.

To a deputation who waited upon him to complain of certain acts of his administration, he made the following response:

"Gentlemen, suppose all the property you were worth was in gold, and you had put it in the hands of Blondin to carry across the Niagara River on a rope, would you shake the cable, or keep shouting out to him: 'Blondin, stand up a little straighter — Blondin, stoop a little more — go a little faster — lean a little more to the north — lean a little more to the south'? No, you would hold your breath as well as your tongue, and keep your hands off until he was safe over. The Government are carrying an immense weight. Untold treasures are in their hands. They are doing the very best they can. Don't badger them. Keep silence, and we'll get you safe across."

How he earned his First Dollar.

He gave the following account to Mr. Seward of how he earned his first dollar:

"I was contemplating my new flatboat, and wondering whether I could make it stronger or improve it in any particular, when two men came down to the shore in carriages with trunks, and looking at the different boats singled out mine, and asked: 'Who owns this?' I answered, somewhat modestly, 'I do.' 'Will you,' said one of them, 'take us and our trunks out to the steamer?' 'Certainly,' said I. I was very glad to have the chance of earning something. I supposed that each of them would give me two or three bits. The trunks were put on my flatboat, the passengers seated themselves on the trunks, and I sculled them out to the steamboat.

"They got on board, and I lifted up their heavy trunks and put them on deck. The steamer was about to put on steam again, when I called out that they had forgotten to pay me. Each of them took from his pocket a silver half-dollar and threw it on the floor of my boat. I could scarcely believe my eyes as I picked up the money. Gentlemen, you may think it was a very little thing, and in these days it seems to me a trifle; but it was a most important incident in my life. I could scarcely credit that I, a poor boy, had earned a dollar in less than a day — that by honest work I had earned a dollar. The world seemed wider and fairer before me. I was a more hopeful and confident being from that time."

"He is intrenching."

A short time after the Democratic Convention of 1864, Mr. Charles A. Dana asked Mr. Lincoln why the nominee of the convention, General McClellan, had not replied to the letter notifying him of his nomination. "Oh," said Mr. Lincoln, with a twinkle in his eye, "he is intrenching."

Garrison in Baltimore.

An account given in the *Independent* of a visit of William Lloyd Garrison, and others, to Baltimore, to find the old jail where Garrison was imprisoned, states that when Mr. Garrison subsequently told Mr. Lincoln of it, the President remarked: "Well, Mr. Garrison, when you first went to Baltimore you could not get out of prison, but the second time you could not get in."

"Let him go."

To his Cabinet who asked him whether it would be right to allow the archtraitor, Jacob Thompson, to slip out of the country disguised, Mr. Lincoln replied:

"Well, let me tell you a story. There was an Irish soldier here last summer, who wanted something to drink stronger than water, and stopped at a drug shop, where he espied a soda fountain. 'Mr. Doctor,' said he, 'give me plaze, a glass of soda-wather, an' if you can put in a few drops of whisky unbeknown to any one I'll be obleeged.' Now," continued Mr. Lincoln, "if Jake Thompson is permitted to go through Maine unbeknown to any one, what's the harm? So don't have him arrested."

His Reply to a Verbal Criticism.

In one of his messages after his first inauguration Mr. Lincoln had this sentence:

"With rebellion thus sugar-coated, they have been drugging the public mind of their section for more than thirty years, until at length they have brought many good men to a willingness to take up arms against the Government."

The public printer did not like the use of the word *sugar-coated*, and went to the President about it, and said to Mr. Lincoln: "You used an undignified expression in the message. I would alter the structure of it if I were you."

"Defrees," replied Mr. Lincoln, "that word expresses precisely my idea, and I am not going to change it. The time will never come in this country when the people won't know exactly what sugar-coated means!"

How a Sentence was Improved.

On another occasion the public printer called the President's attention to a sentence in one of his messages which he thought awkwardly constructed. The President acknowledged the point of the criticism, and said: "Go home, Defrees, and see if you can better it." The next day Mr. Defrees took in to him his amendment. Mr. Lincoln met him by saying: "Seward found the same fault that you did, and he has been rewriting the paragraph also." Then, reading Mr. Defrees's version, he said: "I believe you have beat Seward; but, 'I jings'" (a common expression with him), "I think I can beat you both." Then, taking up his pen, he wrote the sentence as it was finally printed.

Mr. Lincoln's Vow.

Just before the Emancipation Proclamation was issued, immediately after the battle of Antietam, President Lincoln said to his Cabinet that "the time for the enunciation of the Emancipation Proclamation can no longer be delayed. Public sentiment will sustain it, and I have promised my God that I will do it." Secretary Chase, who heard the last words, which were uttered in a low tone, asked the President if he correctly understood him. Mr. Lincoln replied: "I made a solemn vow before God that if General Lee were driven back from Maryland I would crown the result by declaration of freedom to the slaves."

Anticipations of a Happy Second Term.

The Hon. Henry Wilson, who was on the ticket with General Grant in his second campaign as Vice-President, says that on the day before his death the President said to his wife:

"We have had a hard time together since we came to Washington: but now the War is over, and, with God's blessing upon us, we may hope for four years of happiness, and then we will go back to Illinois and pass the remainder of our lives in peace."

His Possessions in 1860.

It is related that on his visit to New York to deliver the famous Cooper Institute speech, the following incident occurred:

He met an Illinois acquaintance of former years, to whom he said, in his dry, good-natured way: "Well, B., how have you fared since you left Illinois?" to which B. replied: "I have made $100,000 and lost it all; how is it with you, Mr. Lincoln?" "Oh, very well," said Mr. Lincoln; "I have the cottage at Springfield and about $3000 in money. If they make me Vice-President with Seward, as some say they will, I hope I shall be able to increase it to $20,000, and that is as much as any man ought to want."

How he got a Knife.

Mr. Lincoln enjoyed jokes at the expense of his personal appearance, and used himself to tell this incident:

"In the days when I used to be 'on the circuit,' I was once accosted in the cars by a stranger, who said, 'Excuse me, sir, but I have an article in my possession which belongs to you.' 'How is that?' I asked, considerably astonished. The stranger took a jack-knife from his pocket. 'This knife,' said he, 'was placed in my hands some years ago, with the injunction that I was to keep it until I found a man *uglier* than myself. I have carried it from that time to this. Allow me *now* to say, sir, that I think *you* are fairly entitled to the property.'"

An Illustration from the Poultry Yard.

To a deputation who urged that his Cabinet should be reconstructed after the retirement of Secretary Cameron, the President told this story:

"Gentlemen, when I was a young man, I used to know very well one Joe Wilson, who built himself a log-cabin not far from where I lived. Joe was very fond of eggs and chickens, and he took a good deal of pains in fitting up a poultry shed. Having at length got together a choice lot of young fowls — of which he was very proud — he began to be much annoyed by the depredations of those little black and white spotted animals, which it is not necessary to name. One night Joe was awakened by an unusual cackling and fluttering among his chickens. Getting up, he crept out to see what was going on. It was a bright moonlight night, and he soon caught sight of half a dozen of the little pests, which with their dam were running in and out of the shadow of the shed. Very wrathy, Joe put a double charge into his old musket, and thought he would 'clean' out the whole tribe at one shot. Somehow he only killed *one*, and the balance scampered off across the field. In telling the story, Joe would always pause here, and hold his nose. 'Why didn't you follow them up and kill the rest?' inquired his neighbors. 'Blast it,' said Joe, 'why, it was eleven weeks before I got over killin' *one*. If you want any more skirmishing in that line you can just do it yourselves!'"

A Non-committal Opinion.

Mr. Lincoln's good nature was such that, even in the busy war times he received almost everybody who had a grievance, and would even give precious time to those who had no particular claim upon his attention. On one occasion Robert Dale Owen called upon him to read him a long manuscript on one of the abstruse subjects with which that rather erratic thinker loved to deal. Mr. Lincoln heard him patiently all through, and when the author looked up to him for his opinion, responded: "Well, for those who like that sort of thing I should think that is just the sort of thing they would like."

A Witty Reply.

On one occasion it is said that some of Mr. Lincoln's friends were talking about him and Stephen A. Douglas. The conversation led to the physical proportions of the respective men, and an argument arose as to the proper length of a man's leg. During the discussion on the subject Mr. Lincoln came in and quietly settled himself, and it was agreed that the question should be referred to him for settlement. They told him what they had been talking about and asked him what, in his opinion, was the proper length of a man's legs. "Well," said he reflectively, "I should think that they ought to be long enough to reach from his body to the ground."

A Characteristic Letter.

"Executive Mansion, October 17th, 1861.
"Major Ramsey:
"*My dear Sir:* — The lady — bearer of this — says she has two sons who want to work. Set them at it, if possible. Wanting to work is so rare a merit that it should be encouraged. A. Lincoln."

His Speech to a Sunday-school

On his first visit to New York he called at the Five Points House of Industry, and the following account of what occurred is given by a teacher there:

"Our Sunday-school in the Five Points was assembled, one Sabbath morning, when I noticed a tall, remarkable-looking man enter the room and take a seat among us. He listened with fixed attention to our exercises, and his countenance expressed such genuine interest that I approached him and suggested that he might be willing to say something to the children. He accepted the invitation with evident pleasure; and, coming forward, began a simple address, which at once fascinated every little hearer and hushed the room into silence. His language was strikingly beautiful, and his tones musical with intensest feeling. The little faces around him would droop into sad conviction as he uttered sentences of warning, and would brighten into sunshine as he spoke cheerful words of promise. Once or twice he attempted to close his remarks, but the imperative shout of 'Go on!' 'Oh, do go on!' would compel him to resume. As I looked upon the gaunt and sinewy frame of the stranger and marked his powerful head and determined features, now touched into softness by the impressions of the moment, I felt an irresistible curiosity to learn something more about him, and when he was quietly leaving the room I begged to know his name. He courteously replied: 'It is Abraham Lincoln, from Illinois.'"

Once, only, a Seeker for Office.

In 1849 Mr. Lincoln was an applicant for office. He wanted to be made Commissioner of the General Land Office; but, according to Nicolay and Hay, "a suitor for office so laggard and so scrupulous as he stood very little chance of success in contests like those which periodically raged in Washington." He failed, and thus "escaped one of the greatest dangers of his life," and afterwards congratulated himself on his happy deliverance. He was subsequently offered the Governorship of the Territory of Oregon, but declined it.

The Snake Illustration.

In his speeches at New Haven and Norwich, Mr. Lincoln used this illustration of slavery in the States and Territories:

"If I saw a venomous snake crawling in the road, any man would say I might seize the nearest stick and kill it; but if I found that snake in bed with my children, that would be another question. I might hurt the children more than the snake, and it might bite them. Much more, if I found it in bed with my neighbor's children, and I had bound myself by a solemn compact not to meddle with his children under any circumstances, it would become me to let that particular mode of getting rid of the gentleman alone. But if there was a bed newly made up, to which the children were to be taken, and it was proposed to take a batch of young snakes and put them there with them, I take it no man would say there was any question how I ought to decide."

The late Prof. John P. Gulliver, who heard the speech at Norwich, said the effect of the snake illustration on the audience was wonderful. Democrats applauded as vigorously as Republicans. He characterized the story as at once "queer and comical, tragic and argumentative."

The New Hat.

After Mr. Lincoln's nomination in 1860, an admiring hatter sent him a new silk hat. Mr. Lincoln put it on and walked to the glass to see if it fitted, and remarked to his wife: "Well, wife, we are going to have some new clothes, anyway."

Difficult Bridge Building.

"I once knew a sound Churchman by the name of Brown, who was a member of a very sober and pious committee, having in charge the erection of a bridge over a dangerous and rapid river. Several architects failed, and at last Brown said he had a friend named Jones, who had built several bridges and undoubtedly could build that one. So Mr. Jones was called in. 'Can you build this bridge?' inquired the committee. 'Yes,' replied Jones, 'or any other. I could build a bridge to the infernal regions, if necessary!' The committee were shocked, and Brown felt called upon to defend his friend. 'I know Jones so well,' said he, 'and he is so honest a man and so good an architect, that if he states soberly and positively that he can build a bridge to — to ——, why, I believe it: but I feel bound to say that I have my doubts about the abutment on the infernal side.' So," said Mr. Lincoln, "when politicians told me that the Northern and Southern wings of Democracy could be harmonized, why I believed them of course; but I always had my doubts about the 'abutment' on the *other* side."

A Happy Illustration.

In one of his debates with Judge Douglas he claimed that his opponent ascribed some things to him by "mere burlesques on the art and name of argument — by such fantastic arrangements of words as prove horse-chestnuts to be chestnut horses."

Mr. Lincoln's Confession of Faith.

On one occasion he said that the reason he had never joined the Church was that he did not like the long, complicated statements of Christian doctrines which characterized the Confessions of the Churches:

"When any Church will inscribe over its altar, as its sole qualification for membership, the Saviour's condensed statement of the substance of both Law and Gospel, 'Thou shalt love the Lord thy God with all thy heart, and with all thy soul, and with all thy mind, and thy neighbor as thyself,' that Church will I join with all my heart and all my soul."

As a Temperance Man.

When the committee of a Chicago convention waited upon Mr. Lincoln to inform him of his nomination, he treated them to ice water, with these remarks:

"Gentlemen, we must pledge our mutual healths in the most healthy beverage which God has given to man. It is the only beverage I have ever used or allowed in my family, and I cannot conscientiously depart from it on the present occasion. It is pure Adam's ale from the spring."

He was strictly temperate. Mr. John Hay, one of his biographers, says:

"Mr. Lincoln was a man of extremely temperate

habits. He made no use of either whisky or tobacco during all the years that I knew him."

Mr. John G. Nicolay, one of his private secretaries, says:

"During all the five years of my service as his private secretary I never saw him drink a glass of whisky, and never knew or heard of his taking one."

LINCOLN EPIGRAMS.

SENTENCES WORTH REMEMBERING.

We cannot escape history.

Let none falter who thinks he is right.

If slavery is not wrong, then nothing is wrong.

Come what will, I will keep my faith with friend and foe.

All that I am, all that I hope to be, I owe to my angel mother.

There is no grievance that is a fit object of redress by mob law.

This country, with its institutions, belongs to the people who inhabit it.

I authorize no bargains for the Presidency, and will be bound by none.

For thirty years I have been a temperance man, and I am too old to change.

No man is good enough to govern another man without that other's consent.

I believe this Government cannot permanently endure half slave and half free.

Gold is good in its place; but living, brave and patriotic men are better than gold.

This Government must be preserved in spite of the acts of any man, or set of men.

Nowhere in the world is presented a Government of so much liberty and equality.

Slavery is founded in the selfishness of man's nature — opposition to it in his love of justice.

If I live, this accursed system of robbery and shame in our treatment of the Indians shall be reformed.

In law it is good policy never to plead what you need not, lest you oblige yourself to prove what you cannot.

Understanding the spirit of our institutions to aim at the elevation of men, I am opposed to whatever tends to degrade them.

The reasonable man has long since agreed that intemperance is one of the greatest, if not the greatest, of all evils among mankind.

The purposes of the Almighty are perfect, and must prevail, though we erring mortals may fail accurately to perceive them in advance.

I protest against the counterfeit logic which concludes, because I do not want a black woman for a slave I must necessarily want her for a wife.

I know that the Lord is always on the side of the right; but it is my constant anxiety and prayer that I and this nation should be on the Lord's side.

Many free countries have lost their liberty, and ours may lose hers; but, if she shall, be it my proudest plume, not that I was the last to desert, but that I never deserted her.

By a course of reasoning, Euclid proves that all the angles in a triangle are equal to two right angles. Now, if you undertake to disprove that proposition, would you prove it false by calling Euclid a liar?

I am profitably engaged reading the Bible. Take all of this book upon reason that you can, and the balance on faith, and you will live and die a better man. — Said to Joshua Speed about a year before the President's assassination.

LINCOLN'S SECOND INAUGURAL ADDRESS.

AT this second appearing to take the oath of Presidential office there is less occasion for an extended address than there was at the first. Then a statement, somewhat in detail, of a course to be pursued, seemed fitting and proper. Now, at the expiration of four years, during which public declarations have been constantly called forth on every point and phase of the great contest which still absorbs the attention and engrosses the energies of the nation, little that is new could be presented. The progress of our arms, on which all else chiefly depends, is as well known to the public as myself; and it is, I trust, reasonably satisfactory and encouraging to all. With high hope for the future, no prediction in regard to it is ventured.

On the occasion corresponding to this four years ago, all thoughts were anxiously directed to an impending civil war. All dreaded it — all sought to avert it. While the Inaugural Address was being delivered from this place, devoted altogether to saving the Union without war, insurgent agents were in the city seeking to destroy it without war — seeking to dissolve the Union and divide effects by negotiation. Both parties deprecated war; but one of them would make war rather than let the nation survive; and the other would accept war rather than let it perish. And the war came.

One eighth of the whole population were colored slaves, not distributed generally over the Union, but localized in the southern part of it. These slaves constituted a peculiar and powerful interest. All knew that this interest was, somehow, the cause of the war. To strengthen, perpetuate and extend this interest was the object for which the insurgents would rend the Union, even by war; while the Government claimed no right to do more than to restrict the territorial enlargement of it.

Neither party expected for the war the magnitude or the duration which it has already attained: neither anticipated that the cause of the conflict might cease with or even before the conflict itself should cease. Each looked for an easier triumph, and a result less fundamental and astounding. Both read the same Bible and pray to the same God, and each invokes his aid against the other. It may seem strange that any men should dare to ask a just God's assistance in wringing their bread from the sweat of other men's faces; but let us judge not, that we be not judged. The prayers of both could not be answered; that of neither has been answered fully.

The Almighty has his own purposes. " Woe unto the world because of offences! For it must needs be that offences come; but woe to that man by whom the offence cometh." If we shall suppose that American slavery is one of those offences which, in the providence of God, must needs come, but which, having continued through his appointed time, he now wills to remove, and that he gives to both North and South this terrible war, as the woe due to those by whom the offence came, shall we discern therein any departure from those divine attributes which the believers in a living God always ascribe to him? Fondly do we hope — fervently do we pray — that this mighty scourge of war may speedily pass away. Yet, if God wills that it continue until all the wealth piled by the bondman's two hundred and fifty years of unrequited toil shall be sunk, and until every drop of blood drawn with a lash shall be paid with another drawn by a sword, as was said three thousand years ago, so still it must be said, "The judgments of the Lord are true and righteous altogether."

With malice toward none; with charity for all; with firmness in the right, as God gives us to see the right, let us strive on to finish the work we are in; to bind up the nation's wounds; to care for him who shall have borne the battle, and for his widow, and his orphan — to do all which may achieve and cherish a just and lasting peace among ourselves and with all nations.

THE END.

www.ingramcontent.com/pod-product-compliance
Lightning Source LLC
Chambersburg PA
CBHW022101230426
43672CB00008B/1244